Praise for *Writing the TV Drama Series, 4th Edition*

"Pam Douglas takes her invaluable book *Writing the TV Drama Series* and makes it even more compelling. New sections on streaming, and on the international market, supplement this already-essential read. It's the book I'd recommend first to anyone looking to launch a career as a writer in television drama."

—**Howard A. Rodman**, Past President, Writers Guild of America West; Artistic Director, Sundance Screenwriting Labs

"Pamela Douglas continues to surpass herself with her outstanding 4th edition, which includes important chapters on the growth of international television. Not only is it a roadmap for writing all aspects of dramatic television, but it's a roadmap for a career. *Writing the TV Drama Series* continues to be the definitive work on writing for television. A must-read if you are serious about a career in television."

—**Jack Epps, Jr., Ph.D.**, Professor and Chair, The John Wells Division of Writing for Screen and Television, USC School of Cinematic Arts; author, *Screenwriting Is Rewriting*; writer, *Top Gun, Dick Tracy*

"Literally a state-of-the-art study of contemporary TV drama writing, not to mention the skills needed to navigate the new global marketplace of streaming."

—**David Isaacs**, writer / producer, *M*A*S*H, Cheers, Frasier, Mad Men*

"Pam Douglas taught me the difference between writing a scene, and writing a scene that *matters*. She is a master at finding the heart of any story. Her perspective as both a professional writer and educator offers anyone wanting to shape a career in TV writing a unique view into the evolving landscape of the business."

—**Brian Peterson**, showrunner, executive producer, *Smallville*; consulting producer, *National Geographic*'s Emmy-nominated *Genius* anthology; screenwriter, *But I'm a Cheerleader*

"If you're curious about the world, and the thrilling confluence of storytelling, business, and values in television drama, the 4th edition of Pam Douglas's definitive work now charts the global waters of international television. A brilliant guide to the familiar (UK, Brazil); the fashionable (Denmark, Israel); and the future (Nigeria, South Korea)!"

—**Ted Braun**, writer / director, *Darfur Now*, *Betting On Zero*

"Pam Douglas lays out the state of the television industry today. For those of us already making television, she offers an insightful guide to where we are going. For those considering TV as a career, she offers even more—encouragement and an invitation to join in."

—**Chip Johannessen**, Past Governor of Writers' Branch, Television Academy; executive producer, *Homeland*, *Dexter*, *24*

"How to write, navigate, and succeed. Pamela Douglas has shown us how to make it in Hollywood and, most importantly, express yourself as a writer in dramatic form in the most accessible medium. Indispensable."

—**Dave Watson**, author, *Walkabout Undone*; editor, Movies Matter blog

"If writing for television is in your future, grab this book. Pamela Douglas shows you what you need to know and do. She brings you into the writing room and lets you decide if you've got what it takes. You'll get the gambit, from lessons on how TV scripts are written and formatted to how to get along with fellow coworkers once you get the job. Learn the lessons taught in this book; you'll fast-track your career."

—**Forris Day Jr.**, host, "Rolling Tape"; guest commentator, "Hitch 20" webseries

"*Writing the TV Drama Series* has always been of great value to my students—both undergraduate and graduate. This new edition, with an entire chapter devoted to international television, is invaluable to students and screenwriters alike."

—**Alexis Krasilovsky**, screenwriting professor, California State University, Northridge; author, *Great Adaptations: Screenwriting and Global Storytelling*

"Great style, a fun read, and a solid overview of the craft and journey involved in writing the TV drama series. An excellent textbook for TV writing courses, or for anyone interested in the field."

—**Terry Borst**, screenwriter; professor, Santa Fe University of Art and Design

4TH EDITION

TV DRAMA
SERIES

HOW TO SUCCEED AS A PROFESSIONAL WRITER IN TV

PAMELA DOUGLAS

MICHAEL WIESE PRODUCTIONS

Published by Michael Wiese Productions
12400 Ventura Blvd. #1111
Studio City, CA 91604
(818) 379-8799, (818) 986-3408 (FAX)
mw@mwp.com
www.mwp.com

Cover design by Johnny Ink. www.johnnyink.com
Interior design by William Morosi
Copyediting by Ross Plotkin

Names: Douglas, Pamela, author.
Title: Writing the TV drama series / by Pamela Douglas.
Description: 4th edition. | Studio City, CA : Michael Wiese Productions, [2018] | Includes bibliographical references and index.
Identifi ers: LCCN 2017060283 | ISBN 9781615932931
Subjects: LCSH: Television authorship. | Television series--Authorship.
Classification: LCC PN1992.7 .D68 2018 | DDC 808.2/25--dc23
LC record available at https://lccn.loc.gov/2017060283

TABLE OF CONTENTS

CHAPTER FIVE:
IT'S WHO YOU KNOW: WORKING ON STAFF 128

CHAPTER SIX:
HOW TO BREAK IN 147

PREFACE

Help! Too much great stuff is on TV! I just went to my Netflix to see one hour of one show and up pops an announcement that they've added 35 more. Since lunch. And it's the middle of the afternoon. No! I don't have time. Still, a new show lures me because all I have to do is click and the whole season is instantly mine — all 12 hours — for free (except for the monthly subscription, but I pay that anyway). No, I'll resist . . . for now. Even someone like me whose job involves knowing what's current can't keep up.

I'd like to thank *Game of Thrones* for the long hiatus between its final seasons on HBO, and then ending, so I could have my Sunday nights back. Of course I could have watched the *Thrones* episodes any other day, or even binged the entire series long after it finished, as many people still do with *The Wire*, more than a decade after its run. But who can wait? We've come to expect everything all at once whenever we want it. And the next great shows keep coming from everywhere. This is awful.

The sense of being overwhelmed laps over into daily life. Do texts clamor for replies on your iPhone? Do your hundreds of "friends" on Facebook and Instagram really need your attention? Do you react to "breaking news" all day long? Are you screaming for it all to stop?

We live in a time of irony. Parallel to the apparent abundance is stark reality, sometimes reflected in the content of the best television dramas. The often-quoted opening of Dickens's *A Tale of Two Cities* comes to mind: "It was the best of times, it was the worst of times, it was the age of wisdom, it was the age of foolishness, it was the epoch of belief, it was the epoch of incredulity, it was the season of Light, it was the season of Darkness, it was the spring of hope, it was the winter of despair, we had everything before us, we had nothing before us . . ."

As I write the fourth edition of this book, madmen who have power threaten life itself while whipping up fear, hatred, greed, distrust, and denying science while at the same time scientific advances enable the blind to see, the paralyzed to walk, and we can go on missions off our planet that we recognize as our shared home in a photo of Earth taken in space. It's our contemporary paradox.

From my travels to faraway lands giving lectures and seminars, I've realized how much experience is universally human. People everywhere want to tell their stories and learn how to shape them for television. That's why earlier editions of this book have been published in translation in Spain, Germany, Italy, France, and China as of 2017.

Now with the international reach of streaming by satellite and the Internet, we are approaching the original definition of "television": *tele* from Ancient Greek meaning "far" and Latin *visio* meaning "sight." That ideal of distant vision goes back to the 1900 World's Fair in Paris when a Russian scientist presented a theoretical device described in French as *television*. Decades later when Philo Farnsworth, an American scientist, developed electronic television, he declared it would bring peace to the world. He believed that when people everywhere could see each other, countries would abandon war. Clearly, we haven't done well with that since the 1920s. But neither has television approached its global capacity until recently.

From my travels, I remember rows of one-room houses on the outskirts of an African city that have no electricity and no plumbing. For toilets they use "long drops" — extremely deep holes in the ground. Yet, each one-room house — every single one — has a TV dish on its roof. They run on car batteries, I was told, and satellite service costs the equivalent of $100 U.S. That may be a quarter of a month's pay for some of these families. But it's the way to access quality shows — mostly from America and (increasingly) China.

I asked my insightful African guide, "Why are they willing to pay for television when they can't afford a toilet?"

"Priorities," she answered.

So it isn't just me in my American bubble trying to keep up. Experiencing 21st century television feels like witnessing the Big Bang. Maybe the explosion began when HBO launched original series with *OZ* in 1997 and followed with *The Sopranos* in 2000. Or it began when Netflix streamed *House of Cards* in 2013 and followed with *Orange Is the New Black* so all episodes could be downloaded at once, anytime, anywhere. Or it happened when Amazon that isn't even an entertainment company surprised everyone with quality original shows like *Transparent*, followed by every other entity you can imagine leaping into the originals pool. Or was it really signaled when television lifted off from Earth via satellites and scripted series reached the entire globe? Does it all come down to "the great convergence" of broadcast with the Internet? Or is it something more that has to do with evolving human consciousness? It's all those happening at once. So rather than a single bang, we're in the midst of fireworks, one after another, and more are on the way.

I remember a simpler time when the first edition of *Writing the TV Drama Series* was published in 2005. The rules of TV were knowable and clear. Hour dramas had four acts with commercial breaks every 13 minutes or so. A network TV season was usually 22 episodes that ran from September to May. And viewers sat on living room couches to watch their TV sets, tuning in their favorite programs when they were scheduled.

Back then, I wanted to tell you how to get into this field and do good work once you're here. That much remains.

By the second edition in 2007, many of the rules had changed — but the rules were still clear. On broadcast TV, hour drama shows went to five or six acts; basic cable was offering scripted series that followed traditional paradigms; on premium cable, HBO and Showtime always won the critical awards, and their commercial-free model had become a distinct form of its own. Pilot opportunities for new writers had blown open, but the pilots themselves were written and made the same way they'd always been.

Back then, I wanted to tell you how to use the new rules to write well and succeed. That remains also.

For the third edition in 2011, I discovered that almost everyone — from showrunners to struggling writers to industry executives to new media creators — was no longer merely adjusting the rules. Now they were asking basic questions: What is television? What is drama? What is a series? What are the delivery options? What are our obligations to the audience? Does a mass audience exist? Even what is reality?

And yet, after the smoke cleared, more remained than had first appeared. The writer's skill at storytelling, understanding what drives human beings, the guts to touch the passions, fears, and aspirations of viewers, and honestly portray the universal issues of our lives — that content always relies on the art, craft, and insight of people who write.

Sure, particular shows came and went, but the basics were the same. I wanted to tell you how to write well and succeed. It seemed all right to leave it that way for a while.

But two years later, I was blindsided. I hadn't seen Netflix originals coming or the streaming revolution. It became uncomfortable for me to advise my students to plan for television that consisted of the traditional networks and a few cable channels. Something had to be done.

So I wrote *The Future of Television: Your Guide to Creating TV in the New World*. I had a delightful interview with Ted Sarandos of Netflix, and tried to delve into what was emerging at Amazon, and spoke with creators working on YouTube and in various new media. The excitement everywhere in television was palpable and it was fun to explore.

But in retrospect, calling any book "The Future of Television" was hubris when the industry was evolving so fast. By the time it was published in 2015, it might have been called "The Present of Television." And another year later, some of it was "The Past of Television." This was especially the case in underestimating Amazon Studios, not anticipating new energy at Hulu, and most of all not foreseeing that cable and even broadcast stations would turn to streaming. What had been described as the "New Golden Age" of television — as if what was going on was comparable to the old Golden Age — or some sort of "Platinum Age," became known as "Peak TV," having run out of precious metals, I guess.

Portions of *The Future of Television* are integrated in this fourth edition. You'll get the best of some the research from that book. And I'll be updating until we go to press.

This fourth edition features an extraordinary section on International Television and fresh analyses of some great writing. And of course, I want to tell you how to use the new rules to write well and succeed. That remains.

The abundance of today's television can be good for you because it generates more opportunity. Now screenwriters who know how to create serialized scripts are in demand all over the world.

INTRODUCTION

WHAT IS TELEVISION NOW?

Imagine the power.

Picture the whole world dotted with hundreds of millions of screens glowing with the light from television images. Inside each flat screen, computer, or phone — your own, for example — visitors tell stories about their dreams and problems, loves and rages, their thrills and their losses. You care about them, probably more than you admit; you even talk about them when they're not around — after all, they come as often as you invite them.

Sometimes they're broiling over issues in the news. Or sick and scared about that, or lying, or brave. At one time, they were attacked and fought back and barely survived. But no matter what, they'll be back next time, your same friends, there with you in your most vulnerable places, at home after work and on weekends, on your phone while you wait alone for a plane, on your computer when you can't sleep at night. Intimate.

Think about the impact. Once you understand the way viewers relate to their favorite shows, you'll get a feel for the kinds of stories that work and how to wield this awesome power.

The ability of episodic storytelling to lure audiences into a fictional world, and the power to make that world seem real runs deep in human history. It reaches from cave dwellers around a fire to *Game of Thrones*, and ripples throughout television. Always, compelling characters have created compelling relationships with their audience, and the more honestly, more insightfully people's true motives and feelings are written the more deeply the audience commits to them.

That kind of intense, personal serialized storytelling is the strength of television today and in the future.

I hear some people confusing television with pieces of equipment. Television shows have never been limited to the wires and tubes inside a box.

1

Programming long ago passed from analog to digital, from antennas to cable to Internet, and from broadcast to streaming and everything else. So if television is no longer defined as a box in the living room, what is it now?

Bruce Rosenblum, former Chair of the Academy of Television Arts and Sciences, told me: "Television is content. Television is the opportunity for very talented, creative people both in front and behind the cameras to tell stories in an episodic environment. Whether stories are being experienced on a 55-inch flat-screen television or a laptop computer or mobile device or tablet, they are experiencing that story, interacting with that story, talking about that story. It's the episodic storytelling that's television."

At its core, our relationship to television is emotional, not only as nostalgia but as a component of our current lives.

So "What is television?" According to Chuck Slocum, Assistant Executive Director of the Writers Guild of America, West: "Television is everything that is not a feature film."

Some aspiring writers are struggling with the breadth of that. As I read applications to the USC School of Cinematic Arts, I see statements from students who say they want to be "screenwriters" and then I realize they intend that word to mean writers of theatrical features only. Apparently they don't yet realize that much of the great writing today is on television.

Lynda Obst, who produced features including *Sleepless in Seattle*, *Contact*, and *The Fisher King* commented, "Those of us who loved writing . . . we started saying, 'Well, where are characters?' We looked and we found ourselves watching *Homeland* and *Mad Men* and *The Sopranos*. Where were all the great characters being developed? On television. What was the water cooler talk about? Television. Things that we could never do in movies, we could suddenly do in television, so all the great writers that could sell their wares in this new market created a diaspora . . . and moved to television."

Writers have been transitioning from movies to TV for a long time. Back in 1974, critic Horace Newcomb wrote, "Intimacy, continuity, and history were the elements that distinguished television and earned its status as a popular art. These characteristics differentiated television storytelling from cinema."

Then television, itself, started to change.

Once upon a time, in the 20th century, television writers had to appeal to mass audiences with what Paul Klein, former CBS V.P. of Programming, called "Least Objectionable Programming." "LOP" not only prevented creators from airing dirty words and nudity, but more significantly, the policy constricted the kinds of characters you could create and interfered with honestly depicting how people live and relate to each other.

On *Orange Is the New Black*, consider how women of all ethnicities are portrayed, especially those from backgrounds that are rarely given full characterizations elsewhere. Think of the range of ways these women relate to each other sexually, psychologically, politically, and as families. No traditional network would have permitted any of that.

LOP shows do continue on traditional networks (and working on those shows is still an option for writers). But by the mid-2000s, U.S. television became more like publishing, where magazines are customized for readers with specific interests. The parallel shift in television happened when economics met up with technology.

Back in the network era, with limited screen real estate — only three hours of prime time on only three or four channels — everyone had to watch what was available and the competition was all about massive numbers. Two evolvements changed that: Advertiser-sponsored outlets (including basic cable) realized that large numbers of viewers were not as valuable as desired viewers — niche fans who were more likely to buy the products being advertised. It's logical: What's better, one viewer in 100 buying your fancy car or two people out of ten who are watching the show driving off in it? Allegiance to a show by its few adoring fans might also translate into warm-and-fuzzies for a product, advertisers figured. But advertising explains only part of the metamorphosis.

Subscriptions turned everything around. Suddenly people could watch quality original shows with no ads interrupting the episodes at all, whoopee! Thus spoke HBO, Showtime, Starz, Netflix, Amazon, and others. You pay for what you want. And those outlets don't care if you want everything they run — you only have to want something enough to subscribe. Women who had loved the *Outlander* novels added Starz to their cable packages purely to watch the *Outlander* series, though Starz had previously attracted mostly male audiences. For years, I'd felt no need to subscribe to Hulu since I could access most of their offerings elsewhere . . . and then in 2017 they broke through with their original scripted drama, *The Handmaid's Tale*, and I was in. And I'm happy to pay my monthly fee for the joy of seeing *Transparent*, an Amazon original series, even if I rarely check out their catalog, and even if they make a flop.

Tiny passionate audiences have power now. In her book *The Television Will Be Revolutionized*, scholar Amanda D. Lotz analyzed: "In the new environment consisting of fragmented audiences and niche-programming strategies, edgy programming produced in clear affront to some viewers can more than succeed: it can become particularly attractive to certain advertisers and accrues value from distinguishing itself so clearly in the cluttered and intensely competitive programming field."

That's great news for you as a creator. Don't believe people who tell you to water down your material. Write with honesty and courage, not just because that's good for you as an artist; suddenly it may be practical too.

But are we all permanently separated in our shrinking bubbles? Well, an opposite trend is happening at the same time. While we are identifying with our separate tribes, we are paradoxically interacting more within a kind of global tribe.

We all know, by now, that the shared warmth of the "electronic hearth" (as television was called in the 20th century) has diminished. That is, the time when a nation felt unified because everyone was watching the same program at the same time is over (except for major events like sports, significant news, and a very few shows). But there's a new version of community where people connect across the globe by nothing more than shared tastes or interests. In effect, these are larger tribes. As the old connections are lost, new communities are forming that are even more potent. In the future, how will you create for a community that is no longer described by time or place? Well, take a breath, and look at how television has morphed to fit its space before.

Television has always opened new creative possibilities, and has always moved forward through content. As *Wired* Magazine observed, "Some of the very first programs were created so networks would have something to air between soap commercials; HBO came up with ambitious series like *The Sopranos* because it wanted to attract more subscribers. Now Netflix, on a quest to grow its audience, is . . . [giving] us wilder TV than we've seen before. Not bad for a company created to rent DVDs."

It's not as if we're blasting off now in a vacuum of history. Television has experienced some sort of upheaval every decade. The curators at The Paley Center for Media wrote, "Despite the dazzling pace of technological change, it is our belief that content will continue to drive viewer interest, and thus play the dominant role in shaping the future of television, just as it has throughout the medium's history. Content is the reason people rushed out in the '40s to purchase televisions sets, to watch *Texaco Star Theater* and *Your Show of Shows*, or turned to *Friends* and *Seinfeld* and the rest of NBC's "Must See TV" Thursday-night lineup in the '90s, or ponied up extra dollars for addictive, buzzed-about cable shows like *The Sopranos* and *Mad Men*, and are now purchasing subscriptions to Netflix.

"Of course how and when people watch will continue to evolve but what people watch will continue to be driven by the quality of the content itself, just as it always has."

It's encouraging to think that we as "content creators" are so important. In the chapters that follow, we'll get *you* ready to write that content.

This can be the best of times.

FROM JOHN WELLS

John Wells is the showrunner on *Shameless*, and previously ran *ER* and *The West Wing*. He was also past president of the Writers Guild of America, West. In 2017, he honored the USC School of Cinematic Arts by naming the screenwriting division that is now The John Wells Division of Writing for Screen and Television.

PD: If you could go back in time and talk to your own young self when you were a student in film school or college, what do you know now that you wish you'd known then about writing and producing television series?

JW: I wish I'd known how long it was going to take. You come out and you sort of assume it's going to be a couple of year process and you don't really start making any headway until you've written about a foot and a half of material, measured up off the floor. That's when you really start to think of yourself as a writer in the way you look at the world. It's a craft that takes a tremendous amount of time.

I wish I had more of a sense that it was much more like learning to play a musical instrument. After four or five years, you start to not embarrass yourself. It takes ten years before you can even begin to call yourself proficient. And that's very difficult for students because they've been through twelve years of primary school, four years of college, and often a couple of years of graduate school and they think they've already done sixteen, eighteen years of education, so they want to go do it right now, though they've actually just started.

It looks deceptively easy from the outside. If you look at the lowest common denominator, you think, "I can do that." The craft that's necessary — the time it takes to have enough trial and error and to keep going with it — that takes a very long time to develop. I'm very suspicious of writers who haven't been writing for ten years. I will often ask people for three or four or five pieces of material if I've read one thing of theirs that I like. I know they've given me the thing they're proudest of, and I'm looking to see the growth, and how much they've done and how much they've committed themselves to the long-term process of writing.

I've supervised well over 600 scripts, and personally written well over a hundred, and I still finish each one disappointed in my work. It's a lifelong endeavor, never something you succeed at. I've been working professionally for twenty years and I'm always learning something new every day about writing.

PD: You could have chosen to write in any medium. Why TV?

JW: The feature world, which I remain involved in, is not a medium, generally, where you're able to write about character in the depth I like to write about character. There are characters now on *ER* whose growth I've been writing about for years. I don't mean to compare myself to Dickens, but I heard Steven Bochco talk about that years ago, when he explained that what he was trying to do on *Hill Street* was like the way Dickens published a chapter a week.

And subject matter is different in television. The kinds of things we can write about seriously are more appealing than most of what you're offered to do in features.

Beyond that, it's much easier to be involved creatively in your work in television than in feature films. It happens a lot faster, so there's not time for as many cooks in the kitchen. But also, you get to see your work and see it quickly. I've done work on features that haven't been produced for years, and [when asked for another draft] it becomes hard to remember what you had in mind when you first wrote it three years ago. In television, you'll finish a script and see dailies on it ten days later.

PD: People talk about how television is changing now with cable, the internet, and the influence of DVR. What does the future hold for the art of television drama?

JW: The technology makes for short-term changes, but we're still doing what Chaucer was doing a thousand years ago. We're still writing stories. I think we are structured in such a way that we're interested in people, and we're interested in hearing their stories and metaphors for our own lives and going through cathartic experiences. That hasn't changed.

I actually think it's a more exciting time for a writer because there are many more ways for your material to get made. You can write something and make it on a digital videocam that you buy at a store. You have an opportunity to work on shows on cable which have content you can't do on broadcast television. The opportunities are limitless. There isn't as much money to be made doing it, but you have thoughts and impressions about the human experience you want to share with others. This is the way to share it, and now there are more opportunities than ever.

PD: Any final words of wisdom for a beginning writer?

JW: It's going to take a lot longer than you think, and don't give up. Just keep writing.

There was a guy I went to USC with who I used to see every year at a New Year's party. And every year I'd ask him what he was doing. He told me what he was working on, and I realized it was the same thing he was working on last year. That went on for three or four years. You need to be writing, at the minimum three or four specs a year, different shows. And you need to do that while you've got whatever day job you have to keep you alive. That's the sort of commitment you need to really succeed.

Even my friends who came out of school and immediately got jobs or sold screenplays — within three or four years they ended up having to do their period of four or five or six years slogging. I really don't know any talented writers who ended up being successful who haven't had a struggle. That's just what being an artist is all about.

CHAPTER ONE

WHAT'S SO SPECIAL ABOUT TV DRAMA SERIES?

Once you understand the way viewers relate to their favorite shows, you'll get a feel for the kinds of stories that work and how to wield this awesome power.

THREE QUALITIES OF EPISODIC TV SERIES

Among the traits that distinguish dramatic series from other kinds of screenwriting, three are especially significant for writers: endless character arcs, the "long narrative" for serials, and the collaborative process.

EPISODIC CHARACTERIZATION:

In feature writing you were probably told to create an arc for your protagonist from one state to its opposite; the character struggles towards a goal and once that is attained, your story ends. Someone who is unable to love is changed when a mate/child/friend appears and, through fighting the relationship, the character is finally able to love. Or someone who has been wronged seeks revenge and either achieves it or dies for the cause. All fine for movies that end. But series don't — or at least they don't end in two hours.

So how do you progress a narrative without an arc? Well, you create a different kind of arc. Remember what I said about series characters being more like people you know than figures in a plot. If your friend has an extreme experience, you continue knowing that person after the event. You're invested in the process, not just the outcome.

But watch out — this does not mean the characters are flat. Your continuing cast should never be mere witnesses to the challenge of the week. On the contrary, characters who are not transformed by the plot need something instead: dimension. Think of it like this: instead of developing horizontally towards a goal, the character develops vertically, exploring secrets and internal conflicts that create tension. The character may be revealed incrementally within each episode and throughout the series, but viewers need to depend that Tyrion Lannister and Jessica Jones are the same people they knew last week. Does that mean those characters are without range or variation? Of course not, and neither are your friends.

THE "LONG NARRATIVE":

Episodic drama comes in three forms: anthologies (including season-long and limited series), series with "closure," and "serials."

Traditional Anthologies are freestanding stories, like short movies, unconnected to other installments except by a frame. *Black Mirror* has a continuing attitude and franchise, but the casts are different each week. As the precursor of today's episodic television, anthologies like *Twilight Zone* flourished in the 1950s and early '60s when showcases like *Playhouse 90* presented literature more like stage plays. Now limited series like *American Crime* arrive at a satisfying conclusion eight hours later, after building layers of storytelling that could not have happened in two hours and would not benefit from extending any longer. When the story is done, it's done.

Series with closure have continuing main casts but they also have new situations that conclude at the end of each episode: they close. This is especially true of procedurals like *CSI* and *NCIS*. In the past, procedurals were almost all that was offered on traditional broadcast networks. Before our current era when anything is available online at any time, syndicators and cable channels that ran repeats preferred this kind of show because they could buy large packages (the first four seasons, or 88 episodes was typical) and sell them to local and overseas stations that could rerun in any order. If the episodes have no "memory," that is, no significant development of ongoing relationships, the order of the episodes isn't supposed to matter. Or so the thinking went.

Now most series have some closure, even if they continue other storylines. But when a series is well developed, the writers and fans follow the characters and find it hard to resist their history as it inevitably builds over time. In its early seasons, *X-Files* had a new alien or paranormal event each week, and though the romantic tension between Mulder and Scully simmered, it didn't escalate. Then interest from viewers pushed more and more of a relationship and turned the partners into lovers by the end of the series. Most *X-Files* episodes can still be enjoyed in any order, but serial storytelling is beguiling.

Today, the best shows that close each episode also have ongoing dramatic stories and build followings on their continuing characters. From a writing point of view, they are constructed as procedurals (more about that term later), but the categories have blurred.

Some great serials include award-winning dramas on Netflix, Amazon, HBO, Showtime, AMC, and plenty of other outlets: *Game of Thrones*, *Orange Is the New Black*, *The Americans*, *Mad Men*, *Breaking Bad*, *The Wire*, *The Sopranos*, and so many more. In fact, most of the acclaimed series on streaming and cable outlets use serialized storytelling along with closed stories.

A serial is any drama whose stories continue across many episodes in which the main cast develops over time. It's called the "long narrative," the epitome of what episodic television can offer: not one tale that ties up in an hour or two but lives that may play out over 8, 12, 36, even hundreds of hours. If you calculate 12 years of *The Walking Dead* at 12 episodes per year, for example, you would get 144 hours of living with these characters and their struggles, 144 hours dealing with the consequences of twelve years of experiences. Think about it — as a writer you have the opportunity to tell a story that is so rich that it expands for years.

As you watch television, look for the way closed stories mingle with the long narrative. Not only will that give you insight into the show's construction, but also a larger sense of what a story can be.

COLLABORATION:

If you go on to write for television, you'll never work alone. Series are like families and even though an individual episode is written by one writer, the process is collaborative at every step. Writers sit around a table to "break" each story then review the outline and all the drafts together. Sometimes a writer may be placing a long arc in many episodes rather than writing a single episode. On medical, legal, and police shows, real doctors, lawyers, and cops act as consultants, and might even supply essential scenes if the consultants are also writers. How would *Mr. Robot* fare if the writing staff didn't have inside knowledge of hacking? And sometimes one writer may do a revision or dialogue polish on another's script. The image of the isolated artist creating his precious screenplay secretly in the night isn't the reality of life on a series. (Though that's not to say staff members don't write their drafts privately, or that they aren't artists.)

You may have heard the comment that happy families are all alike but each unhappy family is unhappy in its own way. Television staffs are full of writers, so how normal can they be? Dysfunctional staff families abound, but so do creative mixes that are encouraging and inspiring. As a beginner, you'll learn tremendously on a staff. Read Chapter Five for how staffs function, and for tips on getting along and getting ahead.

But first, if you're going to write for TV, you need to dump some misconceptions.

FOUR MYTHS ABOUT TELEVISION

• MYTH 1: TV IS SMALL MOVIES

Not really, though that may seem to make sense on the surface. Both TV dramas and movies deliver stories played by actors who are filmed and shown on screens. And many filmmakers — writers, directors, actors, cinematographers, editors, and so forth — work in both theatricals and television. For example, John Ridley who wrote and produced the award-winning movie *12 Years a Slave* also created and ran *American Crime* and other television series. Melissa Rosenberg, showrunner at *Jessica Jones* wrote the theatrical hit *Twilight*.

A funny experience on a series brought home how connected film and TV writing can be. My agent told me that several writers had quit the staff of a show I admired. I couldn't figure out why — the series was winning awards, it was renewed, and the characters had plenty of potential. Not to mention the writers were making a bundle. Maybe the showrunner was a monster. But I met him, a bright guy, no crazier than anyone else in town. So I went to work.

First day in my new cubicle, I waited to be called to a story meeting, or given an assignment, or a script to rewrite. Nothing. I read everything on Facebook and all my catch-up emails. Second day, I observed everyone else writing furiously on their office computers. Why was I left out? Had I offended someone? My mind fell to dark ruminations.

Finally, I popped into the cubicle next to me — "What are you writing?" The writer looked up, wide-eyed, didn't I know? Everyone was working on their features. "He wants to do it all himself," my fellow staffer said about the executive producer. "He keeps us around to bounce ideas and read his drafts. But he thinks it's quicker if he just writes the show." There I was on a TV staff and everyone was writing a movie. Pretty soon the studio pulled the plug on our feature scholarships, and that was the end of that job. But that illustrates an axiom: a writer is a writer, whether television or feature or for any new media.

Still, the more you know about features and television, the more unique each is. People go to movies to escape into a fantasy larger than life with spectacular stunts, effects, and locations. At around $20 per ticket, audiences demand lots of bang for their bucks. And teenage boys — a prime target for features — relish the vicarious actions and special effects that big screens do so well. If you stream a *Godzilla* remake on your cell, the giant lizard becomes a toy and armies of thousands are reduced to ants. Some bubbles are not meant to be burst.

From the beginning, theatrical features grew out of shared entertainment — think of crowds watching vaudeville. Television didn't intend that kind of experience. In fact, the parent of TV is more likely radio. A generation before television, families gathered around their radios for vital information, whether the farm report or the war. And radio dramas were character-driven: beloved familiar personalities scrapping and coping with each other, bringing someone (often women, hardly ever teen boys) to tears or laughter every day. Close, personal, at home.

And real. Before radio, people got their information about the world from newspapers. That lineage continues in what we expect of television. Television became fused with what people need to know and what they believe is fact. So it's not an escape, not fantasy, more like the fabric of daily life.

Oh, you're saying what about a legacy franchise like *Star Trek* or the current Netflix series *Stranger Things* for just two examples — they're hardly real. Well, when I was a beginner I did a brief turn on *Star Trek: The Next Generation*, and I can tell you the producers were interested in stories about people — people who lived in a distant environment with futuristic gadgets, yes, but the core was relationships among the crew, testing personal limits; and, at its best, the exploration wasn't distant galaxies but what it means to be human. As for *Stranger Things*, the young cast, especially the character "Elle" is a metaphor for every kid who struggles with being different, figuring out who they are and how to be with their friends. This is heart stuff, not spectacle alone.

That's not to say you should write without cinematic qualities. The pilot of *Lost* opened with visually tantalizing images that drew the viewer into the mood and quest of the series. But even there, the focus was personal jeopardy: It began on Jack's eyeball, then an odd sneaker on a tree, then a dog out of nowhere, and took its time placing us in a jungle before following Jack as he discovered where he was, moving without dialogue to the beach. Still tight in Jack's point of view, only gradually do we see the crashed plane, and the first word from a distance, "Help!" Immediate, direct, close.

Screenwriting students are taught to write visually and minimize talk — "play it don't say it." Generally, that's good advice, so I was writing that way when I started in television. Then a producer pointed to a chunk of description (which I'd thought was a clever way of replacing exposition) and said, "Give me a line for this — they may not be watching." Not watching? That's my brilliant image up there!

But come back to the reality of the medium. You might be watching on your phone or laptop, usually at home, not in a darkened theater. No one is captured, and the viewers might be eating, painting toenails, doing homework, typing texts — you know how it goes. As the creator, of course you want to make the screen so beguiling they won't turn their eyes away, but if the "viewers" have to get a point, put it in dialogue. People may be listening to the TV as much as watching it. That's not such a bad thing. Whereas the audience is distanced from the screen in theatrical films, voyeurs to other people's stories, television drama has the effect of people talking to you, or at least talking to each other close to you. It's compelling in a different way.

When students ask whether I advise them to write for features or television, after I tell them to try both, I ask about their talent. Do they have an ear for the way people speak naturally? Are they able to convey the illusion of today's speech while actually writing tight, withheld lines? Can they write distinct voices for dissimilar characters? If they don't have the talent for effective dialogue, I nudge them away from TV because action would be easier for them.

As you contemplate the differences between gigantic theatrical entertainment and what works well on a personal computer, take the next step: what sort of storytelling and filmmaking is likely to be successful on a screen the size of a cell phone?

So, no, television is not a small version of movies; it's a different medium; and it's bigger. Yes, bigger. The most successful features are seen by millions of people in theaters, and more when the movies are later streamed.

In contrast, here's the audience for *The Walking Dead* premiere — which represents a fraction of the numbers it got later. In November 2010, its pilot episode reached more U.S. adults 18–49 than any other show in the history of cable television. *Simultaneously*, its international distributor at that time, FIC (Fox International Channels) announced that the show had record-breaking premiere ratings in 120 countries in Europe, Latin America, Asia, and the Middle East. FIC's international distribution is carried in 35 languages, reaching around 875 million people worldwide. Meanwhile, Americans viewed the show across all platforms including on-air, online, on demand, and mobile. That's for just one hour. So, yes, TV is bigger than movies.

Still, from a writer's viewpoint, *The Walking Dead* is entirely traditional. It's a scripted hour drama telling a "long narrative" serial through professional actors, skillfully creating suspense and character conflict, written in the same act structure as 20th-century network dramas. If you time-traveled from the 1980s to watch this show, you'd understand how it works.

I mention that not to diminish this successful production but to keep television in perspective. International distribution is essential to affording shows like this one, and if you're creating a new series, you might keep in mind its potential worldwide appeal. But day-to-day as writers, good work is what it has always been.

• MYTH 2: TV IS CHEAP

Well, I don't think four to five million dollars to produce one episode is all that cheap. That's the cost of an average episode and it doesn't begin to count epics like *Game of Thrones* that are in the stratosphere of finance. But big budgets for shows don't tell you what's going on behind the scenes. The business side of this industry is complex.

The six major conglomerates that own all U.S. studios and television networks reported $51 billion in profits in 2016. At the same time, writers' salaries were stagnant, or declining. This is part of the industry-wide change from 22-episode seasons to 12 or fewer episodes on streaming platforms, cable, and even traditional networks. TV writers are paid per episode, so it's easy to see that fewer episodes make fewer paydays. If you look at this as a proportion of costs, a decade ago when most shows cost around $2 million per episode, around ten percent — $200,000 — went to writers. Now a show that costs $4 million per episode pays out 8% — $300,000 — to its writing staff.

These are heady numbers for beginning writers. It's true that the average TV writer on the staff of a show earns around $250,000 per year, and those with top titles get much more. Someone scraping up their rent money might think TV writers are all getting rich. But that impression is incomplete. Limited series may end after only 8 episodes and then writers are out looking for new jobs having only a few months of paid work; and would-be writers may not make the leap onto a staff all season in an era when freelance assignments are no longer available. The business side of television is more like a manufacturing company than an entrepreneurial venture. There may be a lot of money but it's all allocated.

So towards the end of a season, some shows do tighten their belts. One showrunner instructed me as I joined his series: "It doesn't rain in this town." After he had sprung for high profile guest stars and overtime shooting, he couldn't afford to make rain on the set for the rest of the year. You may have noticed another sign of budget overrun: the "wrap-around" episode. That's the one where the main character relives his previous episodes. Chances are, those memories were triggered not by nostalgia but by the need to use clips instead of spending on production. Then there's the "bottle" episode in which two characters spend the hour in a single location. Funny thing — those tight episodes may create the show's best writing. If you have a chance, check out "The Fly" episode of *Breaking Bad*, "The Fight" episode of *Masters of Sex*, and "Here's Not Here," episode 604 of *The Walking Dead*.

That said, series budgets are usually sufficient for what you want dramatically within the world of the show. As a writer, your investment needs to be in the quality of the story and depth of feelings you can elicit rather than production dazzle, so for medium-budget shows that are not on premium cable like HBO or high-end streamers like Netflix, try to avoid: distant or difficult locations, special effects, extreme stunts, large guest casts, crowd scenes, and CGI (computer-generated images) unless those are part of your series. By tightening, you gain focus on the main characters, which are the strength of television drama.

• MYTH 3: YOU CAN'T DO THAT ON TV

Come on, you can do anything on streaming networks and premium cable — language, nudity, controversial subjects or lifestyles, experiments in ways of telling stories. If you look no further than *Game of Thrones* (HBO), *Transparent* (Amazon), *Orange Is the New Black* (Netflix), *Masters of Sex* (Showtime), and *Empire* (ABC), none of which are new, the freedom is evident, and some more recent series go further.

However, broadcast stations are licensed by the FCC (Federal Communications Commission) which obligates them to operate in the public interest. So local stations are susceptible to pressure from groups that might threaten their licenses when they're up for renewal; and the networks, which also own stations, are sensitive to public mores — though those cultural standards change with time. Certainly, public norms have come a long way since the 1950s when married couples had to be shown fully dressed and sleeping in separate beds. Now even the least adventurous television is closer to real life. And none of this applies to non-broadcast outlets.

The old days of censorship are past . . . but not entirely. Kenya Barris, creator of the hit ABC network comedy *Black-ish*, often teases the boundaries on his series. He did a whole episode on the "N-word" and considered using it in full. He told *Written By* (the monthly magazine of the Writers Guild of America) that he decided a bleeped version with the characters' mouths pixelated "sounded louder" than the literal curse.

And yet, *Written By* continued, "when he sought to televise an image of the Sandy Hook Elementary School *sign*, as a way to illustrate hard conversations parents must broach with their kids, he was told absolutely no."

Barris says he mostly gets "carte noir" because when suits try to press him about notes, "I drop in the phrase 'Well, culturally speaking,'" which, he says is a hole into which white men are loathe to jump.

So, yes, on broadcast television some limits still exist. But here's my advice: Don't censor yourself as you write your first draft. Have your characters talk and behave the way people actually do today. Stay real. If a word or image has to be edited, fix it later, but keep the pipeline open to how people truly are because that's the source of powerful writing.

• MYTH 4: TV IS A WASTELAND

In 1961, Newton Minnow, an FCC Commissioner, declared television a "vast wasteland," and the epithet stuck. Minnow was referring to shows such as *Bonanza*, *The Flintstones*, and *Mr. Ed* in an era when three networks, each smaller than now, shared airwaves that were considered a scarce commodity dedicated to informing or elevating the public. The talking horse just didn't do it for him.

Well, more than half a century later, part of the wasteland has become a garbage dump strewn with fake jilted lovers beating up on each other on so-called "unscripted" shows. The rest ranges from televangelists to pornography, political pundits to purveyors of snake oil, sports to scientific discoveries, wannabe singers to singing animals, and includes fiction of all kinds that may be funny, freaky, fascinating, or familiar. And some is brilliant literature, on a par with the greatest writing and filmmaking created anywhere. Those are the shows I focus on when teaching hour drama because I believe you learn best if you learn from the best. As to the wasteland — with thousands of channels and sites, and access to programming from every era of television history and from all over the world, television is whatever you choose to watch.

I've heard people disparage TV as aimed at 12-year-olds. I answer: *Yes, TV shows are aimed at 12-year-olds if you watch certain shows.* Preteen and teen programming on the CW, Fox, cable outlets like Freeform, and YouTube channels like AwesomenessTV attract viewers who advertisers believe are especially susceptible to their commercials. Some of those shows even link to websites where viewers can buy the styles worn by the actors.

I don't recommend emulating those shows as you learn to write, but I do understand that very young writers may be more comfortable with characters close to their own age. If a student sincerely tells me she hasn't had enough life experience to deal with adult issues or relationships, but wants to learn the craft, I direct her to a well-written show with young cast. *Friday Night Lights* was a perfect case of honestly observed high school students written with insight. *Stranger Things* is a newer excellent model.

Some of you may have grown up watching *Buffy the Vampire Slayer*, either in its original airing as a syndicated series from 1997 to 2003 or in its decades of reruns. Students have told me this is the show that convinced them to write for television or opened their eyes to the possibilities of storytelling on screen. Unfortunately, that enthusiasm has led to generations of first pilot scripts that imitate *Buffy*. Instead, create something unique to your own experience by understanding *why* the show succeeded so well.

It's not the allure of fantasy action or superheroes who save the world, even if they're women. After all, the *Wonder Woman* comic books and TV series arrived earlier. The pull of *Buffy* was creator/writer Joss Whedon's ability to hear the emotional concerns of young viewers and convey their relationships with family and friends, their internal struggles, and most of all their natural dialogue. The strength of this fantasy show turned out to be its realness. If you want to use this show as a model then use its authenticity rather than its premise.

Sometimes people who aim at young audiences impose images drawn from earlier teen fare like *Freaks and Geeks* or *Wonder Years* or something on the Disney Channel. Take a step back and ask if your own junior highs or high schools looked like that. Were there truly no people of color? No one whose families migrated from other countries? No one whose families struggled with poverty? No one whose sexual identification was a question? For a reality check, watch the teenagers in *The Wire*. Even though you didn't grow up in that world, the experience of *The Wire* might balance the stereotypes of teen life (besides being great writing, of course).

If you dare, think about the controversy surrounding *Thirteen Reasons Why* on Netflix. Would you write something like that? Why, and if not, why not or how would you do it differently?

So if you'd like to write teen television, go ahead. If you choose truth as your guide, your script will ring true at any age.

THE RULES OF SERIES TV

• AN HOUR SHOW HAS TO FIT IN AN HOUR.

Sort of.

Traditional networks have always scheduled their primetime shows in hour and half hour blocks. It's purely a matter of fitting programming and ads into available slots, not serving the unique needs of a story. That's one of the rules challenged by streaming.

Though streamed dramatic episodes still feel like they're an hour long (and comedies feel like half hours when they run 22 minutes), loosening the clock affects what you can do as writers. Ted Sarandos, Chief Content Officer at Netflix, spoke with me after *House of Cards* premiered and offered this advice:

"Don't feel limitations because it's a TV show. On one level *House of Cards* is a 13-hour movie, or a 39-hour movie. I want people to write the perfect story in the perfect time. *Arrested Development* is 15 episodes, which is kind of an oddball number. Every episode has a different running time. The less they are connected to a linear grid for creativity, the more the show is like a novel. If every novel had to be the same number of pages, books would be pretty lousy."

Still, regardless of platform, when you sit at your keyboard you need to know certain techniques. In general, one page of a drama script equals one minute of airtime. If you really had an hour for an hour drama, your script would be around 60 pages. That happens on HBO, but not networks with commercial breaks. Actually the dramatic content in network shows tends to run around 42 to 44 minutes. So you'd think I'd advise you to write 44-page episodes. That's logical, but if you're speculating a sample episode, or new to an assignment, aim closer to 50 pages. That will probably be tightened after the script is timed during the table read (if not before), but you want to demonstrate depth and caring in your first offering.

On networks that break shows into five or six acts plus a teaser, writers may find themselves with the later acts running only six to eight pages each, and a final act that has just two 2-page scenes for a total around 4 pages. I'll walk you through those structure prototypes later in the book, but for now we're conceptualizing the sense of an hour.

In networks that require exact lengths, if a script runs long after a read-through timed by a stopwatch, the writer needs to know what to trim in dialogue or which action to ellipse; if it runs short, where a new beat could add depth or a twist, not padding. And you need the craft to get it revised overnight, which leads to the next rule:

• SERIES DEADLINES ARE FOR REAL.

Your show is on every week, and that means there's no waiting for your muse, no honing the fine art of writing-avoidance, no allowing angst to delay handing in your draft. If you can't make the deadline, the showrunner has to turn over your work to another writer.

From the time your episode is assigned, you'll probably have one week to come in with an outline, a few days to revise it, two weeks to deliver the first draft teleplay, a gap of a couple of days for notes, then one week to write your second draft — a total of around six weeks from pitch to second draft (though polishes and production revisions may add another couple of weeks or so). Maybe that sounds daunting, but once you're on a staff you're living the series, and the pace can be exhilarating. You'll hear your words spoken by the actors, watch the show put together, and see it on screen quickly too.

It's fun until the nightmare strikes. On a series, the nightmare is a script that "falls out" at the last minute. It may happen like this: the story seems to make sense when it's pitched. The outline comes in with holes, but the staff thinks it can be made to work. Then they read the first draft and see the problems aren't solved. It's given to another writer to fix. Meanwhile the clock is ticking. Preproduction, including sets, locations, casting have to go ahead if the script is going to shoot next week. Tick tock. Another draft, and the flaw — maybe an action the lead character really wouldn't do, or a plot element that contradicts the episode just before or after, or a forced resolution that's not credible — now glares out at everyone around the table. Yet another draft, this time by the supervising producer. Tick tock. Or maybe it's not the writer's fault: the exact fictional crisis about a hostage has suddenly occurred in real life so the episode cannot be aired. The script has to be abandoned — it "falls out." Meanwhile, the production manager is waiting to prep, and publicity has gone out.

I once heard a panel discussion where a respected showrunner told this very nightmare. The cast and crew were literally on the set and absolutely had to start shooting that day for the episode to make the airdate. But they had no script. In desperation, the showrunner, renowned as a great writer, commenced dictating as a secretary transcribed and runners dashed to the set bringing one page at a time. A hand shot up from an admirer in the panel audience, "Was it the best thing you ever wrote?" "No," he laughed, "it didn't make sense."

• TV SERIES HAVE SPECIFIC STRUCTURES

Television — on any platform — has a rhythm that's different from theatrical features. In a movie theater you might sit through ten or even fifteen minutes establishing the "world" before the first real dramatic beat, the special effects may present a thrill ride that doesn't advance character development, or the scenery is appreciated slowly, and there you sit in the dark waiting for an urgent cause to initiate the character's personal mission or quest. Those kinds of theatrical rhythms (that television writers sometimes think are "auteur" indulgences by certain movie directors) don't tend to fit television dramas. It's too easy to change channels.

Many traditional feature-writing formulas you may have been taught don't apply to screenwriting on contemporary platforms. So put away your books on three-act structure. Television dramas on networks have for decades been written in four acts, though many broadcast and cable shows now use five or six acts. As you'll see later, dramas on streaming platforms and premium cable are structured by character arcs rather than act breaks. You'll learn more about script structure in Chapters Three and Four.

For now, think about what happens every 12 to 15 minutes (or so) on a traditional network show. You know: a commercial break. These breaks aren't random; they provide a grid for constructing the episode in which action rises to a cliffhanger or twist ("plot point" may be a familiar term if you've studied feature structure). Each of the four segments are "acts" in the same sense as plays have real acts rather than the theoretical acts used in analyzing features. At a stage play, at the end of an act the curtain comes down, theater lights come up, and the audience heads for refreshments or restrooms. That's the kind of hard act break that occurs in broadcast television. Writers plan towards those breaks and use them to build tension.

Once you get the hang of it, you'll discover act breaks don't hamper your creativity; they can free you to be inventive within a rhythmic grid. And once you work with that ten-to-fifteen minute block, you may want to use it off-network and in movies. In fact, next time you're in a movie theater, notice the audience every fifteen minutes. You may see them shifting in their seats. I don't know whether 15-minute chunks have been carved into contemporary consciousness by the media, or if they're aspects of the human biorhythm that somehow evolved with us, but the 15-minute span existed before television.

In the early 20th century, motion pictures were distributed on reels that projectionists had to change every 15 minutes. Then, building on that historical pattern, some screenwriting theorists began interpreting features as eight 15-minute sequences. Whatever the origin, 15-minute acts became the original template for drama series on the networks: 60 minutes divided by 15 minutes equals 4 acts.

Today, virtually all broadcast and basic-cable shows are still written in acts to accommodate commercials and the stories are structured to write up to the act break and down from it. That includes critically praised writing on AMC and FX. But as the value of advertising segments declined on traditional networks, more commercials began to be inserted to make up for the loss, leading to series written in five or six acts. These may also have a teaser (explained in Chapter Three) that is sometimes almost as long as an act, giving an impression of six or even seven short acts.

Despite the push to crowd more advertising into shows, the effort is doomed. Most shows can be streamed after their initial broadcast, avoiding ads that break into the story altogether. And, of course, premium cable, such as HBO as well as streaming services never had commercial interruptions and therefore no apparent act breaks at all.

Notice I said "apparent." Partly in an effort to differentiate their shows from network fare, some series adopt an "indie film" (or "art film") sensibility, exemplified by *Girls* (HBO) and *Transparent* and *I Love Dick* (both on Amazon). Funny thing, despite the avowed aversion to act break structure on premium cable and streaming, a surprising reversal has occurred. If you had a chance to see the writer's first drafts of many non-network hour dramas you'd see the four-act structure back again. I once asked the great writer David Milch about the construction of *Deadwood* that had no visible act breaks on HBO, and he told me candidly his initial scripts are always 4 acts because he's comfortable with that rhythm. I also asked Ron Moore (showrunner of *Battlestar Galactica* on Syfy and *Outlander* on Starz) and he said the staff generally writes four-plus-teaser and then drops out the act breaks later. From a construction viewpoint, it just plain works, even if it is adjusted in the final drafts.

When you get to the grid in chapter Three, you'll be able to try out the structure of any existing series and experiment with forming your own script.

• MANY SERIES USE "FRANCHISES"

Not Starbucks, though enough caffeine is downed on late rewrites to earn that franchise too. Some typical television franchises include police/detective, legal, medical, sci-fi, action-adventure, and family. Each brings expectations from the audience that you should know, even if you challenge them. For series creators, franchises are both boundaries and opportunities. You'll find more about how shows are created in Chapter Two, but you can get a clue why franchises are useful if you ask how hundreds of stories can derive from a single premise.

The solution is to find "springboards" that propel dramatic conflicts or adventures each episode. Those catalysts occur naturally in most of the franchises: a crime sets the cop on a quest for the perp; someone in trouble beseeches lawyers who must mount a case; a patient is brought for a doctor to save. The hook for each episode is rooted in a specific world in which sympathetic main characters must take immediate action. In other franchises — family, workplace, high school, and romantic dramas, for example — springboards are less obvious, relying on conflicts between characters rather than outside provocations. In these, a personal inciting incident (even if it's internal) sets each episode in motion.

Decades ago, audiences expected the franchises to deliver predictable storytelling where any problem could be resolved within the hour, as many procedural shows still do. Take Westerns, for example. The template was the frontier town threatened by bad guys (black hats). The good guy marshal (a star in a white hat) wrangles with weak or corrupt townspeople, gets a few on his side, defends the town against the black hats, and rides off into the sunset.

With that old formula in mind, consider *Westworld* (HBO 2016), about a technologically advanced Wild West theme park populated by android hosts. Westworld caters to high-paying guests who indulge their brutal fantasies without fear of retaliation from the hosts. In this series, who is "good?" What does it mean to be human or part human? What does freedom mean for someone controlled by technology? Whom do you root for among these characters struggling to make sense of life in a moral wilderness? The differences between this show and the traditional western franchise are not only results of a switch to the sci-fi franchise, but a deeper questioning of history and values that marks the change from 20th-century television to the 21st.

Does a "high tech" franchise exist now? We could point to *Mr. Robot*, *Silicon Valley*, and *The Big Bang Theory*, among others. But just because shows share certain worlds don't make them "franchisable." To do that, a franchise requires more of a template with shared expectations.

Clearly, *Grey's Anatomy* and *Nurse Jackie* use the medical franchise, where doctors and nurses must deal with new cases each week. But if you compare them to examples of the historic franchise such as *Marcus Welby, M.D.*, you'll see how far they've stretched to reflect contemporary life. Welby, the kindly doctor, free of deep introspection, worked alone in his nice little office and cured someone by the end of each episode. But real doctors and nurses face ethical and legal issues as they treat both the victim of a gunshot and the man who shot him, and they cope with their own humanity — guilt, exhaustion, ambition, and the competing pulls of the job and the rest of life. These realities include addiction on *Nurse Jackie* and *The Knick*, a doctor's deep psychological issues on *House*, and romance on *Grey's*.

From the moment ABC slotted *Grey's Anatomy* to follow *Desperate House-wives*, the network mandated the tone: "Sex and the Surgery." Executive Producer Shonda Rhimes responded in *Los Angeles Magazine*, "I don't think of it as a medical drama. It's a relationship show with some surgery thrown in. That's how I've always seen it."

Meanwhile, the family drama franchise is flourishing — like *Weeds*, *Jane the Virgin*, and *Empire*. Some families. I suppose you could call *Orange Is the New Black* a family drama too because episodes emanate from relation-ships among the continuing cast (some of whom are related or "living" together) as much as external events. Not exactly *Leave It to Beaver*.

In the detective franchise, you'll still see an occasional light show like *Monk* on USA that played out the traditional form: one detective gets one new crime mystery each week and, after investigating red herrings that fall mostly at the act breaks, cleverly solves it by the end of the hour. Though Monk's obsessive-compulsive characterization was a fresh element, struc-turally this was a basic "A" story series (more about A-B-C storytelling in Chapter Three). Check out the shows this basic-cable channel mounted after the end of *Monk* to ride that popularity: quirky main characters in predictable plots.

When I was a beginner, freelancing any show that would give me a break, I landed an assignment on *Mike Hammer*, a network detective series. At my first meeting, the producer handed me two pages of guidelines. The first was titled "Mike Hammer Formulaic Structure." On the second were rules for writing Mike, for example, "Mike speaks only in declarative sentences." To be a strong man, he could never ask questions, you see.

The formula went something like this: At the top of the show, a sympa-thetic character approaches Mike for help. At the end of Act One, the sympathetic character is found dead. In Act Two Mike is on the trail of the killer, only to find him dead at the Act break, and yet someone else has been killed (proving there's a different killer). In Act Three the real bad guy goes after Mike, and at the Act Three break, Mike is in mortal jeopardy. Act Four is entirely resolution, one-to-one, Mike against the killer. And guess who wins. As I started, I thought such a rigid form would be stultifying, but I discovered it was fun. Relieved of certain structure choices, I felt free to be inventive with the guest cast and the kinds of situations that could lead to the turns and twists.

If you find yourself in one of those formulaic shows, here's my advice: use the formula but inhabit it with people and their true feelings set amidst honest social concerns. If you fulfill the minimum expectations, executives may never notice how much further you've gone, and you'll have a better writing sample for yourself (not to mention doing your soul some good).

Some traditional detective shows differentiate themselves with cutting edge technology, as in *CSI*, where the real star is forensic science that engages the intellect. Detectives have always solved puzzles, of course, but *CSI*'s audience seems fascinated with futuristic tools that try the bounds of human capability. Like all traditional procedurals, the various *CSI* incarnations (and *NCIS* and many others) rely on stories that are solved by clues to wrap up a new case each week.

Ann Donahue, one of the creators and executive producers of *CSI* explained the franchise this way: "Every person your characters investigate — and it has to be based on forensic evidence — doesn't have to be guilty but they have to give you something else so the story builds, builds, builds. The other rule is you have to have a warm body by the end of Act One, within the first 17 pages. You have to have a real suspect that informs the audience about the story they're watching.

"A show's job is to entertain. It's plot-driven, and the writer should commit, tell the story, and let nothing get in the way — not educating the audience or political ideas. The hero must have desire. He must be thwarted. There must be complications.

"The difference the *CSI* franchise brought in was our production values. Each show, if it's done right, is always going to be visually intriguing and ultimately satisfying. The filmmaking is changing, but filmmaking will never replace storytelling. What I find heartening is what's always going to matter is the story and the execution of the story. When you get to the end, a good ending is surprising and yet inevitable. That's what people are waiting for.

"So every story, whether it's a medical show or a cop show or a soap opera is a mystery. A secret is going to be revealed. When are other people going to find it out? How do we see a certain person get a comeuppance? And I don't think that's ever going to change. We want it the way we always wanted it to be. We want the ending we couldn't get in our formative years."

That's still typical network fare. But on streaming and premium-cable channels, you'll see mostly ensemble casts and complex intertwining plots that are propelled by issues in the news or social concerns. Along with the many casually watched procedurals, viewers are following densely plotted novelized series with the kind of passion studio executives crave. Examples include *Better Call Saul* (AMC), *The Americans* (FX), and the limited hybrid series including *American Crime* (ABC) and *American Crime Story* (FX).

None of those shows are procedurals in the old sense. Nor could a great drama like *The Wire* be defined by its franchise, though it had cops-and-robbers. And a family drama built on personal relationships among the ensemble. And a spiritual quest built on confronting mortality and the will to survive, even in hell. It was all of those and more, which is part of what happens when creative possibilities are allowed to expand.

Are shows built from the Marvel Comics universe a franchise of their own? Think about what *Jessica Jones* and *Luke Cage* (both on Netflix) have in common with *The Shield* on ABC. How does the platform influence the content?

If I had to guess the frontier of science fiction writing on television, I would look towards the characters. In 20th century, sci-fi series (and comic books and movies), the leading edge was technology or "powers" as used by fantasy heroes, usually "perfect," in action-heavy battles between good and evil, which tended to play to children and adolescents. Though contemporary sci-fi/fantasy shows are as different as *Outlander* or *Mr. Robot* are from *The Walking Dead*, they all follow flawed human beings, and the questions they explore involve both relationships and serious issues about what it is to be a citizen of this planet; and they're watched by wide demographics. With so much range in this franchise, if you're interested in trying it, I suggest reaching up towards real dramatic writing.

The vitality of 21st century television drama has reinterpreted traditional franchises. But that doesn't mean they'll disappear.

Producer Trey Calloway, whose credits include *CSI: NY*, *Messengers*, *Revolution*, and *Supernatural*, says "franchisable" shows are essential to sell a new series to networks today. "It's not enough to have a great original idea for a series. It's as often as important to have source materials behind it — a book, a comic book, a previous television series, 'based on a . . .' It gives networks and studios a comfort level, feeling like they're plugging into an existing track record. There are certain cases when I'll have an original idea that I'll then reverse-engineer to a certain extent and go find source materials that can semi-support the idea. I can make my whole pitch and then throw the book down on the table and say oh, by the way, here's this historical figure's biography that functions as a bible for eleven seasons of the series.

"I find with increasing frequency I get phone calls from screenwriter friends of mine in the feature business who want to take me out for coffee and talk about the TV business because the feature business has dried up. So there's increased competition. How do you rise above the din?"

Calloway concludes, "I tell them networks and studios are about what's the big franchisable idea, what's going to justify our costs and run 12 seasons. They're focused on that."

When you're ready to write your own pilot or plan a script as your showpiece for a series, ask yourself what the underlying franchise is. Even if the show is innovative and evolved beyond the tradition, the franchise may give you tips for constructing your outline (more on outlines in Chapter Four).

CONCLUSION

Writing TV drama series is an adventure into an expanding universe. If you rise above outdated ideas about television, and have pride in your talent so you never write down, you can create for the most powerful medium in the world. In the next chapters, you'll find the tools you'll need, so get ready to jump on a moving rocket!

CHAPTER TWO

HOW SHOWS GET ON TV AND THE TV SEASON

Fasten your seatbelt — here comes a heady two-year ride from the first glimmer of a new series twisting through one year of development and then barreling through its first season. We'll start by touring the traditional network cycle, though you already know from Chapter One that TV is changing.

Currently, 10 to 13 episodes are typical for a season, so a season no longer takes almost a year to write, produce, and air. On top of that, streaming outlets complete entire seasons in advance and may release the episodes all at once. This new programming approach revolutionized both the production calendar and the relationship of creators to the audience.

It started with *House of Cards*. The Chief Creative Officer of Netflix, Ted Sarandos, told *The Hollywood Reporter*, "When we launched our series 13 episodes at a time the one thing everybody agreed on in this town was that it was insane. I got a call from every network executive I knew who said: 'Don't be crazy. You've got this huge investment; drag it out. Make 'em come back every week, and you could launch new things off of them.' It just sounded to me like  the same kind of managed dissatisfaction that is the entire entertainment business. I believe there's a bigger business in customer satisfaction than managing business satisfaction."

Cindy Holland, VP for Original Programming, explained that releasing all the episodes of a show at once frees them from the traditional structure of episodes designed to get audiences to return the next week. "Part of the conversation early on is thinking about it as a 13-hour movie. We don't need recaps. We don't need cliffhangers at the end. You can write differently knowing that in all likelihood the next episode is going to be viewed right away."

Sarandos agreed, "Because of our 'watch them all at once' mentality, we were able to allow them to create a dense and complicated world." He told the London-based *Guardian*: "We think we can build a better product by giving people what they want. In the world of weekly serialized TV, you get 50 minutes of joy watching the show you've been waiting for, and then 10,000 minutes of waiting for the next one. The chances are that something else is going to happen. There is too much noise in the world to depend that people are just going to come back every week."

Nevertheless, most shows on networks and cable continue to release episodes weekly, and as of 2018, they continue to boast larger audiences — viewers who do wait expectantly for their next installment. So we'll begin with a chart I included in earlier editions of this book, and as I talk you through, I'll point out each component that's in flux.

To get grounded in the long-established network pattern, look at Chart 2.1.

Chart 2.1   Traditional Two-Year Development and Production of a New Show

	Year One - Developing a new show												
	Apr	May	June	July	Aug	Sept	Oct	Nov	Dec	Jan	Feb	Mar	Apr
Create Proposal	▓												▨
Production Co.		▓											
Go to Studio			▓										
Go to Network				▓	▓								
Pilot Script						▓	▓	▓					
Green-Light									▓				
Pilot Season												▓	▓
Pick-Ups													
Staffing													
Write Like Crazy													
Debut Show													
Finish Season													
Hiatus													

"Year One" represents the months of forming and selling a new series. See the dividing line before May? That's when a new show first gets picked up by a network. In "Year Two," we'll follow a series that's in production. Month by month, you'll experience the process as if watching your own project grow up.

Let's begin by making believe you have a great idea for a television series. Screech! That was the sound of brakes. You're not likely to get your original show made if you're a beginner. At least, you're not going to do it by yourself. For decades, the custom has been to climb the ladder: You'd join a staff and go up the ranks until a network invites you to propose a series of your own. By then, the reasoning goes, you'd understand the way things work so you could reliably deliver an episode every week. No novice could have enough experience. Simply, no one would listen to you no matter how interesting your idea might be.

So let's back up and understand why beginners don't create new series. (I know, we haven't even gotten to the first month, but hold on, you will get

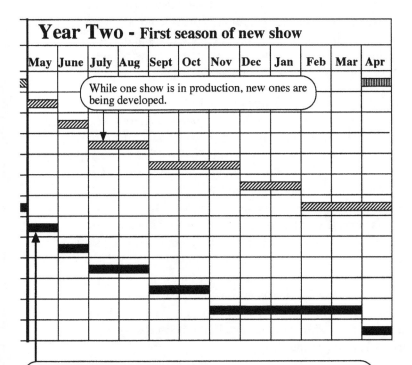

Year Two - First season of new show

While one show is in production, new ones are being developed.

In May networks announce which pilots are picked up for next season. If "yes" go to second year-- production. If "no" start over with another proposal.

on the track.) Consider what a drama series does: It manufactures hour-long films that usually air every week and continue (the producers hope) for years. Your ability to come up with a pilot (the first episode) doesn't prove you can write episode five, or 12 or the 48th episode at the end of four years. It doesn't necessarily demonstrate that the series has the "legs" for anyone else to derive a full season, either. (Having "legs" means a show has the potential to generate enough stories to last a long time.) And it surely doesn't guarantee that you would know how to run a multimillion-dollar business with hundreds of specialized employees (actors, set builders, editors, office staff, directors, truckers, camera-people, electricians, composers . . . without even counting writers).

Television series aren't bought or sold on ideas, but the ability to deliver on those ideas.

Now, don't freak. There are ways. The closed loop of staff writers becoming showrunners who hire staff writers who will one day be showrunners is loosening. Some current TV outlets are interested in twentysomething writer-producers, whose track records may be only YouTube series that have large followings or credits in award-winning independent films, journalism, or published fiction including graphic novels (comics). Since some outlets pursue teen audiences, they tend to prefer writers under 30. That's been going on for decades. But could these beginners have the experience to run a show? Here's how it worked at *The O.C.*

At 27 years old, Josh Schwartz, creator of *The O.C.*, became the youngest person in network history to produce his own one-hour series. He was a junior at the USC School of Cinematic Arts when he sold a feature script for half a million dollars. A few months later, he sold his first TV pilot. And suddenly he was a TV producer, though he never spent a day on the staff of a series. Fox supplemented him with *Sex and the City* writer Allan Heinberg, who helped structure stories for the first 13 episodes, and Bob DeLaurentis, who'd spent two decades running shows. DeLaurentis oversaw all aspects of production while Heinberg ran the writing staff. As for Schwartz, he wrote or rewrote episodes. In an article in the *New York Times*, Schwartz commented, "It's not like writing a movie — you still have to learn how to map out a season, how to track characters. It's not something I could've done by myself for the first time. You need people . . . who've been through it. Who know how to build to sweeps, or this is how a teaser works. I had to get educated."

That brings us to your starting point on:

YEAR ONE

APRIL

Your Proposal

So, here you are with your fresh idea — though I hope you have more going for you than that, even if you've never worked in television. The genesis of new shows ranges from the sublime to the ridiculous. On the high end, fifteen years of journalism covering Baltimore's police department led to a fact-based book titled *Homicide*, which was bought by experienced television producers and turned into the series *Homicide*. And a decade later, that journalist, David Simon, created *The Wire*, then *Treme*, and *The Deuce* in 2017. On the other end of the spectrum, the comedy show *$#*! My Father Says* originated in a series of tweets. You might not have years of journalism or an audience following you on Twitter, but do arm yourself with something, at least accomplishment as a screenwriter.

One of my former students, Brian Peterson, parlayed his credit on a quirky indie film *But I'm a Cheerleader* into several steps that led to writing a pilot for the WB (that became the CW). On the strength of that pilot (not produced), Peterson and his partner Kelly Souders were invited to join the writing staff of WB's show *Smallville*, and after nine years they became the showrunners. Years later, in 2017, after stints on other shows, Peterson was a writer on Nat Geo's first scripted drama series, *Genius*, about Albert Einstein, and at the same time is developing an original series. Peterson's path demonstrates TV's development as much as his own: writing an indie film led to a network series, then to an acclaimed limited series on a cable platform that was new to original dramas, and finally to an original series. For Peterson, that path covered 20 years.

In this early stage, you're not aiming to shoot a series, only to land a meeting with a production company that has a track record. So your first goal is to be "adopted." For this, you'll need the same tool that will carry you all the way to the network, so everything else rests on square one, when you're on your own. Let's assume your idea has been percolating all winter, and now in April you're ready to form it into a presentation of some kind. But what kind? Actually, this stage doesn't offer the clear guidelines you'll find in the other steps. You'll need to discover the most compelling way to put across your unique concept. With that in mind, here are six possibilities:

(1) Write a TV Format/Bible/Pitch

The term "format" can be confusing because it's used in different ways throughout filmmaking. "Format" may refer to a film stock or camera lens, to the way a script is laid out on a page, or even a genre or franchise. In this context, it means a series proposal generally referred to as a series "bible." Though a format or bible isn't an exact process, I recommend creating certain components because you'll be asked about them in meetings anyway. In reality, many proposals aren't even written except as notes for a network pitch. But I suggest you write everything, for now, to clarify your show for yourself and a production company. Lay it out this way:

Cover page: Find a title that grabs attention and suggests the tone of the show (funny, scary, dramatic, provocative, comforting, whatever). The title will probably change; think of it as a toe in a doorway. Underneath, identify the franchise or general category (i.e., teen drama, comedy-drama, political thriller, sci-fi . . .). If it's based on something (book, play, movie, comic) you'd better say so, but make sure you have clear rights to the underlying work. Your credit is "Written By" or "Created By" and that goes on a separate line. Place your contact information at the bottom of the page. If you're represented by an agent or manager, of course, the cover is done by their office and your agent will be the contact.

Do register the completed format with the Writers Guild (specifics on that are at www.wga.org). But do not put your WGA registration number on the cover — it's tacky. Also don't include any dates or draft numbers. Every draft you deliver is the first, untrammeled and never before revealed to human eyes — or that's what you'd like the producer to think. (No one wants something that's been rejected or gathering dust.)

On the top of page one, write a "logline." You've encountered that term in screenwriting classes, but did you know it originated in television? For decades, television station owners have been required by the FCC to keep a log of everything they broadcast. These had to fit on a line, like "Lassie finds lost boy." Then *TV Guide* and newspapers began printing short episode summaries like this one for *Better Call Saul*: "Jimmy takes a case he thinks will make his brother proud of him only to discover Chuck has sabotaged it to fail."

Soon the promotional tag found its way to movie posters, as in: "Tom Cruise stars as Nathan Algren, a heroic American military officer hired by the Emperor of Japan to train the country's first army. After being captured by his Samurai enemies, Algren becomes unexpectedly inspired by their way of life and fights to defend what he has come to love." Or, for a simpler example: "A singing, dancing celebration of Hollywood." Before long, either full loglines (like the one from *The Last Samurai*) or "hooks" (like the one from *La La Land*) became necessary to pitch films, episodes, and series, not merely to log them or advertise.

A logline for a series may be less specific than the story summaries you'll use for individual episodes. The goal is to orient a listener (yes, listener, not reader) to your project, to catch an executive's attention. "MTV Cops" is a famous logline for *Miami Vice* from a long-ago era when MTV was new and hot. *Grey's Anatomy*, on the heels of the success of *Sex and the City* was described as "Sex and the Surgery." Practice making loglines for current shows that you admire.

Once your logline sizzles, take the first couple of pages of your bible for an overview. This is not a summary of the pilot (a common mistake) but an introduction to the world and the quest of the whole series, including location, style, tone, context, and, most of all, characters. Though full characterizations come later, the main cast must be mentioned up front. Use brief tags like "a single, middle-aged probation officer who adopts a child from one of her cases" (from Allison Anders's series proposal *In the Echo*); or "a 29-year-old Congressional aide running against her boss" (from Rod Lurie's proposed *The Capital City*).

Within this overview, suggest springboards for future episodes so decision-makers believe the series has legs. That is, state the source of future episodes, for example: Each week the character must balance the tension of her marriage with the intrigue and politics of a legal case; each week the detectives pursue three cases, walking a thin line between vigilante justice and the job; each week we fall in love with the vampire, only to discover we're bitten again. As in any fiction writing, make 'em laugh, cry, be scared or angry or fall in love. The overview may be as far as you get in a pitch, so make it soar.

Follow the overview with the centerpiece of any series: characters. If viewers don't root for your main cast, if they're not compelled to find out how the people are coping or loving or fighting back each week, you don't have anything. Remember, TV drama isn't really about the concept; it runs on the emotional fuel of endless character arcs.

Take one page each for the few leading roles. I said few. Yes, you've seen excellent ensemble shows with casts in double digits, but in a proposal, the listener's eyes will glaze over after you get past your fourth or fifth character. So focus on one fascinating, eminently castable character, and engage us in her spirit and goals. You can do that again with roles for antagonists or partners, providing their connections to the protagonist are gripping. Beyond those few, summarize the secondary cast with only a tag for each, even if those parts will grow later.

After the characters, you need to tell some stories. You might summarize a potential pilot in a couple of pages. (More about pilot writing in a second.) But networks really need the sense of a midseason episode because that's a window to how the show functions every week. Some list loglines for all 10 or 12 potential episodes in the first season. Some describe the long arc and the end of the quest after five years on the air. Whichever method suits your series best, be sure you communicate an arena so rich that its possibilities seem endless.

That's it for standard components, but that's not it for a proposal. People refer to series pitches as dog-and-pony shows, and so far I haven't suggested any special enticements, furry or otherwise. Try photos, videos, artwork, clippings, endorsements, biographies — come up with something intriguing. If your subject is "inspired by" a true event or character, or an extraordinary experience of your own, say so. If you have a massive YouTube following, say that several times. But don't do the baked goods angle; it's been tried, and readers get annoyed — you know, placing your proposal in a cake so the executive is sure to notice it. Just don't.

TWO CAUTIONARY TALES

Before you invest too much time pitching bibles for your original shows, step back and consider the real-life experiences of "Max" and "Laurie."

Max is a former student of mine who kept in touch through the adventure that follows. He seemed to have everything going for him as he collected his fresh MFA in screenwriting. Intelligent, articulate, and savvy about the industry (or so he thought), he was quickly signed to an excellent agency on the strength of the well-polished scripts he'd written at USC. Better yet, the agent engineered a meeting with a studio that was interested in one of Max's subjects. And lo and behold, in his very first year out of school, that studio optioned Max's pilot, including a nice deal paying him to rewrite it.

He was on his way to riches and a "created by" credit on his own original show! An Emmy was being engraved with his name.

Or not. Revision notes came from various producers and studio execs that didn't always agree, and the first rewrite became a second, third . . . By the end of the six-month option period, the bloom was off the fresh script, and the studio passed. But Max had made money as a professional writer and surely he'd learned so much from this early experience his next original project would go all the way. The agent (who after all had made some money too) was game to send Max out again.

At this juncture, Max had a few choices: 1. He could ask the agent to set up appointments on existing shows in the hope of getting on a staff. 2. He could try to raise a million dollars on Kickstarter to produce his own pilot based on the rejected script and see if he could sell it that way. 3. He could write a new pilot on a different subject. 4. Or he could prepare pitches based on other ideas and see if he could get a deal to develop them.

I advised him to try to join a staff and pursue a real career, while writing fresh scripts in his off time, and return to original pitches after he was more established. But Max took option 4. He worked hard creating bibles and he pitched them, once getting as far as a network meeting. After a year, he could still have turned around and tried to join an existing staff. The money from his early option was gone by now and he was working a part-time computer job to survive. But he was sure one of these pitches was going to lead to a sale.

Five years went by. Five years. Max was writing all the time. He's a hard-working guy. But none of that work was writing a script. It was all bibles, presentations, packages, performances at meetings, and more pitches. One of his bibles ran 50 pages and detailed intricate workings of the show for years ahead, as well as a full treatment for a pilot. I told him just writing the pilot would have been less work, and then he'd have a new writing sample. But he was stuck on the dream of creating his own show and he couldn't figure out why he was failing. Then one day at the end of an especially good pitch meeting, the executive did him a favor by saying honestly, "Who are you? Your idea is good. If you were someone I'd worked with before, or I'd seen your shows or something, I'd probably put it into development. But I don't know you."

That hard truth finally sent Max back to being a writer instead of a salesman. Now he's on the staff of a series that's not his own, and he's becoming a writer that a producer might "know."

Of course, Max's experience is not the only possible outcome of a pitch. Here's a different tale — a different caution — about Laurie. She contacted me after reading the third edition of this book, and that's how I know her story, though by the time we spoke it was too late to help her.

Unlike Max, Laurie was new in town and naïve. Since childhood, she'd loved television and wanted to be part of that world, though she had written only one script on her own for a short movie. She couldn't afford to enroll in a film school but she was dedicated to learn. In Los Angeles, one-day and weekend workshops, seminars, pitch fests, and all sorts of meet-ups abound where hopefuls have a chance to pitch to people who work at various levels in television. Usually, these "special events" charge the attendees quite a lot and at best, they yield some feedback, education, and contacts. No one expects to sell a television series there. That would be like winning the Publishers Clearinghouse Sweepstakes. No one ever really makes a deal . . .

. . . Except the time Laurie pitched. She loved her TV series idea — her enthusiasm was palpable and attractive — and she told it clearly, including well-observed characters in a fresh arena and a narrative with legs. On this occasion a young producer exclaimed, "I'll buy it!" At least, that's how Laurie remembered the moment when she told it to me. Whatever he actually said, he wasn't kidding. His company was looking for a subject like hers and the elements she offered were sufficiently compelling for him to pitch it up the line. An offer was eventually made to buy her rights to the story and characters and all the other elements she presented. She was thrilled. Like Max, she was on her way to riches and a "created by" credit on her own original show! An Emmy was being engraved with her name. Right.

Too excited (and too daunted) to question the contract, she signed it as presented and deposited the check, happy that it covered her rent long enough to quit her waitress job for almost a year. And she waited for the calls to work on her own project. The calls never came. It was a simple buyout. The project was already in the hands of seasoned writers and producers who were working on the pilot. They didn't want her around.

Had she sought advice earlier (whether from me or anyone else experienced in the business) she would have been told to hire an entertainment attorney before signing anything. The lawyer might have negotiated some kind of continuing involvement, preferably a chance for Laurie to write the first draft of the pilot. Ultimately, the show was made and it aired for one season before being cancelled. As for Laurie, with no produced writing in her name, she received no screen credit and no residuals, nothing. Now she is taking a workshop in TV writing and is beginning to learn her craft by writing a spec script with guidance.

These cautionary tales don't mean you shouldn't create pitches and bibles for your original shows. You must do them. They are necessary, just not sufficient. If you are a beginner, you also need a finished pilot. And that leads us to your next task:

(2) Write a Pilot

Often, pilot scripts are assigned by networks in the course of development, and I'll tell you how that works when we get to September on the chart. (We're still only in April.) Many producers proposing a new series don't go in with a pilot already written because it's too expensive for something not likely to succeed (most proposals die, and so do most pilots). Also, network reactions might change the series. But if your writing is not yet known, and you believe a sample could motivate producers to work with you, then speculating a pilot is your smart strategy.

Matt Weiner, creator of *Mad Men*, wrote the pilot of that show while he was toiling away on sitcoms. At the time no one would buy it, but the quality of the writing landed him on the writing staff of *The Sopranos*. Years honing his skills on that great show and winning awards finally made it possible for him to produce the *Mad Men* pilot exactly as he'd envisioned it long before.

J. Michael Straczynski, creator of *Babylon 5*, is said to have written all five years of his series while he was on the staff of a *Star Trek*, so *Babylon 5* was finished before he ever proposed it. But don't try that at home, folks.

If you write (and rewrite and polish) your pilot, the worst you risk is an unsold script. If it's good, a pilot can serve as a writing sample along with any other screenplays or episodes. And as soon as you have clout (or know someone who does), you can take it off your shelf.

I'll tell you much more about writing a pilot, and take you through every step later in this book.

(3) Write a "Backdoor Pilot"

A backdoor pilot is a two-hour movie, and might be a clever way to propel a series. The game involves writing a pilot that masquerades as a movie, and, in fact, works as a closed story. But the seeds of subsequent tales and promising character developments are embedded in a situation that could easily spring many episodes.

You could offer it as a screenplay and be thunderstruck when someone else observes that it could lead to a series. Or you could come clean with your intentions up front. Depends on who you're dealing with, but you certainly should tell an agent what you have in mind.

If you're coming out of a film school that offered "screenwriting" but very little exposure to television, especially if your department emphasized classic theatrical features and traditional ways of writing, you might benefit from this option. Let's say you have two screenplays from your program. Each of the scripts completed its character and story arcs; maybe the protagonist even died, leaving you with nowhere to go. How can that be adapted to a television series?

One solution lies in the difference between episodic series and movies. Instead of trying to extend the end of your feature script, look towards the middle or even earlier. What if the same finale will be reached, but after ten or twelve hours instead of two? That involves discovering layers of characterization that were unexplored in the feature for both the main and secondary characters. Think about how this can be an opportunity to imagine the stories of minor characters and create B and C arcs in a pilot that can grow to full narratives as the season progresses. Among characters worth developing, the antagonist may offer the richest layers. Why is this person so opposed to your protagonist? Who else is propelling that person's life that was not visible in the two-hour version? These are just starting points for your imagination. In truth, though, some movies are best left as they are.

And some movies are best told in 8 to 10 hours; or looked at from the other side, some television series are movies that run 8 to 10 hours. With critically acclaimed "limited series" such as *American Crime Story*, each separate season of *American Crime*, *The Handmaid's Tale*, and *Big Little*

Lies, it's time to ask anew what the differences are between serialized television dramas and very long movies.

Does that confuse this option? It needn't. Go ahead and write your feature, if that's where you're most comfortable, keeping in mind ways to open it into a series. And if it doesn't go to series, you still have a new script.

(4) Create a Presentation Video

A showrunner once invited me to his office to discuss a series that had suddenly landed in his lap. He didn't have a clue about it, he said uneasily; it was loosely based on a hit movie and had been sold as a series on the basis of a ten-minute trailer made by one of the movie's producers who didn't have time to do the show. So the newly anointed executive producer was hastily interviewing writers to "find" the series. The problem was that ten minutes of "possible scenes" using the movie producer's actor friends (who would not be in the actual series either) didn't add up. Not that the trailer wasn't cinematic — it was beautifully atmospheric — but the group in the office were TV writers looking for the kinds of elements I've told you about: a) springboards suggesting where stories would come from; b) characters with potential for long arcs; c) some sort of quest or motor for the star. The video turned out to be sort of a Rorschach test: everyone came up with a different show . . . which meant no show at all, finally.

Even if you're not a Hollywood movie producer who can sell a series off a few scenes, a video might be helpful if used cleverly. Think of the dog-and-pony show, and imagine an executive in his office. It's 4 o'clock and he's been taking pitches every 20 minutes since his breakfast meeting at 8:00. You walk in with a laptop already cued up to a short "sizzle reel," or a clip from a web series that got great numbers on YouTube, or a 3-minute trailer that serves as a teaser for your series. He might wake up for that.

If you want to try, here are some tips:

Be careful it doesn't scream student film. You know: the long zoom into the doorknob, which is ever so beautifully lit, and the reflective moments laden with symbolism. Often, student films aim at festivals where their style is appreciated. In television, which moves faster, those same qualities may come off indulgent. So make sure your video suits the medium.

Keep it short enough so you have time to pitch before and after the video, including the set-up time. Three minutes is a possible target. You may have only 15 minutes, total, in the meeting.

Do pitch the show. The trailer is only eye candy. Unlike the movie producer, you're not going to get away with not knowing how the series is going to work.

Have fun. Creative, original filmmaking can be an exciting calling card as long as the series would be able to sustain your approach.

(5) Attach a "Package"

A "package" consists of "elements" that enhance your project's profile. Later, the package may include writers who are more credited than you, directors, main cast, possibly some special perks (for example, location, animation, or an underlying source if those are relevant), and maybe even a sponsor. Certain "packaging agencies" (the giants include CAA, William Morris-Endeavor, and so forth) pride themselves in assembling all the creative talent from within their own shop. But for you, at this stage, it might come down to nabbing a star that audiences find interesting, someone they'll tune in to see. These concerns belong to studios and networks, usually not writers, but if you're trying to load the dice, you might see who you can "attach."

Ah, there's another bit of jargon. When a writer, director, or actor is "attached," he has committed to work on your project. It's more than an expression of interest, and must be confirmed in writing. Be careful whom you attach, though. Say you've courted your idol and finally convinced her to come aboard. Then you learn the network is looking for a vehicle for their hot new thing, and will greenlight your series only if Hottie is the star. But now you're stuck with your idol. That's one of many reasons talent is rarely packaged at this point.

(6) Get a Web Following

A friend of mine was thrilled the day a major studio said they were interested in her original series. They had read her pilot and her series bible; she was represented by a respected agent; she even had a few credits. This would be the big break, she believed, as she went to the first meeting with her expected new creative home. And then they dropped the question: "What is your YouTube number?" They were interested in her project all right, but they wanted assurance that an audience would be interested. So they expected her — a writer — to somehow assemble enough of a film crew to post samples of what she was proposing online and gather "heat" before they would go forward.

My friend didn't go for it, but the approach might work for someone else. Michael Ajakwe has culti- vated the excitement around web series in his WebFest that began in Los Angeles and grew into an international festival. Ajakwe is the showrunner of *Basketball Wives*, an original series on BET, and has many other TV credits. I asked him, "With all those traditional credits, why did you make web series?"

He said, "I'm one of the fortunate ones to be able to make a living as a writer. But I do it all. It's all writing and creating — it's expression. When I was starting, I spent a year watching every web series I could find. I learned the shows had to be short, and they focused on a moment versus having a big arc. They still had to have a beginning, middle, and end. Web stories are just like all the others — even commercials have beginnings, middles, and ends. Dramatic structure still applies. Everything is just shorter. Comedies are 5, 6, minutes long; dramas are 7, 8, 9, minutes long. The only difference between a TV series and web series that are on now is length.

"A lot of people in traditional television were poo-pooing web series. But what any writer knows is that it's much more difficult to write short than to write long. You have less time to set things up. You have to get to the point. No fat. The shorter it is, the tighter it is. A lot of traditional televi- sion and movie writers dismiss web series as if they're not real writing but I knew better.

"Web series have become an amazing tool to show people what you can do. Hollywood is a closed shop, really hard to break into. Before web series, you would write a script or put on a play. A play was the cheapest thing you could do to show yourself as a writer. You put it on and invited the industry and kept it up as long as possible. But even if you had it going for months, the difficulty was getting these people who were busy all day to leave their studios and come. Now with web series you don't have that problem. You can send a postcard with a link to the web series and they can watch it. There's no problem with sending unsolicited scripts like before because the Internet is for everyone and everyone can see it."

In 2017, the *New York Times* observed, "As the number of scripted shows has more than doubled in the last several years, networks and streaming services have been mining the improv comedy, theater and digital video worlds, and even hiring people with no Hollywood experience."

Kulap Vilaysack, for example, worked her way up through comedy's improv-podcast culture, writing sketches, performing, and making short videos. Her comedy show "Bajillion" sold to Seeso, NBC's (now-defunct) streaming network devoted to comedy.

Colleen Ballinger was a YouTube star before she took the oddball character she plays online to Netflix. That's part of the migration we're witnessing from YouTube to mainstream platforms. Before you grab this as your own way in, though, keep in mind that the YouTube channel started by Ballinger had 7.7 million followers and nearly 1.3 billion views when Seeso approached her.

The *Times* commented, "All these first-time showrunners are being helped by the voracious appetite for new material fed by streaming services like Hulu, Amazon, and especially Netflix. According to FX Networks data, the combined number of original scripted shows on broadcast, cable, and premium channels has been flat since 2014, while the number of shows on streaming has exploded — to 92 from 32 — during those same years."

So if you're a young comedian with the skills, talent, and resources to make a popular web series, you have a new way to bypass the traditional ladder, especially in comedy. TV drama series tend to require more experience, but with hybrid comedy/dramas, the possibilities are expanding.

Go ahead and try them all — one through six — if you have the time and money. But that would take another year. So to stay on our cycle, let's make believe you've created a terrific bible, and backed it up with impressive writing samples. Now you move ahead to square two:

MAY

THE PRODUCTION COMPANY

You're on the hunt for a production company with your new series as bait. In May, you might get a producer's attention because the previous season has ended and work for the new one not quite begun. If your proposal is ready sooner, you could also "put out feelers" in April during "hiatus." (You'll hear about the hiatus in Year Two.) Now, you need a company that can get you into both a studio and a network. Better yet, try to meet a showrunner who has an "open commitment" or "blind overall deal," which means a network is obligated to buy a show from him. Who knows, the producer just might be searching for something new.

But how are you going to find them? Through your agent or manager; like it or not, that's how this industry works. The professional agencies and top management companies know who's willing to take series pitches, who is between shows, who might spark to your idea, who is willing to deal with a beginner, and who has relationships at the kinds of outlets that fit your show. The agent can put you in the room. So if you already have an agent you can skip this section. NOT! Don't ever lie back and think an agent is going to do it all for you. To paraphrase: Agents help those who help themselves. If you don't have one, see Chapter Six, "How to Break In."

But what if you're determined to plow ahead on your own? It's not impossible to get to production companies, and in some cases they may be more accessible than agents or managers. Comb websites, especially online versions of the *Hollywood Reporter*, *Deadline Hollywood*, *Variety*, and others to scope the companies interested in developing new series. If you have the magic bullet for a company who needs to get with the times and climb back to the top, or if you're young, talented, have some awards or credits, and an aggressive personality, you may well get past the receptionist. Part of the technique is finding the perfect match to your sensibility and your project.

The match-up involves two halves — who are you and who are they? Let's start with you. In the past, television was an exclusive club of white men. Now is a good time for well-prepared writers of all descriptions. The "2017 Hollywood Diversity Report" released by the Ralph J. Bunche Center for African American Studies at UCLA analyzed 1,200 television programs from the 2014–15 season on broadcast, cable, digital, and via syndication. Darnell Hunt, Director of the Center, said, "There is so much original television production. It used to be the big four networks. Now there are all the digital networks. . . . The industry has to fill the space, so they can't go back to the same 15 white guys. It created opportunities."

On broadcast networks, shows such as *Fresh Off the Boat* and *Empire* were staffed by a majority of "minority" writers in 2017. In scripted cable, women accounted for 20.9% of show creators, an increase of almost 3% from the previous year. Showtime's *Masters of Sex* created by Michelle Ashford and HBO's *Girls* by Lena Dunham (both now off the air) are two examples, besides all the series from Shonda Rhimes's company. In digital programming, women improved even more from the previous year. Jill Soloway's *Transparent* and Melissa Rosenberg's *Jessica Jones* and any shows by Jenji Kohan, including *Orange Is the New Black*, are examples of the emerging presence of women as show creators, up by 5 percentage points to 20.4% of all creators on streaming outlets. Since 51% of the U.S. population is female, 20% representation among executive producers is not proportionate, but if you're a woman you have a better chance than in the past to be pitching to a woman producer or for a man to take you seriously. And by the time you read this, the numbers will probably be higher.

As this is written, around 500 scripted television series are in production in Los Angeles right now. That's a lot of work for anybody, no matter who you are if you have mastered your craft. Focus on your strengths and look for the companies that will vibe to what you have to offer.

Seeing who *they* are depends on what you want to see. Maybe that sounds cryptic, but television is not a monolith and neither are the production companies. That's where knowing who you are fits in. For example, the audience for Crackle, Sony's streaming network, is mostly young, male gamers who like action. If that's you, and you have a caper show, research the companies producing for Crackle.

Do you like old shows from the 20th century? Do you avoid challenging or topical issues? Do your stories have happy endings? Have you lived in small towns or rural areas? Well, you may be in luck with production companies that feed traditional networks if their 2017 roster is an indication.

It seems traditional broadcast networks want to be America's security blanket by opting for shows that are safe and familiar to viewers. In 2017, NBC brought back *Will & Grace* that ran from 1996 to 2006. ABC returned *Roseanne*, a hit from 1988 to 1997. The 1980s soap *Dynasty* was revived at the CW. And the 1970s cop drama *S.W.A.T.* ran on CBS.

These programming choices were probably a reaction to the 23% decline in primetime broadcast viewers who are 18 to 49. In fact, the audience for broadcast networks has been growing older for a long time. In 2017, the median age for ABC and NBC was 56, and 60 at CBS. Jason Maltby, president of National Video for Mindshare, said bringing back these titles might be a way of acknowledging that "their bread and butter going forward is going to be on the older end of the audience spectrum." It might not be just a matter of age, though. When people feel anxious about national and world events, they tend to reach for feel-good entertainment.

Considering all those revivals, you might wonder if networks have room for your new show. Well, that depends on what you have to offer. Here's what happened with *This Is Us* on NBC. Dan Fogelman, whose writing-producing credits include the movie *Crazy, Stupid Love* and several TV series, told *Emmy Magazine*, "I'm never going to write something really dark and messed up, because it's not my point of view. . . . I'm going to make people laugh and hit them with something emotional — but hopefully not manipulative."

The project started like the paths we've been discussing. Originally, he saw *This Is Us* as a movie, and began a feature script. But he said that after writing seventy or eighty pages, "it wasn't feeling like a movie." So he dropped it but couldn't get the abandoned characters out of his mind. He realized, "The reason I was struggling with [the film] wasn't the plot; it was about these characters and how I didn't want to 'beginning-middle-and-end' them. I wanted to do this continuous story — which felt very much like the theme of the show." Soon, Fogelman had a 50-page pilot script, which he brought to the studio where he had a deal, and it ultimately found its home at NBC.

The last part is probably not available to you. Fogelman has his own production company and relationships with other producers as well as a deal at a studio. But his show demonstrates an appetite for a kind of material. Ken Olin, one of the producers, told *Emmy*, "I don't know whether *This Is Us* would have been the same success at a time when people feel safer. I think there's a great need for a humanist sensibility and a voice for hope. And not schmaltzy hope. [*This Is Us*] is saying that we can see life for as difficult and sad as it can be at times and still find decency, honor, and truth."

In contrast to traditional networks, streaming and cable outlets have their arms out for innovation. Warren Littlefield, executive producer of *The Handmaid's Tale* for Hulu, told the *Los Angeles Times*, "The digital platforms and streaming platforms have absolutely said, 'we are your home' . . . for groundbreaking, edgier, younger audience appealing content."

The template for premium off-network TV is still HBO. *The Economist* wrote that HBO "has lavished good, smart product on its viewers, and in the process raised the entire industry's creative game. In the late 1990s HBO pioneered an intelligent, patient style of storytelling that gloried in loose ends and morally ambiguous characters, a style *The Sopranos* came to epitomize.

Even with all the innovative breakthroughs on streaming and premium-cable channels today, HBO offers real creative freedom. Alan Ball, who won an Oscar for writing *American Beauty* before joining HBO to create *Six Feet Under*, contrasts HBO with the 'gulag' of broadcast television. He remembers flurries of notes from network executives that squeezed the original ideas out of his scripts. At HBO the notes are fewer and actually helpful."

David Simon, creator of *The Wire*, had a similar writing experience at HBO. He told Alan Sepinwall in *The Revolution Was Televised*: "My rhythms are prose rhythms to an extent. In the beginning the one thing prose could do that TV couldn't do was tell a sophisticated, complicated story. [Network] television couldn't do that because they needed the episodes to stand alone."

When I interviewed Michael Lombardo, HBO's President of Programming, for my earlier book *The Future of Television*, he told me: "The minute we program derivatively or reactively we've lost sight of who we are and what brought us to this place. The HBO brand stands for clear, distinct voices. Our role is to listen to — and believe in — a voice and help the creators do their best work. We don't micromanage. If a show requires us to help craft and execute it, then it's probably not the right show for us. We create a place where we trust the creative vision, and where our number one priority is to keep the creators feeling happy, engaged, and supported.

"HBO starts with great writing. There's no cheat to it. There's nothing except it starts with the writing, and that has been our mantra from early on. Going forward, it continues to be our mantra in a world where there's a lot of noise — 'event television,' 'branded content.' For us, it still comes down to the writing.

"When I think about what has worked for us, it's less about event programming than about passion engagement. What works is something really well told with an authentic voice. We're not in the business of looking to take a swing on a show thinking this is going to get the most eyeballs in the world. Our subscriber is expecting us to do more than that — they can get that on free television. They're expecting singular voices here. They're expecting well-crafted shows here. They're expecting shows that don't cheat, that don't take the easy route, that challenge the viewer. We have to stay true to that."

If that sounds like a perfect fit for you, well, take a breath. You're not likely to sell your first big drama series to HBO. The competition there is too tough. But think about the companies that produce shows you admire for

HBO. Those same producers may also place shows elsewhere, and you can reach out to showrunners who have their own production companies too.

That's what writers Liz Flahive and Carly Mensch did in launching their series *Glow*. They knew each other from a New York writers' group and wrote together on Showtime's *Nurse Jackie*. After seeing a documentary about female wrestlers, they thought it would make great material for a series. Mensch said, "We sent Jenji Kohan (creator of *Orange Is the New Black*) a one-line email asking if she wanted to work on a show about women's wrestling in the '80s, and she wrote back, 'Yes.'"

Whatever your tactic, start by researching. At the tail of each episode, you'll see a list of producing entities. Sometimes several logos appear because an expensive series may spread the cost among various backers, so to find out who is actually developing the series, try phoning the show or the network and asking. Other resources include show websites, Wikipedia, the Library of the Writers Guild of America, the Television Academy, and The Paley Center for Media.

Once you have your targets, email them and follow with a call asking to pitch your series idea. Don't send the bible, but if you can catch the reader with a beguiling a few sentences, you may flush out someone curious enough to take a brief meeting. You don't need to wait for a response from your first choice before hitting up a second place. Contact them all at once.

At the meeting, you need to hook the listener quickly. Of course, you hope that listener is an executive producer or head of the production company. But if you're shunted off to an assistant, go ahead anyway. Make an ally so you'll have a chance to repeat the pitch to the decision maker another day.

What are they looking for? Energy. That's amorphous, I know, but it covers the sense that the series has possibilities. Remember, a series pitch is not the same as telling a movie story where the plot beats need to be in place. This is the first step in a long development process, and if this company becomes involved, they'll probably steer you towards revisions so the project will sell, or so it fits in a specific programming slot, or competes with other series coming down the pike. They'll be watching how flexible you are, wondering if they'd be comfortable working with you for years, kind of a blind date. If you're defensive or reluctant to revise your precious property, they'll wish you luck trying to do it all by yourself — elsewhere.

They'll be checking whether the concept is viable; that is, whether they can physically produce it each week within a likely budget. But they won't ask that question unless you satisfy two other qualifications: (1) The show is completely new and unique, and (2) the show is exactly like what has succeeded before. Yes, it's a paradox. One solution is to be original within a franchise, even if that franchise is reinterpreted, as I discussed in the first chapter.

And, of course, you know what every TV series needs above all. Come on, you know the answer: Characters. The heart of your pitch is how fully you engage the buyer in the people you have created. But you already know that from your bible, because you're well prepared.

So let's imagine you've pitched to a few executive producers and settled on one company that has everything: a studio deal, the juice to take you to a network, the ability to deliver the show, the willingness to keep you in the loop even though you're a beginner; and, most of all, they "get" your idea. You've found a creative home.

Maybe.

JUNE

THE STUDIO

I'll try to guide you gently through a maze of cross-ownerships to a simpler place that's relevant to how a lone writer might interact with these behemoths. After a production company partners on your project, they will take you to the next step — a studio lot where you'll meet with a grand poo-bah. So here comes a little context:

Once upon a time in 1970, rules existed to prevent the Big Three television networks from monopolizing all broadcasting by preventing them from owning any of the programming they aired in prime time. Those rules were repealed in the 1990s. Immediately, media companies like Disney, Viacom, News Corp., and Time Warner made purchases that combined studios and networks to create new kinds of corporate entities. And the networks populated their schedules with new shows purchased from studios they owned, effectively shutting out independents.

That led to where we are today when all networks have their in-house production companies and they own (or co-own) cable outlets. For example, NBC-Universal — NBCU owns not only Universal Studios and NBC network but also cable channels including Telemundo, USA Network,

Syfy, E!, CNBC, MSNBC, Bravo, the Weather Channel, and a 32% interest in Hulu. CBS owns Showtime and CW, among many other businesses. Quickly, Hollywood turned into more of a conglomerate and dominated the global entertainment industry. Now six Hollywood studios exist, each as part of a larger media empire: Sony, 21st Century Fox, Warner Bros., Paramount, NBC/Universal, and ABC/Disney.

The trend towards concentrating power was exacerbated with the threatened end to "Net neutrality." We're going to take a brief detour to put your journey into perspective.

Meanwhile, at this writing in 2017, the Disney Company is buying entertainment assets owned by 21st Century Fox, including the Fox television studio, the FX cable network, and a share of Hulu. According to the *Los Angeles Times*, "The deal would not only transform Hollywood into a land of fewer studio giants, but also fire clear warning shots to technology giants like Netflix, Amazon and Google. The message: Legacy media — or at least Disney, the king of them all — isn't going down without a fight."

Disney's takeover of the majority of Hulu may impact writers most directly. As the Times reports, in a business driven by the volume of quality content, Disney could boost Hulu's standing with more shows. Until now, Hulu has operated only in the U.S. and Japan, but Disney's clout will expand its reach internationally. "Big players like Disney are seeking to get bigger as they follow Netflix into the streaming business, and square off against tech giants like AT&T, which is acquiring Time Warner."

On top of that, Amazon Studios that produces only for Amazon calls itself a studio. Marvel Studios that has a deal with Netflix also sells to other networks and makes movies. And in-house production units such as ABC Studios make shows sold apart from their home bases. The media landscape is too complicated to describe here, but the reach of the studios you're encountering is worth appreciating before you venture to the next step.

Most production companies can't go to the networks by themselves. That's because network series are mostly "deficit financed." That's not the case with online companies like Netflix and Amazon that finance their own shows, but traditional networks pay a fee to broadcast each program, around 75% of the cost of making it. For an hour-long drama, the shortfall can be millions of dollars per week. Every week. Individual production companies don't have that.

Studios do. Think of the studio as the bank. From the point of view of a "suit," every time a studio endorses a series with one of the production companies on their lot they're taking a calculated risk. Years may go by before they see any return on their investment, if they ever do, and most shows are cancelled before that. But, oh, when a show is a hit they can make profitable deals selling the show to cable channels, online platforms, syndication, foreign markets, and ancillary products. A single hit underwrites years of failures. Will yours be that hit?

That brings us back to you. Probably, you have no written agreement with the production company. They're waiting to see if the studio will get behind this project. While you're away, the producer is talking to the Vice President for Dramatic Series Development of the studio where he has a deal. If the producer loves your show, he's pre-pitching it, maybe touting you as the next great thing.

Or not. He may be testing the waters to see if you're approvable before he sticks in his own toe. That might involve sending your writing samples to a studio executive, or even, quietly, to a contact at one of the networks. He may also test the general "arena" of the show, without specifically pitching it: "Any interest in a drama about house plants? I have a great fern." Prepare yourself, because if weak signals start coming back from the studio, he might drop the project; or he might keep the project but begin nudging you aside. You'll know you're being dumped if his conversation includes the term "participating," if he floats names of possible writers who aren't you, and if he talks up the title "associate producer." Sometimes that indicates an actual job, but it might be honorary, a way to shift you off the writing staff. Remember, you do have the right to say no and take your project elsewhere.

Let's imagine someone up there thinks you're interesting, at least enough to let you audition. So on you go to the studio lot. But this time, you and the producer will refine and rehearse your pitch, and together, you'll go to the V.P.

If your producer is powerful, and he has an open commitment or overall deal, the studio may let him make network appointments on his word alone. If he's not that strong, or he's not so confident of your show, he'll ask you to pitch your heart out again, this time to the network. Though your original bible has been revised, you're essentially presenting what you developed in April. But now the producer is sitting next to you, and you're talking to a big desk.

Let's say you pass "Go." You advance to the next squares:

JULY AND AUGUST

THE NETWORK

Traditional network television operates on the lemming model: All the creatures rush to the precipice at the same time and most fall off. You'll observe this behavior in most of the following stages.

This model describes most broadcast and cable, but does not apply to streaming platforms (and some cable) that are open for new shows all year. Since Internet real estate is unlimited, digital networks don't have to program a certain number of hours and cut off development until new slots open for the next season. It's a different way of making television, and we'll explore one example in the Amazon experiment later in this section. Now I'm giving you the traditional schedule because it can help you plan.

The broadcast networks "open" for new series pitches during the summer. They announce an exact opening date to agencies, and sometimes it's in the trade press. Depending on their needs — that is, how many series are returning, how many slots they have to fill for the fall — some might begin meetings in June, and some might be hearing proposals as late as October. You want to get in there as soon as possible, before they're filled, though they're inundated no matter when you go. And the playing field isn't level. The big shots (companies with successful shows on the air) will have scarfed up prime meetings before yours is even scheduled.

The process is well established and organized, though it looks like a shell game to an outsider. Each network may hear around 500 pitches during their open season. Out of those, each chooses fifty to a hundred to become pilot scripts. Of those, ten to twenty might be made into pilot films. Out of those, a few become series. Those numbers vary each year, but here's a simplified example from just one of the four broadcast networks: Take twenty percent at each cut — 500 pitches yield 100 pilot scripts yield 20 pilots, which yield four series. That's a ten percent overall chance of making a sale, if all else was equal, which, of course, it isn't.

Instead of dwelling on the odds, let's stay focused on your own opportunity. First, understand the human side of what you're walking into at a network. The Vice President for New Dramatic Programs and the Director of New Dramatic Programs (along with a lesser title, Manager of New Dramatic Programs) are taking meetings all day, every day, for three or four months. A parade of showrunners come in and out of that office every

20 minutes or so. In fact, your own producer may be fielding other shows besides yours, which means they're in competition with you.

On the day of the meeting, everyone is dressed up. You'll gather in the lobby with your executive producer and possibly someone representing the studio, an agent from a major packaging agency (likely, the producer's agent), and other components of your package. That might mean a network-approved high-power writer who would guarantee the pilot script, or a television star.

I once went to a network pitch on a show where the lead actor was essential. When the day came, the actor was called to a dubbing session. And we couldn't change the appointment. So we went in with a blow-up of his head shot and sat it on a chair.

You'll have a cheering section in your meeting, and the first little while will seem like friendly greetings. Then the moment comes when the producer says, "You're on," the room falls silent, and all eyes are on you. Now, pitching to a network executive is a craft unto itself. Some execs nod, smile, and act interested. With others, it's like talking to Mount Rushmore. Regardless, keep your energy high. With the nice guy, you skip out of the meeting sure you just sold a series. With the mountain, you believe you failed. Neither might be true.

If you haven't heard in a week or two, the studio (or your producer, depending on the network relationship) phones the network. They're usually pretty quick about saying no, and in that case, the studio will set up a meeting at the next network on the list. This can go on a few times, but after two or three networks and a couple of calls to cable, if you're not getting a nibble, they'll probably drop your project. Remember, the property is still yours at this point, and no one owes anybody anything.

THE AMAZON EXPERIMENT

In an industry earthquake, Amazon broke into scripted television with original series in 2013, bringing an outsider's approach. Unlike Hollywood studios and networks, Amazon is a mass merchandiser based in Silicon Valley, home of computer-driven data. Its marketing experience said the number of stars a vacuum cleaner amasses tells customers which one to buy, so they figured the number of stars a television proposal can garner from whoever decides to vote online should determine which shows the network makes.

Fan ratings aren't new even when it comes to art; on broadcast networks singing contests routinely allow audiences to choose winners by voting. But that's not the same as influencing the *creation* of art; viewers don't decide what notes a singer should hit, only who they like best. In contrast, mass "collaboration" on writing a television series — where the public weighs in on how a story should end or how a character should develop — is one of the issues raised by Amazon's crowd-sourcing initiative for their new shows. Should an aggregate of random voices mold artistic expression? Then what is the role of the artist? Ultimately, as you'll see below, Amazon arrived at an epiphany about the value of the individual passion-driven creator, but they didn't get to that until later.

After launching their first pilot orders in 2013, former Amazon Studios director Roy Price was quoted in Deadline.com: "We built Amazon Studios so that customers could help decide which stories would make the very best movies and TV shows."

Price contended in the article that crowd-sourcing is more efficient than the way other media companies make shows and movies by investing big dollars in proven screenwriters, directors, and actors. "By and large, your $80 million is out the door. You're certainly not going to be able to unmake the movie and go make a different movie that people want to see."

What was he suggesting? Was he saying they could avoid spending the money needed to hire capable and experienced writers because amateurs can do it just as well, for a whole lot less money, if guided by haphazard bystanders? I wonder. Would you buy a vacuum from a company that had never made one before? Would you trust a dentist to work on your teeth if he hadn't gone to dental school?

So how did that experiment work out?

Well, around 5,000 pilot scripts were uploaded to Amazon Studios through their open submissions site, almost all from non-professionals (writers who don't have agents or managers and are not members of the Writers Guild). Amazon posted 25 pilots online. Viewers rated them and made development recommendations on the ones to bring to series.

So how many of the open-submission contest entries became series? Zero. Amazon did move forward into production with other shows. But they all came from major talent agencies.

Nevertheless, Joe Lewis, Amazon Studios programming chief, told the *Los Angeles Times*, "We're focused on breaking down the walls of Hollywood. Thanks to our open submission policy anybody in the world can get a script to Amazon development."

Clearly, they're dedicated to appearing populist. *Wired Magazine* described their strategy as actually "a giant decentralized TV focus group. The company planned to use the viewing data and feedback not just to select but to tweak the projects."

Television Critic Robert Lloyd wrote in the *Los Angeles Times*, "The democratic aspect is deceptive. While Amazon wants to know what you think of its pilots, the decisions about which ones to make in the first place took place in executive suites far from your eyes or mouse-clicking fingers. It may bring you in at an earlier-than-usual stage in the process, but it's fundamentally the same as a TV network judging what shows to keep making by viewership, demographic analysis, and buzz.

"Even the public-rating feature, despite being ballyhooed as an innovation is fundamentally old-fashioned, an Internet-age variation on the preview cards and focus groups studios have used for nearly a century. It is not the case, as has been reported that viewers are being asked to 'vote' on the series, as if to pick which will be produced; rather, they are being asked to leave comments and take surveys that will 'help' Amazon give the people what the metrics say the people want."

Still, Roy Price enthusiastically advanced the idea of Amazon Studios as a place for experimentation. In a presentation at the Television Academy, Price explained, "What we want is to have a system that is broadly open to ideas, where we can get as many ideas as possible directly to the actual audience, not a small group of people that are representative of the audience.

"That's why we do pilots. . . . I think pilots allow you to be more experimental. If you're going to order things straight to series, the list of people you're capable of doing that with is very small. You're basically only going to work with 25 people or so. . . . If you have a lot of pilots, you can take chances. You can explore the boundaries of writing something more experimental. So hopefully we can find something new and different."

Price continued, "In an on-demand world the value of the pretty good show is diminished. There's no linear schedule. There's no feed-in show. So you need people to be reaching out to your show in all cases. It creates a some-what different dynamic. You have to really pay attention to the number of people for a given show who are passionate fans. For instance if we had ten people and nine out of ten people think a show is good-ish; but you have another show where six out of ten are pretty indifferent but two or three are really passionate, in an on-demand environment the second may wind up being more distinctive and more valuable and adding value to the set of TV choices people have."

Finally, here's the epiphany: Price concluded that the experience ulti-mately taught them the choices weren't actually about the crowd data. "You have to ask a different question: tell me about where that show is coming from. What people consistently respond to is a show where you have a passionate, talented creator who has a vision for a great show who wants to do a show that is new and interesting. A focus on that has a very strong correlation to success. That is the best thing we learned from the data."

Years later, Amazon's experimental mindset brought them *Transparent* by Jill Soloway and other innovative shows. Soloway is an experienced writer and producer, very much a woman with her own vision; her breakthrough films are not the products of crowd-sourcing. So it might be that Amazon's spirit for experimentation was more powerful than the data-mining process the executives had imagined. And, funny thing, it worked — Amazon became a leading platform for experimental storytelling in the whole televi-sion industry, at least for a while.

Then in 2018, Price was replaced by Jennifer Salke, who championed *This Is Us* as president of NBC Entertainment. At Amazon she quickly signed *Get Out* writer/director Jordan Peele and other major talent. It would seem that Amazon's pioneering experimentation has given way to main-stream economics.

Whether you went through the traditional network system or one of the digital options, now you move on. Let's say in your meetings that you were intriguing and fresh and fun in the room. And the network thinks your show fits their goals. You pass Go again. Of course, you're not greenlighted to make a series — you know better than that by now. The assignment is only to write the pilot. That's the next group of squares:

SEPTEMBER TO NOVEMBER

THE PILOT SCRIPT

Whoever writes the pilot will have at least a "developed by" credit, and may even receive "created by" credit on the series. That will generate a royalty on every episode, and that person's name will appear on screen forever, even if the pilot writer is long gone. Don't assume that's you unless your writing proves that only you can capture the style and world you've proposed.

Or have you already written the pilot? If you took a chance on it, the producer will wonder if it's going to hurt or help your prospects. That's a sticky situation because asking you to set aside your pilot in favor of someone else's draft is emotionally wrenching. But if you lose the whole deal because your pilot is less than mind blowing that's just as wrenching.

Some professional writers have built careers doing pilots for other people's shows. They're savvy about the ingredients any pilot needs, they bring a pedigree of successful series, and they know how to win over network readers. It's an oddity because these special pilot writers, who may earn around half a million dollars for a one-hour script, usually are not the ones who will write the episodes each week, so network decision-makers are evaluating a hyped up version of the show. It's kind of a bait-and-switch where they're buying one writer's voice, but another will write the series.

Let's say they love your project because they love something about you — your writing style, insight into a subculture, your humor, your passion. Or maybe you're just less expensive — $50,000 for the pilot script instead of $500,000. Now the network calls the studio that calls the producer who calls your agent who calls you and you get a contract to write.

So, how do you do this thing? Pilots come in two flavors: *premise* and *midstream*. A premise pilot begins with a "before" and propels the quest or situation the central character will tackle throughout the series. For example, *Orange Is the New Black* opens the day before Piper, the lead character, goes to prison. Life in her upscale Manhattan townhouse crashes into her new reality as we experience being processed into Litchfield Women's Prison moment by moment through her viewpoint. Drawn into this new world, we meet characters who will become Piper's new relationships, and their arcs are set in motion.

In the pilot of *The Walking Dead*, Rick wakes up from a coma to a world of zombies. We discover the horror along with him, and worry how to survive. In the many seasons that follow, human characters are tested by their own humanity, more than by zombies, so the pilot had to root us in credible characters that viewers would care about, while introducing a premise that is not actually credible.

Similarly, the premise pilot of *Outlander* delivers Claire from 1942 to 1742 through a time travel device that would be unbelievable except that the characters and romance that follow feel so natural and compelling to viewers that the leap becomes part of the experience.

In contrast, a midstream pilot presents the world of the show already in place and characters that are entrenched in their dramatic missions. The challenge is to reveal these characters and relationships without the aid of an introduction, which we had with Piper, Rick, and Claire.

An example of a midstream pilot is *Jessica Jones*. We meet her as a young woman full of angst, lust, and alcohol working as a private detective, who, incidentally, has some super-powers. Her world is well established. A first assignment reopens the revenge she seeks against a past oppressor, and thus begins both the procedural and serial elements that roll out from the pilot.

In *Empire*, another midstream pilot, palace rivalries are already in play as Cookie rejoins the Lyon music kingdom after years in prison. That's an inciting incident within the pilot, and the style of the show is new to viewers, but this world has always existed for this family.

The same can be said of *The Wire* and other dense serials including *Game of Thrones*. We are plunged into the deep end of an environment filled with characters we don't yet know, and somehow we have to swim. It's like real life if you suddenly found yourself a stranger in Baltimore or Winterfell and had to navigate the layers of society in place before you arrived.

Whichever type of pilot you choose, you'll need the same ingredients. In addition to terrific writing, which includes building tension and creating rich and provocative characters, just as you would in any episode (see Chapter Three for more about this), pilots have a special burden of exposition. Without the audience feeling they're being informed, you need to establish the rules of your world, the engine for future stories (springboards), and enough "backstory" (history) on the characters so their current situation is understandable. You want viewers riveted by the characters. Simply, your pilot has to make people tune into episode two.

Some techniques are similar to beginning a feature, where audiences don't yet know the characters either. But features are easier because once people have bought tickets and are sitting in the dark, they'll give a movie time to unveil itself. Television has to grab people in the first minutes or they're clicking off. So, sure, use everything you know from theatrical screenplays in terms of presenting a new character, but start the story faster. Also, use everything you've learned about avoiding clunky exposition (bury it in an argument, play it in a scene instead of explaining, use visual evidence, parse it out in bits, reveal it as part of the plot instead of for its own sake, and so forth). If you're "living" your writing, instead of manipulating it, some of these problems may solve themselves. And if those central characters and your idea are as vibrant as the bible you pitched, the pilot might come naturally.

Easy or difficult, approximately 50 pages are going to be due at the network around Thanksgiving. From a network's point of view, it will be the first draft. Of course, it won't. You will have gone through every step with your producer, and the studio may have read drafts as well. No one wants to take a chance this won't work, so if your drafts aren't delivering the spirit that landed this assignment, they'll bring in another writer, who will share the writing credit. So all through October and November you're rewriting like crazy — you and everyone else who's doing a pilot. And, true to the lemmings, everyone else's pilot is due at all the networks the same time as yours. All over town, everyone is anticipating:

DECEMBER AND JANUARY

THE GREENLIGHT

Several possibilities: The network may send notes for a second draft of the pilot. If so, you'll gnash your teeth: What do they mean they don't like the central character — that's exactly who I pitched, and that's who they bought! They wait until *now* to tell me they have another pilot too close to this, so we have to change everything! What am I supposed to do with a note like "not funny enough" when this drama was never supposed to be funny at all! No, I can't turn this drama about men in prison into a vehicle for Lady Gaga!

This is the world of traditional networks that tend to be extremely involved in the creative process. We will follow the network system here because it represents most of what gets on mainstream television. But for perspective, here's a reminder of the alternate universe off-network:

How *House of Cards* Happened on Netflix

Screenwriter Beau Willimon told Dina Gachman of *Studio System News*, "When we first started talking I think we envisioned a show that was made for cable most likely and those were the outlets we were aiming for. At the same time, it came to our attention that Netflix was interested and wanted to meet. We had no idea what to really expect of the meeting, but in that very first meeting, they said, 'We want to get into the originals game; we want *House of Cards* to be our first show.'

"So we said we wanted a first season guarantee from the get-go, and they said, 'We'll not only give you one season, we'll give you two. And we'll give you creative freedom.' When you have that sort of offer, it's one that you can't really refuse. It's one that the competing suitors couldn't match or weren't willing to match because they have their mandates for how they do business, and that's a scary proposition. It's a scary offer for a lot of people, but in our case, it seems to have worked out."

Willimon explained, "They have access to the scripts, and we share dailies with them. They come to the table reads. After a table read, I might get some coffee with Cindy Holland [VP for Original Programming] or Jonathan Friedland [Chief Communications Officer] and say, 'Hey, what did you think, do you have any thoughts?' There's no corporate dictate. It's a conversation, and they're smart, insightful people. I'm interested to hear what they think, and sometimes I incorporate some of those thoughts, but . . . I've never received a document with a list of notes on it. Every conversation we have is all in service of the show.

"It's not as though we disappear into a little bubble, and six months later, say, 'Here you go, Netflix.' They know what's in the pipeline, Ted Sarandos said in that first meeting, 'We want you to make the show you want to make; we trust you.' We take that responsibility very seriously. When you get to make what you want to make, if something is bad there's no one to blame but yourself. With that kind of encouragement, they're getting the very best work out of the artists that they trust. I don't think any network executive could be as rigorous with notes as we are on ourselves."

Back to the world of traditional network television, we rejoin your path after the post-notes teeth gnashing. You'll sit with the producer and maybe your studio development person and figure out what you can fix, and what, if anything, may be left alone or argued. If they believe your situation is precarious, the studio may ask for a major rewrite. In any case, your finished script is due by Christmas — the same as everyone else.

And like everyone else, you're hoping your pilot script will be plucked out as one of the twenty or thirty percent that get "greenlighted." That means the network gives the production company the go-ahead to produce the pilot. These greenlights may be announced anytime from December through January. They lead to:

FEBRUARY TO APRIL

PILOT SEASON

Instead of snow, a climate of anxiety hangs in the sunny skies of Los Angeles in winter. It's accompanied by a giant sound of vacuuming, inhaling all unclaimed film crews down to the last grip and gaffer, all the soundstages, every available television director, and all the actors who cycle through pilots year after year in "holding deals" (contracts which hold an actor exclusive to a potential series). George Clooney was cast in fifteen failed pilots before *ER*. Welcome to pilot season.

Though it begins with your script, the produced pilot is enhanced by "production values" (locations, techniques, or personnel) that make it much more expensive than a normal episode.

When fully edited, a typical pilot will be 44 minutes long, the length of a broadcast or cable hour without ads. But once in a while a network asks for a 20 or 25-minute "presentation" instead, like a demo for a record company. That's bad news for you as the writer, because your finely honed 50-page script must be slashed to 25 pages, losing secondary storylines, nuance, and sometimes risking the sense of the show. Networks order these presentations anyway because they might cost roughly a third the possible cost of a pilot. If this befalls you, just sit down and cut the pages. You really don't have a choice.

Except for production revisions (for casting, location, timing, and so forth), the writer's work is essentially finished by February. Still, I advise you to stick as close as you can to the production. If the producers will let you, be on the set, see the "dailies," go to meetings. Of course, you know better than to breathe down the director's neck or stand in the way of rolling cameras. Just don't fade out after you write "fade out."

By April, all the pilots in all genres at all the networks are edited and tested at the same time. This testing, incidentally, is a tribal ritual in itself. Unwitting tourists in Las Vegas (chosen because Vegas attracts visitors from all over the country) are given gift certificates in exchange for registering their reactions on an electronic dial while viewing a pilot. If something scores poorly, it may be reedited; it's way too late to rewrite, though. With the pilots done, it's time for:

MAY

PICK-UPS

All the lemmings arrive at the edge of the precipice at once — and off they go to New York by May. Isn't it strange that shows are (usually) produced in Los Angeles, and network and studio executives are based here, and the entire creation of the pilot happens on the West Coast, yet the verdict is rendered 3,000 miles away? That's because the decision is corporate, involving huge investments that impact parent companies and involve advertisers who (they hope) offset those costs. It's Big Brother time.

If you dig into financial sources, you'll discover not all shows are actually financed through New York, or anywhere in the United States, for that matter. The BBC is behind much of what is on Starz premium cable, and shows like *Orphan Black* and *Sherlock* are also British productions or co-productions. Their green lights (and sometimes notes) are filtered through London. Meanwhile, colossal series like *Game of Thrones* require the kind of international financial consortium you'd imagine backing a slate of blockbuster movies or massive construction projects. And, as we've discussed, online sites like Amazon and Netflix have a financial base in Silicon Valley — West Coast, not East — a geographic difference that hints at differences in their attitudes towards television.

Still, we're following your project's journey through the long-established mainstream American pattern.

Once the pilots have gone, no one can do anything but wait. That doesn't stop studio executives from checking into top New York hotels and haunting lobbies where screenings are in progress upstairs. They can't really influence the outcome, can't attend screenings or discussions, so what do they hope to gain? Gossip — leaks, hints, a raised eyebrow that their show may go. Or die.

I once wrote a pilot for a company whose glory days were memorialized in posters of hit series lining the corridors. But the rooms off the corridors were empty. Every one of their series had concluded or been cancelled the season before. They fielded a number of possibilities, but only one went to pilot — mine. It was early May, and only one light was on in one office — the executive producer's. He went there every day and sat at the desk in case a call came through reception. He ate lunch in the office. Waiting. Waiting for the call from New York. He sent his secretary to the city to listen for rumors, but she hadn't heard anything. I brought him lunch one day, but we didn't have much to talk about, staring at the phone.

Finally, in mid-May the call came: "We're not going to pick you up." There was no explanation — there never is — but post-game analysis guessed that too many similar shows were offered, or too many competing shops had early commitments, or too few slots were open, or none of the above.

But let's make believe your phone call is some version of "Yes!" Your order will probably be in one of four categories:

FULL SEASON

Until May 2016, a full season meant 22 episodes on the air. I'm exaggerating that the curtain came down on all "full season" shows on that date, but it's significant because that's when *The Good Wife*, ended its 7-season run, having competed for awards — and won — against shows that had to deliver only ten or thirteen episodes all year. Robert and Michelle King, the showrunners, remarkably had delivered 156 episodes without ever diminishing the quality or repeating tropes. Few top drama series do that many anymore.

NCIS (the classic version) produced 24 episodes per season for 14 years as of 2017. *The Blacklist* on NBC still does long seasons — 22 per year as of 2018. So the "full season" template isn't fully over. You might run into a show like that, so here's how it works:

Think of a traditional network season as 22 episodes. In reality, even an order for a full season is hedged: The pick-up (commitment to air) is "13 plus the back 9." That means 13 episodes will be broadcast, with the decision on the final 9 contingent on their performance.

You are not going to get an order for 22 episodes. Be glad. The pressure would be enormous. Instead, your dream order would be the new kind of "full season" that is 10 to 15 episodes guaranteed on the air which would allow time for both you and the episodes to breathe.

SHORT ORDER

In a world where a season is 22 episodes long, networks and studios take an expensive risk. Sometimes they hedge with a "short order," which is bad news for show creators. It means the network agrees to produce only a few episodes. Remember, the pilot already exists, so if they pay for two or three more you might have just three or four on the air. If those hook an audience quickly, more episodes are ordered. But how many shows find their audience in three weeks? With so many options, viewers might not even visit the newborn until week three. And some series take a while to get their legs. Historically, icons like the original *Star Trek*, *All in the Family*, and other famously successful series took months before word of mouth alerted viewers to check them out.

A powerful example of patience was HBO's *The Wire* that never had a big weekly audience, but was still being discovered on DVD and online years after it finished production. When I interviewed David Simon, creator of *The Wire*, for the third edition of this book in 2010, he told me:

"The thing that happened in the last decade is somebody figured out an economic model where you could be a grown up story teller and do something that has meaning. And if people come, they come, but at least you're still bringing people into the tent. . . . It's a different economic model where I literally don't have to look at the Nielsens. What I do ask is does the thing have a tail? Does it find its audience eventually? *The Wire* DVDs are selling at a faster rate now than ever before, though the show has been off the air for two and a half years. I need to know the show finds an audience or what I'm doing is irrelevant. But I don't need it to find an audience on Sunday night."

Now, on platforms that produce entire seasons of 13 or so and have them all "in the can" before the debut, short orders aren't an issue. The idea would make no sense at Netflix, for example. And subscription-based cable stations are able to let a new show run in the hope it will pick up steam, as long as viewers keep their subscriptions because of the channel's other offerings.

But back at the network, the heap of dead series, killed before people hardly knew they were on, casts a stench over creativity at the networks. Bottom-line network executives tend to avoid risks. That policy backfires because fear-based decisions send some of the most creative producers and writers to digital platforms where it's more likely their show will have the time it needs to find its audience.

SPLIT SEASON

This is not actually a pick-up option, but it can happen to your show, whether or not you're warned in advance; or your show may premiere in another show's hiatus. This is how a divided season works: Maybe 6 to 8 episodes air, and then the show is put on hiatus and comes back months later for the rest of the season. This strategy isn't new. The final "season" of *Lost* trickled out over two years with a very long break in the middle. Everyone knew the series would resolve years of suspense in the final segments. The challenge was how to spin that out — long enough so excitement would build; not so long that people gave up. In other cases, seasons are split so a new show can be piloted in the slot of a successful show, hoping to build on the audience used to watching that channel at that time.

MIDSEASON

Midseason pickups may be the best news, some showrunners think. Though a late debut denies the show a spot on the fall schedule, and probably limits the number of episodes that would air the first year, some producers like it: Their show is removed from the crowd of September premieres and saved from the insistent pressure to be on the air in a few months. Networks also like midseason shows because they create an illusion of year-round programming which helps the network compete with year-round cable and streaming. And midseason replacements are a cushion against inevitable cancellations. If the network lets the show go ahead and produce a few episodes, pending a slot, you'll have the time to write as well as you did in the pilot.

That said, as the writer, you'll feel disappointed. You have to wait until winter to find out when you're on the air. And it's hard not to wonder if you'll ever be given a place at all.

BACKUP SCRIPTS

Backups are the smallest pick-up, accompanied by a better-than-nothing sigh. It means the network won't let you produce any episodes but would like to see additional scripts. They're holding on to the show because the concept interests them, but something in the pilot didn't work. It might be casting, tone, location, or something at the core — the direction of the stories themselves. This is a second opportunity to prove the series can work by actually writing two or three more episodes, sometimes called "backup pilots." You, the writer, are in the spotlight, and assuming they haven't held back because the writing is weak, this can be your chance to shine.

Let's make believe you got a pick-up for whatever amounts to a "full season" on your network. See the chute from May on the outer circle in the diagram? Well, hold on because you're about to be swept down it to:

YEAR TWO

JUNE

Staffing

Hurtled out of the development chute, still tumbling, you land in June with three months to put an hour series on the air every week. That doesn't mean producing the first hour. It often means scripts for the first five episodes, plus two "in the can" (ready to air) in addition to the pilot. But you have next to nothing. The sets have been struck and need to be rebuilt. You have no crew, no office, no production facility, only your personal iPhone. And you urgently need a writing staff right now.

Shows that are ongoing or announced early aren't in this fix. Neither are premium cable and streaming series, but you already know about that. At new network shows, optimistic showrunners started reading sample scripts and speaking with agents as far back as February, especially if the pilot was attracting an industry "buzz." But without an actual order, they couldn't staff. And some producers are taken by surprise.

I was once hired on a staff in June and we didn't gather until the first week in July, though we were scheduled to premiere the first week of September. The executive producer, a highly regarded writer-producer, had written a personal pilot that didn't fit neatly into a usual franchise (sometimes called a "passion project") and everyone thought it was a long shot. I think he was actually out of town on vacation when the pick-ups were announced; that's how unlikely he thought this would be. So there we sat in a temporary office lent by the studio — four adrift writers and the surprised showrunner. He opened with "Anyone have ideas for stories?"

But that's rare. With months to imagine winning this lottery, most showrunners are ready, and the instant the series goes, negotiations commence with writers. If you were in the mix from the beginning (if the concept was yours or you wrote the pilot), your deal is already in place. If you're trying to join a staff, June is when those jobs open and fill quickly, so your agent should have been pitching you in the months before.

The next chapter tells how a writing staff works, so we'll skip over that and assume by the end of June everyone is in place and writing has begun. It continues:

JULY AND AUGUST

Write Like Crazy

Ditch the idea that summer is vacation time if you're writing for network television. July and August are the crazy-making months when the staff is turning out scripts as fast as they can. Though each show has its own rhythm, if you're in any writers' room, you'll be "breaking stories" around the table, dissecting outlines as they come in, and discussing early drafts by the other writers every week at the same time as you write your own. (In Chapter Four, I explain the steps of writing.)

Probably, the first episode exists: It's the pilot. But the audience might not discover your series the first week, or even the second. So in a way, the first three episodes will function as pilots. Episodes Two and Three have to reach a balance between orienting first-time viewers by reprising the overall "mission" and identifying the cast, while progressing the stories to hold people who watched before. If the pilot was a premise that deposited a character in a new environment or quest, then Episode Two is expected to deliver what happens there. It may be the most difficult and least rewarding episode on a show.

Think about it — the audience doesn't know the characters, so viewers are not yet emotionally invested. But neither do you have the benefit of the inciting situation or curiosity that sets the series in motion, since that happened the first week. Nevertheless, this "development" episode must sizzle with the tension and anticipation of the pilot. That calls for one of the more experienced writers — not you. Your earliest assignment might be Episode Four or Five, depending on the size of the staff and the length of your season.

While the staff is writing, production is rolling out shows. Probably, you'll be invited to sit in on casting guest stars in your own episode. Once shooting starts, "dailies" (unedited scenes) are screened almost every day. Go to the screenings, no matter how hard you're writing. After you hear how the dialogue plays, you might want to rework the cadence of a scene you're writing. Dailies also reveal the strengths of the actors. If chemistry between actors burns through the screen, you'll want to use it.

But don't get beguiled by stars. In television, writers have power, and smart actors know it. They'll want to have lunch with you to pitch stories for their character. I was on one show where an actor researched each writer's birthday and sent exquisite handmade cards; on another, an actor distributed coffee mugs personalized with each writer's name. Some showrunners warn new writers not to hang out with the actors, fearing they'll be too easily influenced. I say, go for it — talented actors contemplate their characters, and that can inspire you.

As the series evolves, the head writer must decide whether to let characters develop in a way the creators didn't foresee, or stick to the original plan. If the series has an underlying source — examples include books for *Game of Thrones*, *Big Little Lies*, *Outlander*, *The Handmaid's Tale*, and a graphic novel for *The Walking Dead* — the showrunner considers how close to stay to the source. Some showrunners begin with a chart of story arcs for the whole season. In fact, many established series invite their writing staff to a retreat in early June (or whichever month precedes their season). On a whiteboard, they might assign each character a color coded marker and track the five-or-so main roles from episode one to the season finale in a stack of horizontal lines. After all arcs are complete, they slice vertically, showing how the stories intersect (see Chart 2.2). If you work for that executive producer, no one can abscond with the series.

Chart 2.2   Sample Character Arcs for a Season on One Series

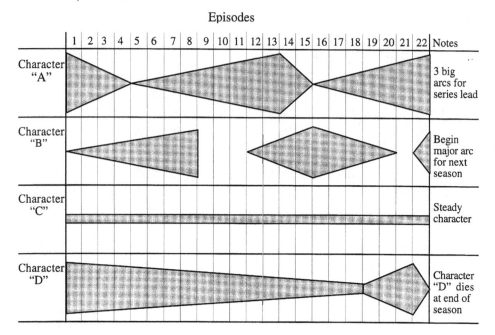

Other showrunners have a freer approach. In Season 5 of *Orange Is the New Black* (2017–2018), Jenji Kohan took a storytelling gamble: all 13 episodes happen over the course of a three-day riot in the wake of a beloved character's death. The writing staff began as they always do, binge-watching the previous season together and discussing how to move forward. "We wanted to slow things down a little bit," Kohan told the *L.A. Times*. "We felt really excited by the notion of a riot in almost real time." That led to 72 fictional hours filmed over the course of many months.

Every series has its own origins tale, and the gestation of *Breaking Bad* has become a classic. The pilot by Vince Gilligan had promise from the start, but outside events intervened before the show had a chance to develop. The 100-day Writers Guild strike of 2014–2015 stopped production. At that point, the writing staff had planned to kill off Jesse in the early episodes. Hard to imagine, right? For those of us who admire this series, that would have devastated the narrative, depriving the show of its father/son dynamics and core tensions throughout its five seasons. But the enforced break gave the writers time to reconsider. They saved Jesse and made other adjustments that brought us the show that became one of television's greats.

Back to the genesis of your own project, the staff writes and rewrites through the summer while network notes trickle down. Each episode is read by the network — Legal, and Standards and Practices, on top of the executive assigned to your show. Those notes go to the showrunner, so if you're a beginning writer they will be filtered and interpreted before they get to you; you won't interface directly with the network. Your boss is choosing when to fight the network brass and when to accommodate the notes. It's just part of the network landscape.

All this work leads to:

SEPTEMBER AND OCTOBER

THE DEBUT

If it were a stage play, you'd have flowers and a party opening night. But in television, you're doing "post" on a later episode by the time the pilot airs. (Postproduction means everything after filming, like editing and scoring.) And that pilot was written a year ago, before the series was a glimmer in the eye of any of the current staff. Still, send up the fireworks in the parking lot after you watch it on TV like it was new.

AMC showcased *The Walking Dead* on Halloween after a weeklong festival of the best feature films in the genre. For the staff involved it was a full-out Halloween party, costumes and all.

So even though the show is no longer new to the people who worked on it for months, it seems new anyway because once the show is broadcast, it becomes public property, out of the creative cocoon. "Overnights," which are quick national ratings, are on the showrunner's desk the next morning. He'll tell the staff to pay no attention to the numbers, just keep writing; and, indeed, lower level writers are shielded from marketplace pressures, temporarily. But how can you not feel buoyant if the show is liked, or disappointed if you played to an empty house? Just remember, it's not going to do any good to blame the network (look what they put us up against — of course we have no numbers), or blame viewers (they don't appreciate us because they're all . . . insert adjective), or blame your producer (he should've known the title sequence/opening scene/music/actor/whatever wouldn't work), or blame yourself (I have no talent). Hey, probably none of those are true. It takes time for a series to catch on. If a few critics recommend the show in reviews, and the marketing people do their thing, and the audience does join you in Episode Two or Three, and they become involved in the characters — then you'll have an entire first season for the series to grow and stake its turf. Breathe out now.

NOVEMBER THROUGH MARCH

COMPLETING THE SEASON

Writing continues steadily until all episodes are in final drafts. Don't make Thanksgiving plans except dinnertime. As for the winter break you had in school, you're not going anywhere this year. You'll have a few days off at Christmas and New Year's. Or maybe you'll be finishing a draft at home before the wrapping paper is off the floor.

Depending how well your series is pulled together (and that depends largely on the skill of the showrunner), and how many episodes are in your season, you'll be slowing down at the end of February or sooner. Your own episodes are probably finished, so you're sticking around for polishes of scripts by other writers. Even if you're done, follow everything through "post." Not only is the series very much alive with new episodes airing every week, but you want to preserve your position for the next year.

If the first season was a resounding success, the showrunner will have early notice it's been renewed. But plenty of first-time series are uncertain down to the wire, just like pilots. It's awful, from a writer's point of view. You want to create a season ender that entices viewers to watch in the fall, and yet if you're not being picked up for a second season, the impulse is to go out bravely and close the story arc.

Something like that happened at the end of the first season of *Mad Men*. This is how I heard the story: Now, keep in mind that this cable show was off the network grid so they were hearing news on a different timetable or the tale might not have unfolded like this. Anyway, the showrunner (Matt Weiner) thought *Mad Men* didn't have a chance for a second season. At the point he planned the arc, it was so far ahead of announcements that he configured the episodes leading to the end of Don Draper's core question of whether he could be a family man, loving and loved, not unknown and alone. In the original script, Don goes home to Thanksgiving and finds his family waiting for him, and the through-line of the series is resolved. The producers wrote it, shot it, packed it up, and that was that.

Except it wasn't. On the walk to the gallows, the award nominations started flooding in. Critical acclaim. People wanted more. But what more? As the industry tale goes, one of the interns on the staff (who later became a writer/producer, herself) wrote a new scene. Don goes home and there's the family waiting, just as in the early draft. But it's in his imagination. The house is empty. Don sits alone on the stairs of his empty house. And tune in for next season because his troubles are only just beginning.

More often, the producer bets on the show and opts for the cliffhanger, while the staff hangs on their own cliff. This happens during:

APRIL

HIATUS

Vacation — yay! For a network series writer, spring is like summer and winter holidays rolled into a mass getaway. The hiatus might last three months from March until July, or be as limited as a month and a half — April to late May. If your season has only 13 episodes, your whole writing job may last as little as four or five months. If the staff is assured they're coming back, this is a fling of freedom. If everyone's worried, the agents sniff around for another staff. In any case, the break is total. Many shows lock their offices and leave nothing but an answering machine; even the receptionist is gone after intense weeks of long hours, non-stop.

This brings us all the way back to where we started, as the cycle spins around and around and around.

CHAPTER THREE

HOW A SCRIPT IS CRAFTED

Constructing your episode may seem daunting at first, but hour dramas — especially primetime network shows — tend to follow a general template. Your insights into character, talent with dialogue, inventiveness in storytelling, and the depth of meaning are all creative qualities beyond any system. But I've found that using a basic pattern can actually release your artistry because you don't have to worry whether the underlying skeleton will hold up.

Initially, I even advise students to try to separate their right brain and left brain functions — the creative and the analytical. We know how we are as artists, ready to run off with the circus, or an emotional explosion. Those moments when passion takes over are gifts, and if you're touched by a cinematically hot encounter between characters, go ahead and write it down. The best writing is like trying to catch the wind anyway. But then put that piece of writing aside and return to engineering your script in the cold light of the left brain.

Even if you could somehow begin at page one and steam your way through to page 50 in a single creative breath (and I don't think anyone can), television series don't work like that. As you'll discover in Chapter Five, you'll be collaborating with a staff and will have to submit an outline or beat sheet (more about those in Chapter Four) prior to writing your teleplay.

THE DRAMATIC BEAT

Before we go further, keep in mind the nature of a screenplay scene, as I'm sure you've learned in screenwriting classes or books. A dramatic scene is the essential building block of storytelling on screen and should have a complete dramatic structure. That means each scene has a motivated protagonist who wants something and drives the action to get it through conflict with an opposition, usually an equally motivated antagonist. That's just a basic statement of story plotting. If you're stuck on this point, then take a break and refresh yourself on screenwriting before you move on to TV. Seriously. Writing television drama isn't easier than movies, even though each episode is shorter than a theatrical film; it's more difficult because it requires all the same elements compressed in a tighter form.

When you look at the script pages that follow you'll notice that television dramas use the same format as theatrical screenplays, and it's the same whether you're writing for traditional networks, basic or premium cable, or streaming. Notice the capitalized locations. These are "sluglines," also called "scene headings," but they are not scenes in the dramatic sense. For example, an establishing shot outside a building is not a full dramatic scene, though it is a location that physical production needs to plan. For our purposes, a dramatic beat may encompass one or more sluglines; the key is identifying a step of the story, not a shot. You'll see examples later in this chapter, but don't stop with those. You should read as many well-written scripts as you can find and study the shows that are made from them.

With a basic Google search, you can easily find episodes of shows that have already run, especially if the series has won awards. Your first visit might be to the website of the show's network that probably offers the pilot free. Other resources include Amazon, Netflix, Hulu, iTunes, Roku, Apple TV, and DVDs. Some sites require membership for a small monthly fee; some charge a little to "own" the episode. I'm going to ask you to follow along with the analysis of one great pilot by watching simultaneously. You can do this.

Scripts are also available, though not as easily. The Writers Guild Foundation Library in Los Angeles has all the award-nominated scripts and they can be read in the Library (though not removed). Many educational organizations have sample scripts too. I don't want to list all the sites that advertise scripts for sale (and sometimes for free) because I'm wary of copyright infringement. But, hey, the scripts are out there, and if you're going to write for television, you need to be familiar with how the pros put their stories on the page.

THE 2-PAGE SCENE

I use the two-page scene as a target for students partly because inexperienced writers have difficulty accomplishing a complete dramatic beat in fewer pages, and when they write more than two pages, their scenes tend to lose focus or become redundant.

Historically, screen scenes used to be long, more like stage plays. If you look at great movies from the 1940s, like the ones starring Humphrey Bogart, you'll see some scenes that run five or even seven pages. They reflect a different era where the slow evolvement of a dramatic moment, gradually experienced, was part of the pace of life. Currently, that's part of the pendulum swing I mentioned above to longer, slower styles where scenes are paced to explore subtle nuances, and may sometimes be several minutes long.

But we're focusing here on what's useful to developing your craft to work in mainstream outlets. You need to master the skill to write tightly focused moments. Consider the speed of computers, where you're growling at the screen if a function takes two seconds. An electronics-savvy populace is quickly bored. If audience attention drifts, or is way ahead of where you're going with the story, you've lost your moment. On television, a one-minute beat is more welcome than a three-minute scene, and if you're starting page four of a single encounter, that's a red flag.

Notice also that I'm using the words "minute" and "page" interchangeably. That's just shorthand. A minute per page may be an average, but it's not always accurate. Pages of dialogue move faster, while action eats up lots of time. As with all my construction advice, I'm pointing out a general design, not policing whether you color outside the lines!

A, B, C STORIES

For a great example of a show that uses parallel storytelling, screen *American Crime* by John Ridley that aired on ABC from 2015 to 2017. In the pilot of the first season, the three storylines are not subplots, but independent tales each involving a distinct cast. Since they occur within the same area — Modesto, California — and they each open windows to the thematic spine as the series develops, the stories are sometimes interwoven, sometimes blended, sometimes juxtaposed. Clearly, they are part of the same show, though each inhabits a separate culture within the "world" of the show.

We've witnessed this storytelling approach before, notably in *The Wire*, *Treme*, and *The Deuce* all created by David Simon, where the city — Baltimore or New Orleans or 1970s Times Square, New York — is the "world," but within it are cultures that have their own characters and rules. In all cases, the episodes don't shatter into disconnected stories, no matter how separate are the arcs, because the writer's vision creates a unifying attitude and tone. The disparate stories ultimately collide and create layers for each other in *American Crime* as well as in the Simon shows.

The largest (or most resonant) story is called "A." The second most important story is "B." And the third "C" story is sometimes comic relief in an otherwise serious show, or may be a "runner," such as a recurring incident or character issue. However, in the case of *American Crime*, no character or issue is included for comic relief. Like any description of writing methods, those distinctions are flexible. Among variations, you may find A and B stories that are equal in weight, shows where a C story in one episode is a seed beginning a major arc in subsequent episodes, and shows that normally have three stories but might turn up with two or four. Again, I'm giving you a sense of the overall design, not laying down the law.

Some series may have more than three stories — *Orange Is the New Black*, *Transparent*, and *Game of Thrones* are also examples. And some are primarily "A" story only, for example *Better Call Saul*, *Mr. Robot*, and *Jane the Virgin*. Before you speculate a show, carefully study how it's crafted.

Each series has its own ways, but I've come up with a generic grid that fits many shows on broadcast and basic cable, though it does not apply to certain streaming shows especially if the length of each episode varies widely. I use it to analyze sample episodes in my classes, and here's a blank one you can apply to the excerpt printed in this chapter. For practice, try it while you're watching TV. But here's a hint: for five acts look for which two acts are the shortest. Sometimes five acts are simply Act Four divided in half. Other shows divide Act One instead. This creates the appearance of five acts while actually writing a long teaser that is called Act One, though the result is the same as writing a traditional four plus teaser. If you count pages (or time the acts), it's easy to figure out how shows are accommodating themselves to this basic structure. Once you get the hang of it, you can also use this simple chart in the early planning stages of an original script. (Chart 3.1)

Chart 3.1   Basic Four-Act Grid

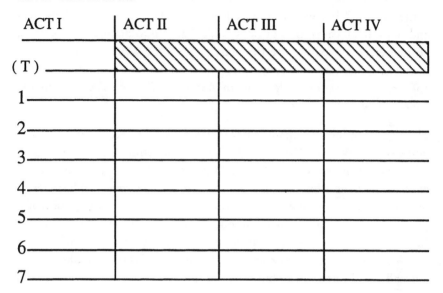

The titles on the top are the teaser ("T") plus four acts of an hour episode. Remember from Chapter One that on network television and basic cable (but not on streaming or premium cable) commercial breaks occur roughly every 10 to 15 minutes. Dividing 15 minutes into 60 minutes gives you the four acts. Now, an hour drama doesn't really run an hour — it's actually less than 50 minutes after commercials. And each act isn't really 15 minutes — more like 12. Dividing 12 minutes into 48 minutes gives you four acts also. But for planning a first draft script, figure that Act One ends around page 17 or 18 if the show has a teaser (more about teasers below); Act Two ends around page 30; Act Three at 45; and Act Four around 60 (or anywhere from 50 to 60).

On the left of the grid, you see numbers one through seven. Those are the scenes in each act. Why seven? Well, you won't always have seven, in fact. Five solid scenes could fill out an act in some cases; and in "vignette" shows where scenes are quick, you might find yourself counting up to nine or ten. The basis for the list of seven is the two-minute scene. Back to arithmetic, if an act is 14 minutes, and each scene is around two minutes, 14 divided by 2 = 7.

USING THE GRID

If you're using the grid to help you understand the form of an episode on TV, I suggest you begin by recording the show or get it online so you can pause and go back. Watch it all the way through and name the A, B, and C stories (or whatever number of stories your show has). Attach each story to one of the main cast, and then summarize that particular arc in a sentence. Keep going, creating a "logline" for each story.

Once you've figured out the stories, re-play the episode. This time, write a letter in each of the boxes on the grid. For example, if Act I, Scene 1 is about the "B" story, put a B in that box. As the grid fills out, it will probably look sort of like a checkerboard with A, B, C (or other) stories following each other in a somewhat random pattern.

You'll notice that the cliffhanger that occurs at the end of an act might not always be a suspenseful moment in the A story; it might be a turning point in the B story, for example. You'll also see that sometimes one of the stories continues for several beats in a row, especially if it's following a "line of interest" the writer didn't want to interrupt. On other occasions, you'll see one story interposed between beats of another; this might be used to convey a sense that time has passed between the beats in the first story (this skipping is also called an "ellipsis").

No rules exist for how this "checkerboard" should look, so don't get hung up trying to match the order of scenes. You're serving the dramatic tension of the stories, not some outside system. The point is to recognize the way parallel stories complement each other.

The grid may also help you track the arcs, and especially if your show is part of a serial, you might be surprised that one of the storylines ends in Act Three, or the C story doesn't begin until Act Two, or Act Four is entirely about resolving the A story. That's all okay. Again, the structure serves the story within the general parameters of a four-act episode with cliffhangers. So learn from other shows but don't copy.

If you're using the grid to create an original script, your first foray into the grid might be to jot notes about key points in the boxes: how the show opens, the "worst case" cliffhanger at the end of Act Three, and how the show will end. You might do that for the A story only, or for both A and B stories, leaving room to think about the C later. Particularly with the act breaks, it's helpful to reverse-engineer, stepping backwards from the cliffhangers to the beats right before to fill in the actions that led to the jeopardy or collision. That reverse technique may help you figure out your outline. (I'll explain more about outlining in the next chapter.)

5- AND 6-ACT STRUCTURES

More than a decade ago, the traditional networks mandated six acts instead of four for all their shows. You can guess why: more commercial breaks. I don't know any writers who liked this change which seemed pushed by desperation to pump revenues when network advertising rates are declining and the audience can watch on sites that omit commercials altogether. After that mandate, the rhythm of shorter acts spread throughout television; you can sense that speeded pace, especially on action shows, even when the commercials are absent.

Like it or not, you need to find out how to reconfigure your structure if the show you're speculating has four, five, or six acts. I suggest you begin with the four-act idea. Then take what used to be the teaser and lengthen it to around ten pages to create a new Act One. Be sure you open directly into the story with jeopardy or action or a provocative issue because this is where you need to hook the audience (and the reader).

Each of the succeeding acts will be shorter than in a four-act plan — roughly ten pages each. In a six-act structure, with acts only around eight pages long, think in terms of Act Six being a tag or the final shoe dropping, or a twist. You might see an Act Six that runs as short as five minutes. Look at *The Walking Dead* as aired on AMC (rather than streaming it) and time the amount of dramatic material that plays between selling cars. Hint: it's not much, maybe only three scenes fit in an act towards the end.

THE MORE THINGS CHANGE . . .

. . . The more they remain the same. After all the uproar about going to five, six, even seven acts in an hour series, the pendulum has swung back to the template in the grid. I asked around and discovered two phenomena: First — writers are planning their stories in the traditional four acts and adjusting to five or six in a later draft. In some cases when the series has no commercial breaks, the writer simply drops out the act break headings when the finished script goes to the next production phase. (More about off-network structure later.) Second (and this amazed me) — writers I've never met on shows I don't know were turning up at meetings with the grid from this book. Sometimes they knew where it came from, sometimes a colleague had just handed it to them on a piece of paper. So this little grid I invented for myself — and for you — has taken on a life of its own.

As useful as the grid may be, you always want to be flexible to find the form that best expresses the story.

I asked some friends on the staffs of current shows how they handle act breaks in the writers' room. One who works on a long-running heavy action series explained: "The show used to be in four acts and we had a very long Act One. So we split Act One in half — three scenes and four scenes. It used to be six to seven scenes for Act One. Now it's a teaser and two small acts. We do that because at the end of Act One we need an action beat."

I also put the question to Peter Blake, a writer on the staff of *House*, which is no longer running but is still an outstanding model of procedural drama. He said: "What I do and I recommend to all the other writers on *House* is write in a four-act structure and then add two act breaks. The doctors will go down a path — what is this disease? Then you have a diagnosis. They have a theory and at some time a treatment for that theory. And at the end of the act, it doesn't work. That's a really simple way to break the act. The audience has to be involved enough that they're not going to turn off at the act breaks. Generally, I would beat out a very simple medicine story. Then I'd beat out the personal story. I use index cards and shuffle them around. I'd see which of the later acts is the longest and I'd divide that in half."

CHARACTER-DRIVEN STRUCTURE

Writers on streaming platforms and premium cable — shows with no commercial breaks — have mostly abandoned the traditional act structure in favor of breaking stories according to character. That approach affects the rhythm of the hour and can allow a slower development.

The swing to a slower pace began with *Mad Men* (that did have act breaks on AMC). Now check the length of scenes in *Transparent* and other shows that recall the rhythms of art films formerly seen mainly at indie festivals.

Queen Sugar embodies that style. Creator Ava DuVernay, known for *Selma* (which was nominated for a best picture Oscar), wrote the pilot and first two episodes of the show's first season on OWN. Asked about her decision to hire only women directors, DuVernay said, "I wanted people with my sensibility, who care about things I care about. People who make films that I love and I knew would embrace the luxurious pace and the attention to detail and the love of nuanced characters."

I asked a friend who is on a prestige series (that she asked me not to identify) how her writers' room breaks stories. Her show has no commercials so the episodes have no visible acts. Keep in mind that movies have often been discussed as having three acts (beginning, middle, end), in which Act Two is twice as long as Acts One and Three, so in old fashioned terms, Act One of a movie is 30 minutes, Act Two is 60 minutes and Act Three is 30 minutes. Translating to hour drama, Act One would be 15 minutes, Act Two would be 30 minutes, and Act Three would be 15 minutes. But as soon as you add a midpoint in the center of the second act (a usual dramatic turning point) you get a regular four-act structure. With that context, here is her answer to how her writers' room navigates without act breaks:

"The show reverts to a three-act structure. We break the beats by character and then do a weave. We put everything up on whiteboards where each character has a beginning, middle, and end, which is why I say it has kind of a three-act structure. Although in truth, we don't break anything by acts at all. We break it by character. Typically the big reversals are in the A story so we break that first, and don't worry how the other characters' stories fit into it if they're not inherently a part of it. The reversals are built into what journey the main character takes in each episode. The reversals tend to come where you'd expect — page 40 to 45 out of a 55-page script."

For off-network shows, I've made an alternate chart you'll find on page 86. This approach responds to the different goals of these platforms. Consider what a network show needs: viewers who will return after commercials. The challenge there is to build cliffhangers at act breaks to hold on to the audience that can easily switch channels, especially at the half hour. In contrast, Netflix (for example) is concerned only about keeping you watching the next hour. Streaming outlets don't expect the audience to switch channels midway, so they'd avoid an impression of breaking points during the episode. They do care about the cliffhanger at the end of the hour, though, so the character arcs are constructed to lead to that endpoint.

For the next chart imagine your A, B, C stories are built around the main cast, each of whom has an arc within the episode that leads seamlessly to a cliffhanger at the end. The stories can be balanced in many ways. In a hypothetical prototype for an episode that runs close to a full hour (longer than network shows) that might mean planning around 28 beats (scenes) in contrast to 20 to 25 for network episodes. A = 14 beats. B = 9 beats. C = 5 beats. Of course, that's not a recipe for any particular script, just a way of analyzing. In a show with long scenes that average 5 minutes each in 60 minutes you might find yourself planning only 12 beats total (60 divided by 5 = 12). That could lead to something like this: A = 6. B = 4. C = 2. Again, these are not prescriptions, just estimates of how many beats may be available for your outline.

After you know your stories, weave them into a pattern for the episode. No rule exists for their order; it's an intuitive process discovering which story elements move the narrative forward and which scenes complement others. Here's a simple tip: figure out the realistic time frame for each beat — early morning, midday, evening, night. You can be as specific as is useful — some shows count hours and minutes as a dramatic device. Then you can color code the scenes for time. If you have two beats of the A story in the morning, and you realize you've put a night beat from the B between them, either you need to change the scenes so they're all at the same time or move the wrong-time beat elsewhere.

I like to do the weave on paper, either with post-its I can move around or index cards. Others prefer to weave on screen. Some people use different colors of cards or different computer highlighting so they don't lose sight of the story balances. For example, you probably don't want to lose the A story halfway through because it was all clumped at the beginning (unless that's actually your intention for some reason). Usually, you want to be sure the A appears near the beginning and at the end but the artistic decisions are up to you . . . and the showrunner. These systems are meant as a ladder not a limit. Remember, screenwriting is an art.

Chart 3.2   Example of a Character-Driven Episode With No Act Breaks

These are all the scenes in your hour episode (28 is just an estimate)

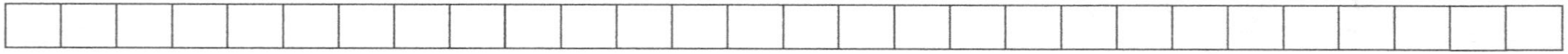

"A" Story: Start with your main character and plan this entire story. Figuring back from the character's goal in this episode, list all the A-story scenes. They are represented here by 14 filled-in squares.

"B" Story: Plan the story for the second important character and list all the scenes. They are represented here by 9 dotted squares.

"C" Story: Plan the least important story. It can be added after the others are in place. It is represented here by 5 squares with lines.

Now weave all the stories, beginning by laying out the main character's path, and keep shifting until the rhythm maximizes the dramatic impact of the whole episode. Of course, the order of scenes will depend on your own stories, so the result won't be the same as this chart. It is only an example!

TEASERS

One of the excerpts you'll read in this chapter is from *Breaking Bad* that opens with a "teaser," though not all series begin with one. A teaser, also called "a cold opening," refers to dramatic material before the titles (before the name of the series and credits). It may be a one-minute "hook," or as long as ten minutes that includes several scenes, making it nearly as full as a traditional whole act. In any style, it exists to grab viewers faster than the enemies, which are the remote, mouse, or esc button. The notion is to open the hour with an action, image, situation, or character that provokes enough anticipation to keep viewers through the title sequence and into the first act.

However, increasingly, networks have dumped title sequences along with theme music, preferring to grab viewers with uninterrupted drama. The "tease" is the story itself, and titles scroll over Act One.

Often, a teaser sets out the problem of an episode. For example, on a detective show, the crime to be solved may be enacted or discovered in the teaser. Other crime procedurals open with the cast arriving at a crime scene after the deed is done. Of course, each show is unique.

In many law and medical shows, a case arrives and incites the events of the episode. But in *Grey's Anatomy*, for example, where emphasis is on the ensemble cast, teasers have sometimes shown the continuing characters waking, getting ready for work, or traveling to work, launching their personal stories that will spin out in the episode.

Even in the Marvel Comics realm that depends on elements of super power action, their best shows including *Jessica Jones* and *Luke Cage* often use their teasers to remind viewers of the show's psychological world instead of beginning a plot.

I Love Dick on Amazon is built on the inner lives of the characters and relies on dissections of the rarified culture of academic critics observed through the eyes of a self-aware woman. Fitting the style of this show, episodes may open with intimacy that is analyzed and even include philosophical dialogue.

If you're a new writer, though, I recommend sticking with story rather than message. A swiftly propelled dramatic tension will lure a reader to turn the page and a viewer to see what happens next. Real storytelling is difficult, and I've seen too many students fool themselves into thinking they can impress by opening with a weighty theme, when they're actually avoiding the challenge of impelling an arc. The best teasers tend to be the best drama.

Before we get into content, remember that a TV drama script looks just like a theatrical screenplay. Most screenwriting software will give you format options, so choose "standard," "screenplay," or whatever term your system uses for writing movies. Final Draft and Celtx are commonly used throughout the industry.

ABOUT THIS EXCERPT FROM *BREAKING BAD*

The pilot of *Breaking Bad* is often cited as the "perfect" model. Vince Gilligan, who wrote the script, involves his audience in the complex reality of Walter White from the first instant and never lets up as this character develops from "Mr. Chips to Scarface," from a meek chemistry teacher to a violent drug lord. Gilligan said, "Television is historically good at keeping its characters in a self-imposed stasis so that shows can go on for years or even decades. When I realized this, the logical next step was to think, how can I do a show in which the fundamental drive is toward change?"

If you haven't watched all five years of this series yet, you should treat yourself. For a writer, the ability to entice viewers into rooting for a protagonist as he morphs into an antagonist requires both skill and the kind of artistry that encourages creative risks. Along with a few other classics (especially *The Wire*), *Breaking Bad* is part of this century's great American literature.

We're going to look at a small portion of the pilot. The pages that follow are from a writer's draft dated May 2005. The show first aired on AMC in 2008 — a three-year gap. Some of that delay was caused by the writer's strike. But I mention the dates so you will take heart if you have an important script on the shelf. It can still happen when the time is right if it's good enough.

Read the Teaser and the first page of Act One. Simultaneously, run the show on a DVD or download. We will compare the written script to the produced version, and then we'll switch to analyzing the rest of Act One from the screen.

TEASER

EXT. COW PASTURE - DAY

Deep blue sky overhead. Fat, scuddy clouds. Below them,
black and white cows graze the rolling hills. This could be
one of those California "It's The Cheese" commercials.

Except those commercials don't normally focus on cow shit.
We do. TILT DOWN to a fat, round PATTY drying olive drab in
the sun. Flies buzz. Peaceful and quiet. Until...

... ZOOOM! WHEELS plow right through the shit with a SPLAT.

NEW ANGLE - AN RV

Is speeding smack-dab through the pasture, no road in sight.
A bit out of place, to say the least. It's an old 70's era
Winnebago with chalky white paint and Bondo spots. A bumper
sticker for the Good Sam Club is stuck to the back.

The Winnebago galumphs across the landscape, scattering cows.
It catches a wheel and sprays a rooster tail of red dirt.

INT. WINNEBAGO - DAY

Inside, the DRIVER's knuckles cling white to the wheel. He's
got the pedal flat. Scared, breathing fast. His eyes bug
wide behind the faceplate of his gas mask.

Oh, by the way, he's wearing a GAS MASK. That, and white
jockey UNDERPANTS. Nothing else.

Buckled in the seat beside him lolls a clothed PASSENGER,
also wearing a gas mask. Blood streaks down from his ear,
blotting his T-shirt. He's passed out cold.

Behind them, the interior is a wreck. Beakers and buckets
and flasks -- some kind of ad-hoc CHEMICAL LAB -- spill their
noxious contents with every bump we hit. Yellow-brown liquid
washes up and down the floor. It foams in a scum around...

... Two DEAD BODIES. Two freshly deceased Mexican guys
tumble like rag dolls, bumping into each other.

Completing this picture is the blizzard of MONEY. A Von's
bag lies leaking twenties. Fifteen, twenty grand in cash
wafts around in the air or floats in the nasty brown soup.

CLOSE on the driver's eyes. He's panting like a steam
engine. His mask FOGS UP until finally he can't see.

2.

EXT. COW PASTURE - CONTINUOUS

The Winnebago comes roaring over a berm and down into a deep
gully. Too deep. BAM! The front bumper bottoms out,
burying itself. WAAAAAAH! The rear wheels spin air.

The engine cuts off. Silence again. The Winnie's door kicks
open and out stumbles underpants man. He yanks off his gas
mask, lets it drop.

He's forty years old. Receding hairline. A bit pasty.
He's not a guy who makes a living working with his hands.
He's not a guy we'd pay attention to if we passed him on the
street. But right now, at this moment, in this pasture?
Right now, we'd step the fuck out of his way.

Underpants man looks at the RV. End of the line for that.
He listens hard. Out of the silence, we hear... SIRENS.

They're faint, a few miles off -- but growing louder. Our
guy knows he's boned with a capital B. He HOLDS HIS BREATH
and leaps back inside the RV.

INT. WINNEBAGO - CONTINUOUS

A chrome 9mm is clutched in the hand of one of the dead
Mexicans. Underpants grabs it, tucks it in his waistband.

His unconscious passenger, still strapped in his seat, lets
out a groan. Underpants leans past him, yanks open the glove
box. He comes up with a WALLET and a tiny Sony CAMCORDER.

EXT. COW PASTURE - CONTINUOUS

Ducking outside, he starts breathing again. A short sleeve
DRESS SHIRT on a hanger dangles from the Winnebago's awning.
Underpants pulls it on. He finds a clip-on tie in the
pocket, snaps it to his collar. No trousers, unfortunately.

He licks his fingers, slicks his hair down with his hands.
He's looking almost pulled together now -- at least from the
waist-up. All the while, the sirens are getting LOUDER.

Underpants figures out how to turn on the camcorder. He
twists the little screen around so he can see himself in it.
Framing himself waist-up, he takes a moment to gather his
thoughts... then presses RECORD.

3.

                    UNDERPANTS MAN
          My name is Walter Hartwell White.
          I live at 308 Belmont Avenue,
          Ontario, California 91764. I am of
          sound mind. To all law enforcement
          entities, this is not an admission
          of guilt. I'm speaking now to my
          family.
                    (swallows hard)
          Skyler... you are... the love of my
          life. I hope you know that.
          Walter Junior. You're my big man.
          I should have told you things, both
          of you. I should have said things.
          But I love you both so much. And
          our unborn child. And I just want
          you to know that these... things
          you're going to learn about me in
          the coming days. These things.
          I just want you to know that...
          no matter what it may look like...
          I had all three of you in my heart.

The sirens are WAILING now, on top of us. WALTER WHITE, the
underpants man, turns off the camcorder. He carefully sets
it on a bare patch of ground by his feet. Next to it he sets
his wallet, lying open where it can be seen.

CLOSE ON the wallet -- a photo ID card is visible. Walt's
smiling face is on it. It identifies him as a teacher at
J.P. Wynne High School, Ontario Unified School District.

Walt pulls the chrome pistol from the back of his waistband,
aiming it across the tall weeds. It glints hard in the sun.

Flashing red LIGHT BARS speed into view, skimming the tops of
the weeds. Heading straight for us.

Walt stands tall in his underpants, not flinching. Off him,
ready to shoot the first cop he sees...

                    END TEASER

4.

ACT ONE

EXT. WHITE HOUSE - NIGHT

No president ever slept here. No millionaire ever visited.
This is a three-bedroom RANCHER in a modest neighborhood.
Weekend trips to Home Depot keep it looking tidy, but it'll
never make the cover of "Architectural Digest."

We're in Ontario, California -- the Inland Empire. LEGEND:
"ONE MONTH EARLIER."

INT. WHITE HOUSE - MASTER BEDROOM - NIGHT

Dark and silent. SKYLER WHITE, late 30s, sleeps peacefully.
Beside her, her husband Walter is wide awake.

Walt reaches over and presses a button on his Sharper Image
alarm clock. It projects the time in glowing blue numbers on
the cottage cheese ceiling: 5:02 AM.

Walt lies motionless. Brain churning. He presses the button
again, staring straight up. 5:02 turns to 5:03.

Close enough. Walt rises without waking his wife. He exits.

INT. WHITE HOUSE - SPARE BEDROOM - NIGHT

We hear an o.s. SQUEAK-SQUEAK as we drift through this room.
We pass an empty crib, Pampers, a baby monitor still in its
box. There's going to be a new addition to the family.

We come upon the source of the SQUEAKING. It's Walt balanced
on a Lillian Vernon stair-stepper, just three easy payments
of $29.95. Walt plods up and down in the darkness like he's
marching to Bataan.

INT. WHITE HOUSE - BATHROOM - NIGHT

Walt sits down on the edge of the tub. We're watching his
face in the bathroom mirror. He masturbates. Judging by his
expression, he might as well be waiting in line at the DMV.

Walt double-takes, catching sight of himself. Distracted, he
examines the sallow bagginess under his eyes. He draws at
the loose skin under his chin.

Staring at himself long and hard, Walt loses his erection.
He gives up trying, pulls up his sweat pants.

5.

INT. WHITE HOUSE - KITCHEN - MORNING

Walt is dressed for work -- Dockers and a short-sleeve dress
shirt courtesy of Target. An American flag pin on his tie.
He and Skyler eat their breakfast in silence.

Skyler glances up, sees Walt puzzling over his bacon.

                    SKYLER
               Sizzle-Lean. We need to think
               about our cholesterol.

                    WALT
               Huh.

Skyler's cute in a way most guys wouldn't have noticed back
in high school. But not soft-cute. Not in the eyes.

She's dressed for staying home -- she's five months pregnant
and just beginning to show.

                    SKYLER
               When'll you be home?

                    WALT
               Same time.

                    SKYLER
               I don't want him dicking you around
               tonight. You get paid till six,
               you work till six. Not seven.

Seventeen year-old WALTER, JR. enters the kitchen, dressed
for school, hair still damp from the shower. The CLICK...
CLICK of his forearm crutches precedes him into the room.

Walt and Skyler's son is a sweet-faced teenager who appears
to have cerebral palsy. He moves slowly and awkwardly, and
grinds his teeth as he labors to talk. But he's a smart kid.

                    WALT
               Hey.

Just seating himself at the table is a trial for Walter, Jr.
His parents don't give him the slightest help. They treat
him as if he were able-bodied, which is how he wants it.

                    SKYLER
               You're late.

He shrugs. She gets up, serves him breakfast. Walter, Jr.
squints at the plate she plops down before him.

6.

                         WALTER, JR.
          What's--that?

                              SKYLER
          Sizzle-lean. We're watching our
          cholesterol.

                         WALTER, JR.
          Not--me! I want--<u>bacon</u>!

                              SKYLER
          Eat it.

Walter, Jr. picks at his breakfast, annoyed.

                         WALTER, JR.
          What's this--even--made of?!

He looks to his dad for backup. Walt shrugs, ambivalent.

                              WALT
          Eat it.

EXT. HIGH SCHOOL - MORNING

J.P. Wynne High School. Home of the Fightin' Skyhawks. Two
thousand-plus students, many of them in overflow trailers.

Into the faculty lot motors a 1991 Nissan wagon. It was a
piece of shit when it rolled off the assembly line, and has
not improved with age. It parks in a handicapped space.
A handicapped placard hangs from the rear-view.

Walt climbs out from behind the wheel, checks his watch.
He's late. Walter, Jr. struggles to get out of the passenger
side. He fumbles with his crutches and his backpack.

                              WALT
          All set?
               (off his son's nod)
          Alright, see you at home.

Walt grabs his briefcase and hurries toward the building,
leaving his son to work it out for himself -- which is,
again, exactly how Walter, Jr. wants it.

INT. HIGH SCHOOL - CLASSROOM - DAY

Hours later. This is a chemistry classroom -- black-topped
lab tables with gas spigots. Walt is lecturing to seniors.

ANALYSIS

THE OPENING

On screen, look at those flying pants! Framed against the rocks and clear blue sky of Albuquerque, this has become an iconic image. Think about why this is impressive. First, it's outrageous. Anything that throws the audience off will raise questions: Why is this happening? What does it mean? Whose pants are those? So the teaser generates involvement immediately. It also previews the attitude of this show. Clearly, it has a sense of humor. Also danger. Also jeopardy. Also a character probably in dire straits (or at least in dire need of pants). All that is accomplished with nothing but the stunning opening image.

Yet, in the early draft of the script, the flying pants are not specified. This is an example how even a brilliant script was improved in a later version. A few other things changed from the draft script to the shooting script. Early in the development process, *Breaking Bad* was set in California. The move to New Mexico was purely a financial decision. Still, location impacts the writing. The beautiful and bleak Southwest desert gives this series additional layers of metaphor as well as opportunities for actions. Everything matters when creating the screen experience.

This teaser is a single dramatic sequence that can be considered one beat, though it's comprised of several scene headings. In planning an important opening like this, I recommend beginning by making a mini-outline, placing each beat to maximize suspense. Make your own list of the turning points in these first pages to the end of the teaser.

Did you get these? 1. A terrified man in a gas mask drives a Winnebago filled with dead bodies, drug paraphernalia, and money as it careens on an empty desert road. 2. The Winnebago gets stuck and the man stumbles out, where he hears sirens approaching. 3. Reacting to the sirens, he goes back in for a gun, his wallet, and camcorder. 4. As sirens get louder, he records an apology to his family. 5. He readies the gun to shoot the first cop he sees. When the rest of this situation plays later in the show, we discover the sirens aren't even coming for him, and pass him by. Meanwhile, notice how much we learn about Walter White through his actions and the urgent message to his wife and son. The dramatic context allays the exposition that could otherwise risk being an information monologue.

Those five short beats quickly ramp up suspense using a basic storytelling progression: Anticipation — Expectation — Surprise. That is, viewers are led to *anticipate* an event, which holds people through the set-up. As the action advances, we come to *expect* certain outcomes. Instead, the story turns (twists), generating a sense of *surprise* that then begins a new sequence of suspense. You can readily create tension on screen that way, as this teaser demonstrates.

Also, consider the use of humor in this heavy episode. Here's another age-old practice: increase the impact of tragedy by setting it against a comic foil. Shakespeare played his fools and foolishness — sometimes for belly laughs from the audience of his day — in his most tragic plays. Here, the episode begins with a moment that is almost comedy even in the presence of death.

This teaser is a flash-forward, as we'll soon discover. *Breaking Bad*'s style of introducing a curious future event in the teaser becomes an ongoing texture of other episodes in this series. It's a risky choice because the audience can get confused, but when the flash-forward is used to intrigue viewers and set the basis for storytelling, it becomes a skillful ploy. This technique is also called a "book end" that applies to a structure that returns to an early scene to complete it later in the episode.

At the start of Act One, we'll discover another reason for starting "a month later."

ACT ONE

(1) Walter White's life a month before the teaser was uninspiring. Nothing in the first page of the first act would lure a casual viewer to continue with this show. Actually, plenty is revealed that becomes essential later — White shared in a Nobel Prize in chemistry, years before; now his world is filled with mundane details of family life. The contrast between the man we saw in the teaser and this one makes this domestic morning provocative. We're still wondering why the teaser happened, anxious to watch until it's revealed.

Continuing with Act One on screen, study the breakfast scene for its craft. Who is driving this scene? Who "wears the pants" in this family? The answer is Skyler, Walter's wife. Starting at this point in their relationship is essential to creating a long arc. In planning character development, once you know where a character will be emotionally and psychologically at the end, you can reverse to establish the opposite in the beginning. At the end of five seasons, Walter will be powerful and Skyler will be powerless. But in the opening of Act One he's thoroughly controlled by his wife and she scolds him, "I don't want him dicking you around — you get paid till five, you work till five." Think about that line. His work schedule is what *she* demands. And her choice of words "I don't want him dicking you around," undermines him specifically as a man.

(2) The second beat is in the high school where Walter teaches chemistry to students who give him as little respect as he gets at home. But here is a peek at the man he can be and who he finally becomes: energized, passionate, someone who has the inner potential to be strong. That's important if you start a character at a low point. No one roots for the pathetic shlub who can't root for himself. Feeling sorry for a victim leads to disgust, not engagement. But if you give the wounded character the spark of potential, people can believe a quest will follow.

This classroom scene signals the theme of the series: "Chemistry is the study of change," he tells the students. "It's the cycle of life . . . growth then decay then transformation." It's not unusual to find a statement of the creator's intent somewhere in a pilot, and as long as it occurs naturally within the world of the show, it can reveal a journey to deeper meaning than the actions on screen at that time might suggest.

3) The car wash. When Walter is told to wipe down the tires of the very students who were rude in class, he has reached the bottom of his humiliation. This character has nowhere to go but up. But how? Think of the parallel in an action film — the hero is chained to an immovable object while the monster approaches. That sort of jeopardy works if (only if) enough spunk has been established that we anticipate the character could somehow escape.

4) In the surprise birthday party, the seeds of Walter's transformation are planted, though he is not yet ready for the man he will become. It's a loaded scene, rich with characterization of secondary roles (especially Hank) that will figure in the entire series. The first essential element is Walter's awkwardness with Hank's gun that Walter is surprised is heavy. "That's why they hire men," Hank quips, to party laughter. Here it is again, the unmanning of Walter White, and that will change by the end of this pilot.

The second crucial element at the party will propel the plot: Walter sees stacks of bills from a drug raid on TV and is struck by what's available. Hank's offer to take Walter on a ride along to "get a little excitement in your life" prepares for Walter's next step.

5) In bed that night, Skyler is uninvolved with the hand job she offers her husband, more interested in her eBay auction. She's even in charge of his sexuality. It could seem as if he will be stuck in this rut forever . . . except that we've seen the teaser. We know change is coming. We know Walter will take a tremendous risk, though we don't know how that will happen. Again, placing suspense in the teaser is essential to every scene that follows.

6) Walter collapses at the car wash. The early script draft ends Act One on this cliffhanger, wondering what's going to happen to Walter, and still wanting to make sense of that teaser. Actually, this is not a case of hitting bottom. The scenes that follow reveal that he has inoperable lung cancer. He's going to die but that's the beginning, not the end of his life. It's the catalyst he needs to be able to change.

Whether the version you see places the first act break at this point or elsewhere, or if you're binging or watching a DVD with no breaks, you can see how much has been loaded in the first act. This accounts for 17 pages out of a 58-page draft, divided traditionally into a teaser plus four acts.

Watch the rest of this pilot! Notice how much that was planted in Act One pays off and how characters accrue dimension with every beat. Look out for the second half of the bookend in the teaser. Think about how the toughest dramatic moments are modulated by a comedic note, as happens in the doctor's office. By the end of the pilot, you will be anxious to binge the next episode, and that means it has done its job.

WHAT YOU SHOULD DO NEXT:

Read and analyze all the good television scripts you can find from many different series. Sure, you've watched TV all your life, but observing how episodes are crafted on the page prepares you to work as a writer.

Once you have a solid sense how the best dramas are constructed, you're ready for the steps to write your own, which I'll show you in the next chapter.

CHAPTER FOUR

WRITING YOUR OWN EPISODE

HEARING VOICES

(The following impressionistic essay appeared in *The Journal* of the Writers Guild of America.)

> ". . . Trumpet at his lips, he listened to the notes bounce from brick rooftop to rooftop until, finally, he knew the rhythm of the echoes. He'd based his music on those intervals. People called him a genius, but he knew what they could not understand — that he had merely listened."

That's from a short story I wrote in college, when I believed music exists before it is played, that a statue is inside the marble block and the sculptor cuts away whatever is not the statue, and that for writers . . . now we come to it . . . characters exist beyond what is written, with larger lives than fit on film. They'll talk to you. You merely have to listen.

You catch a character the way a surfer catches a wave, waiting in still water until it wells up from a source as invisible as it is powerful.

Whaddya want? That was a kid talking.

Okay, okay we know what it's really like. In some scripts, catching a character is more like catching a bug mid-flight on your windshield.

Working writers have to hear other voices. "You want it good or you want it Friday?" Yeah, yeah, I know, good *and* Friday . . . and it better be Friday.

The voice of my first movie business boss plays in a perpetual loop. Greenly arrived from the East Coast, I had landed a studio development job. I brought the boss a script by a New York friend and naively blazoned it with the kiss of death. I called it beautiful. I can hear the boss now, over his thick cigar, "Don't tell me that shit!" He's making boxing moves like Norman Mailer. "Man to man! Action! Action! Get it? Mano a mano!" He's snapping his fingers in my face. "Is it going to make 100 million? Is it? Is it? That's what you tell me.

You come in here and prove it's going to make 100 million." A sucker dare. No one can prove any movie will make a dime. But I didn't know.

He didn't snap his fingers in your face. You're over the top, and that character is running wild. Stop him!

Okay, okay. He didn't snap. But the rest is true. I soon left the studio job for a writing career. The denigrated New York author went on to win a Pulitzer. And the executive retired richer than both of us.

What's that got to do with the voices?

They don't come easy. Sometimes you have to snare them.

My field is television drama. I've had the chance to learn from a few great writer-producers who provoked their staffs to what drives a real person, not just what gets a laugh or twists the plot. Where else do you find a 22-hour narrative of evolving characters? Immediacy. Intimacy. Power. Like a hard-charging river. But we all know what's along the banks: some cesspool shows.

When I was a beginner, I went for an assignment on one. It wasn't exactly a cesspool, just stagnant. The series characters were moved like toys to fit a franchise. While the producer described contrivances he wanted me to write, the characters in my head screamed, "Can we have the bathroom pass?" With enough craft, you can do an assignment like that. Fake it. Kind of like a worn-out love affair, and as deadening.

Then, in the midst of the script, a character surprised me with a line that could only have come from her. Gotcha! The sound of her voice was like having her address. And once I knew how to find her, she forced the characters who answered her to be as real. And they made their world whole. Once you've had it good, you don't want it any other way.

Right, like you do that every day.

No. Staring at the computer screen with a belly full of caffeine and terror, I know what it's like to have nothing on a character besides every <u>thing</u>. Facts. Stuff that has to happen at the act break. Wind whistling on deserted shores. But I've learned something: craft can be a tugboat that pulls you out to where you can hear the voices.

So, you gonna get to Joan of Arc, or what?

Not Joan. But there is a connection. The high when you're flying with a scene rolling out like it's alive — that euphoria is worth putting up with the detractors and distractions. It's like an all-nighter when you can't get enough of each other, you and the characters, and no one wants to sleep again ever, and it's already all there . . . just listen.

* * *

I decided to begin this chapter about preparing you to write your own script by quoting that article so we don't lose sight of the source — where writing really comes from — as we focus on the nuts and bolts of craft.

FINDING YOUR STORIES

Whether you're setting out to write a spec script or you're on a staff vying for an episode assignment, you'll need to choose subjects which (1) fit the medium, (2) complement the specific show, (3) contain events that will play on screen, and (4) express your unique experience or fresh insights. Yes, you can do all four.

Ideas that will work on television have the scale and intimacy I discussed in Chapter One. So look for character-based subjects that benefit from scenes with dialogue.

To fit an existing show, you need to have watched that series so much you can hear the characters' voices in your head. And you'll have figured out the kinds of springboards the show uses to impel stories, and its pace and style.

As you know, externalized actions are basic to any screenwriting. Just as in a feature screenplay, you plan your structure around things that happen. That sounds simplistic, and I wouldn't bring it up but I've seen otherwise-sophisticated students become so involved with the psychology of TV characters they forget that character is expressed in a series of events on screen.

Finally, what do you bring to the party? Of course, you'll consider ongoing relationships among the cast; those kinds of continuing stories are called "on series," and are fine to write, but be warned: the large turns in a season's arc are planned by the showrunners.

It would be naïve to spec an episode of *The Walking Dead* where Rick goes in search of sex-reassignment surgery, or an episode of *Game of Thrones* where warriors from the various kingdoms join hands to sing "It's a Small World," or where the cast of *Outlander* in 18th-century Scotland breaks into a Bollywood dance routine. Ok, you wouldn't write anything that far off, but even lesser misinterpretations of a show's tone and intention would indicate you don't understand how it works (or you didn't do your homework), or that your idea of originality is a show you'd like to write, and it's not theirs. Don't do episodes that change the central characters or the course of the show.

Instead, think about incidents you know (or know of), and then play them out in the world of the show. If that's scary, you're not alone. Even Aaron Sorkin, creator of many series including *The West Wing* and *Newsroom*, and movies including *The Social Network*, *Steve Jobs*, and *A Few Good Men* sometimes has difficulty beginning. He confided at a Writers Guild Foundation seminar: "It's bad enough trying to have ideas. When you really start, you're trying to get one. Every day you're flipping through instantly dismissible ideas, so my head is like the worst movie you've ever seen. Horrible, horrible ideas that go nowhere. . . . It's like being bludgeoned with your own inadequacies."

One way to break the logjam is through research. Some writers maintain files from offbeat Google sites or small-town newspapers, or they shop at swap meets for unusual books. For example, if you were planning a *CSI*, you'd be smart to investigate scientific clues that can be visualized under a microscope, especially if they might reveal a personal secret. For *Better Call Saul*, you might come across a topical issue on an op-ed page but come at it with an unexpected interpretation of the law. If law is not your thing and you're trying to write for *Saul* you might dig up little-known events in the Southwest or find an angle on auto mechanics geared to driving an old car through the desert. Now, none of that means you should rely on gimmicks. Clever bits of information do not make stories. But they might turn your own creative wheels.

And here's how they turn: Make your subject live and breathe through the experiences of your continuing cast. That's key. The most common error is to tell the story through guest cast. I'm going to repeat that in other words because it's so important: Don't write a story that can be told without your continuing cast. If your story could work as a movie without your show, then you haven't made it work for your show.

Here's an example of wrong and right ways to approach your story. Let's make believe you're planning an episode for a series about Jane and Sally, who are detectives, and you've come upon an item about a woman cat burglar who scales tall buildings to steal Manolo Blahnik shoes.

A *wrong* logline would go like this: Portia Pedi, a former rock-climbing champion, attempts to scale the Seattle Needle at night to acquire the world's most expensive stilettos, but her clever plan is foiled when she's caught by Jane and Sally.

A better approach to an episode logline would be more like this: Jane confronts her fear of heights on a ledge of the Needle at night when she must rescue Sally who has been taken hostage by a woman cat burglar, and together Jane and Sally foil the plan to steal the world's most expensive stilettos.

See the difference? In the wrong version, the guest cast drives the action of the show and leaves the main cast as mere witnesses or pawns of the guest. In the second version, the challenge, jeopardy, and viewpoint belong to the main cast, whose decisions create the turning points.

Once you've identified a subject for your spec episode, write it as a logline. (Loglines are discussed in Chapter Two, in case you want to refer back.) That's easier said than done because in order to state your story in a sentence, you need to know the whole dramatic arc. I understand that's difficult, but I advise you not to skip ahead. Once you're clear about your story's conflict you'll be secure you really do have a plot, not only a premise.

If you're working on an A-story series, you can move on as soon as you have a single logline, though you'll need to make sure your one story has sufficient substance for around 25 scenes. If you're doing a show with three or more stories, you'll need separate loglines for the B, C, or other stories, and you do have to figure out each one. With that done, you're now ready to get to work.

BREAKING YOUR STORIES

"Breaking a story" means identifying the main turning points. On network TV it involves structuring the episode so strong cliffhangers occur at the act breaks and the story engine runs all the way from the inciting incident in the Teaser (or the beginning of Act One) to the resolution in Act Four or Five. In shows with no commercials, you can break an episode based on big twists or reversals and surprising reveals in a main character's arc.

It's not a process to take lightly, and even experienced writing staffs wrestle with stories for hours, even days. In addition to placing the act breaks, apply these two basic dramatic tests:

1. Credibility: What would real, normal people do in the situation? Are you forcing the plot twists by contriving actions that stretch believability, or do the actions and responses of the characters follow naturally from the jeopardy or conflict? What's honest here?

2. Rooting interest: Do you care whether the characters succeed? Are the stakes clear enough and high enough to make an audience root for your protagonist? Will people be emotionally involved?

Once you've settled on your essential stories, you can sneak up on the structure by figuring out some tent-poles. The easiest may be your opening because the event that propels the episode is often what attracted you. But even with the most obvious story, you'll have options: Do you want to open with the guest cast who will present the challenge, or with an internal problem for one of your main cast, or with a goal for one of your main cast that becomes subverted once the guest cast arrives?

Aaron Sorkin told the Writers Guild Foundation seminar how he starts: "I have an idea for the first page and a half — which, by the way, no joke, if I know what the first page and a half is of something, I don't want to say I'm halfway home, but I can see the house."

Whatever it takes for you to see the house — the voice of a character, picturing a place, coming upon a crime scene, getting a case, or confronting a conflicted relationship — close your eyes and make that come to life. Then you'll be centered in your show's world, which makes it easier to be real about what happens next.

The second easiest tent-pole is probably the ending. When you chose this subject, the final outcome might have been inherent. The body is found at the beginning and the real killer is the one who reported it, or the nice witness, or the secret lover, or whatever. In a non-procedural serialized drama, the show may have a master plan that prevents you from arriving at any kind of closed ending, even temporarily. But your specific episode still must have its own story engine and a goal, usually in increments of a relationship or decision. Your challenge is how to arrive at that ending through the main character's process of discovery or growth, not mainly to solve a crime or cure a disease or manage to survive. So even when you know the ending, you have to get to it, and therein lies the craft of storytelling.

The third tent-pole occurs at the end of Act Three (in a four-act model). In a show without act breaks, think of this tent pole as around three-quarters of the way to the end. It's the "worst case." Remember, in drama, the worst event is whatever opposes the protagonist's goal (or the triumph of the antagonist), not necessarily bad stuff that happens. For example, in the hypothetical show about detectives Jane, Sally, and Portia the shoe burglar, the worst case might be that Jane, who is afraid of heights, is forced to venture out on a ledge to rescue Sally. The jeopardy here is not only to Sally, who has been taken hostage, but that Jane has to confront her darkest demons in making herself climb out, and is shaking so badly because of her fears she's going to blow her one chance at the rescue. That's the cliffhanger before the Act Three break.

Here's another example: A doctor fears his wife doesn't love him anymore and is struggling hard to win her back. During the episode, he has a patient who needs surgery. At the same time it's raining outside. From a dramatic viewpoint, the worst case is that the wife rejects him, not that the patient dies or the rain turns into a flood, though those circumstances could certainly complicate the character's quest.

When you know the Act Three "worst case," you've nearly solved your basic structure because you can begin figuring backwards to how your characters arrived at this crisis. Even if you can fill in no more than one or two beats prior to the third act break, you'll begin to feel the progression.

Now you want to pin down the cliffhangers at the ends of Act One and Act Two. Developing the antagonist might give you some clues. Often (but, of course, not always) the second act is where the opposition that began in Act One gains strength. You know that at the end of Act Three this opposition will appear to have won, so see if you can come up with two surprises. You might discover that the protagonist underestimated the antagonist in the first act but is forced to fight back after a reveal at the end of Act One. In Act Two, maybe the antagonist is not exactly what was expected, or your characters follow a red herring, or they even believe they've won, when the antagonist (or problem) reasserts itself at the Act Two break.

Using our make-believe Jane and Sally show, you might introduce the challenge that someone is stealing shoes in Act One and reveal at the Act One break that the culprit is a woman cat burglar who scales skyscrapers . . . and that brave Jane is paralyzed by this case because she's afraid of heights. So in Act Two Sally has to go it alone as Portia becomes more and more bold, endangering many shoes. In fact, Jane's inability to work on the case leads to Sally being taken hostage at the Act Two break. As the jeopardy deepens through Act Three, it becomes urgent that only Jane can save Sally, and that she has to go out on that ledge or all is lost at the Act Three break. Act Four is pure resolution, and would emerge naturally from the "worst case."

Of course, that's a silly story, but I'm trying to give you a broad sense of how to find the big bones of your structure. Your writing is more subtle, more complex, and doesn't rely on cartoon-like action, right? Still, these "tent-poles" can help you plan:

THE GRID

Yep, here it is again, doing an encore since the last chapter. This time, though, you're not noting the various stories of someone else's script. Now, you can use the grid for your own rough ideas by filling in the major beats I've just described — opening, ending, worst case, Act One break, and Act Two break.

One caveat: The grid is something I've created for myself because it helps me see the entire hour at a glance in the earliest stages of figuring it out. If this doesn't help you, don't worry about it. The grid is just a planning tool because everybody has to start somewhere, and a blank page might be daunting. Make copies and play with it if you'd like, and vary it for five or six acts if that fits your show.

Chart 4.1   Basic Four-Act Grid

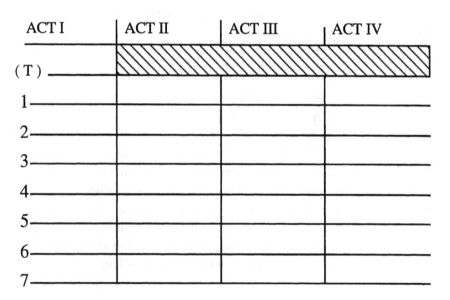

THE OUTLINE

The first step of writing involves listing the scenes in your script. This process has several names in addition to "!@#$%^&*()+," which is what you might want to call it when wrestling down the structure. Actual names include "outline," "step outline," "beat outline," "beat sheet," "treatment," and even "beatment," but they all amount to figuring out the order of events in your teleplay.

"Treatment" has a specific definition, usually observed only in the breach, and it's not a word you'll hear much in television. Technically, a treatment would be a half to two-thirds the length of a finished script written in prose (not screenplay form) that includes every scene in the order it occurs, as well as tone, style, and descriptions, and is virtually the entire script lacking only dialogue. Hardly anybody writes treatments like that. If someone asks you for a "treatment" of your story, what they really mean is a few pages that summarize it. Even for full-length features, I've heard the term "treatment" apply to a three-page pitch. Don't bother with it unless you're asked.

A "beat sheet," as used by some producers, is midway between a treatment and an outline. It parses your show into acts and describes the big story elements, though it doesn't spell out specific scenes. So we're talking about seeing the dramatic turns, not a diagram for writing.

"Beat outline" is sometimes used interchangeably with "outline" because it's a list of what's actually written in the teleplay, and usually those "beats" are scenes. On one show where I worked, the producers asked writers for a very full outline (like a treatment with numbers), but when the staff met, they would reduce the narrative in the outline to a more skeletal list they called a beat outline so the construction could be analyzed.

For example, an outline scene might say something like "While Jane clings to the ledge, frozen in fear, desperately trying to convince Portia to release Sally, Portia taunts Jane to climb out to get her." The simplified beat might say "Jane on ledge — Portia: "Come get her." It's an internal cue used for planning though it might not make sense to an outside reader.

This brings us to your outline. As you know from Chapter Two, an outline is a step in the professional development process. It's a contracted stage of writing that generates "story by" credit and pays almost as much as a whole script. If you have a contract with "cutoffs," you might get no further if the outline doesn't work; but a successful outline means your option for a first draft will be "picked up" (you'll go ahead to write the script).

What if no producer or payments are involved, though? Un-fun though outlines may be, you really should write one, even if you're working alone on your spec. I advise: Don't travel without a road map — hour episodes are too complex, especially if you're juggling multiple storylines. If you're on your own, though, handwritten notes might be enough, and initially you could get away with being vague, noting only what you need to accomplish for the characters within a scene. Personally, I've found that the time it takes to type a complete outline and weigh each beat saves me oodles of time writing because I'm not worrying about being lost or redundant, and it saves me from writing scenes I'll have to delete because they don't move the story ahead. To me, grief-avoidance is worth the effort.

HOW TO WRITE YOUR OUTLINE

Nobody launches into an outline at number one and trucks on to number 25 in a straight line. Instead, start with the tent poles I mentioned and fill in the grid until it's complete enough to write the scenes as an outline. Or you could begin with index cards (physical or digital), as many writers do. Cards are wonderful because they're not threatening. If you don't like an idea, toss it out. If your order doesn't make sense, rearrange the cards. And you can "down-load" your thoughts in any order, which lets you reach creatively to scenes you'd enjoy whether or not they fit next in the script.

One technique is to choose different color cards for each story. If you do all the beats of the yellow story, then the green one, then the blue, and assemble them, you'll see at a glance whether you've lost your green story in the second act, and whether the blue is paying off in Act Four or if it petered out in Act Three (which might be okay, but at least you'll have a chance to ask the question).

Remember, in a multiple-story show, the stories are probably uneven. So, if you'll have around 25 scenes in an hour episode, and your "A" story predominates, it might have as many as 10 to 14 beats; the "B" could have 6 to 10 beats or so, and the "C" has whatever is left, as few as 3 or 4 beats, up to maybe 6. Of course, if you're dealing with vignette writing, with seven or eight parallel stories, you might have a whole little tale in a single beat, though that's not typical of most dramas. Understand, I'm not suggesting exact numbers of scenes that should go with any story. I'm illustrating the kind of planning you might do.

Let's say you start with your "A" story. Make cards for every scene that tells your story. Count them. If you've got 40 cards, you have a problem. Maybe the cards are fragments rather than whole scenes. See if you can condense many of them together until you have 10 to 16 cards. Or maybe your story doesn't fit in an episode. What portion of this story is the essential conflict that could work within an hour? Or maybe you're rambling, including backstory or side incidents that aren't part of the forward motion. Whatever doctoring you need to do, get that A story down to size.

What if your beats are too few? You can troubleshoot by asking the opposite questions. Maybe you have combined a few scenes on one card. See if you can separate them into two-minute blocks, and then see if this story becomes the right size. Or maybe you don't have enough material for a major story. If it truly doesn't have enough meat, then you might look for a larger story to "marry" with it. Or maybe it does have fine potential but you haven't yet spelled out the moments that would unveil it on screen. Again, see if doctoring will get you to a useable scale.

After you do that with one story, go to the next and the next. Some scenes from different stories may play at the same time and place, so you'll actually get more mileage out of your screen time than you'd have if each story were a freestanding little movie. And once you weave them, you'll discover interesting contrasts, where telling one story enables you to ellipse time in another, or a scene from "A" resonates thematically with "B" in an interesting way. Putting the stories together can lead to discoveries, so you want to be flexible here.

After your individual stories are filled out, and you've ball-parked which beats occur at the act breaks, read the cards through with the feeling of watching on screen. Don't kid yourself. If you're bored, the audience will be too. But they're only index cards — change anything you want at this stage.

Once your basic structure is in hand, write it out. Here is a cheat sheet for how a standard outline looks:

"Title of Episode"

TEASER

Summarize the teaser in a few lines, usually with more description or tone than the beats that follow. In shows where the teaser is a single scene, it's one paragraph.

— However, complex ensemble series may begin several stories in the teaser and break them into separate blocks.

— Teasers with two or three (or more) distinct scenes may have two or three (or more) segments like this.

ACT ONE

1. EXT. LOCATION — TIME
The beats of the outline are numbered, beginning with #1 in each act, and headed by sluglines, as in a script. Keep them short like "loglines" for the scenes.

2. INT. LOCATION — TIME
Each step is a scene with dramatic structure. Every scene has a protagonist (a character who drives the scene), a goal, and an antagonist or opposition to the goal, even in scenes one minute long, even where conflict is subtle.

3. INT. SAME LOCATION — LATER
These are dramatic scenes, not production scenes. In other words, beats are determined by the content, not merely by time or location. If in the same location, you have a new conflict it is a new outline beat.

— However, in a show where multiple stories converge at a single moment, and you use a fragment of a different arc, it may be easier to follow if you note it after the scene.

4. EXT./INT. A FEW LOCATIONS — DAY TO NIGHT
A single dramatic scene may cover several places, beginning when characters meet, continuing with them in and out of a car, concluding elsewhere. In this case, use an inclusive slugline, as above, though you wouldn't do it in a script.

5. INT. SQUAD ROOM — DAY
An example: Jane arrives saying a mantra about her fear of heights just as Sally accepts a dare from Pedi to try on the stolen shoes if they meet her on the roof right now.

6. See if you can fit each act in one to three pages. The total hour outline would then run between 4 and 12 pages, approximately. However, every series has its own pace and style and it's not unusual to see 15-page outlines.

If you use that outline form to specify locations and times for each scene, it will help you be real about what's actually on screen. Here's an example of an *incorrect* beat in place of #5 on the sample:

INT. SQUAD ROOM — DAY
Jane says the mantra to herself while driving to work and stopping to feed the pigeons. While petting one, then releasing it, she thinks about how scared she would be to fly like the pigeons. Meanwhile Sally gets a call from Pedi, who is trying on shoes on the roof, inviting Sally and Jane to join her up there, where we can see her dancing in high heels. Sally worries whether Jane would be able to go up there too. When Jane enters, saying her mantra, Sally tells her etc. . . .

That's awful, right? That example is like one of those children's games where kids try to pick out all the things that don't belong in a picture. Before I tell you the answers, find the mistakes, yourself. . . . Okay, ready?

- Engage each scene as close as possible to its conflict or problem. Here, Jane meanders while screen time ticks away before we get to the purpose of this beat.

- Animal wrangling is expensive and consumes production time, so it's an example of the kind of material TV series spend for only when essential to the drama.

- If you're inside the squad room, you can't see Jane outdoors. All that would be exterior (EXT.) action. In an outline, you can use an inclusive slugline, but if you really mean to place the dramatic conflict in the squad room, omit the driving.

- Jane's fear of flying is not visible on screen. Don't put it in the outline if you can't put it in the script. If you do intend to put it in the script, though, indicate how you'll show it.

- A similar problem recurs with visualizing Pedi on the roof. Sure, there should be a place in the script to establish Pedi. If this is it, be clear in the outline — and give it all it's due in its own location as a separate beat — or omit it from this scene and allow Pedi's dare to be heard on the phone or communicated in Sally's dialogue.

Once you delineate your usable beats, you can easily turn your index cards into an outline a producer (or you) could track. Or maybe not so easily. When you move from handwritten notes to a typed structure, you'll probably realize some facts slipped by: You've indicated a scene is in daytime. Oh, it can't be day because the scenes before and after are at night. But it doesn't make sense for the characters to be at work at night. Okay, should you move this scene elsewhere? Or can the other scenes occur in the day? If so, how does that change the tension? What day of the story is this anyway?

That's just a hint at the reality-check awaiting you, but better to resolve it in the outline than after you've written 50 pages!

ALTERNATE OUTLINE FORMS

Not every show, or every writer, does outlines so detailed or specific. Some prefer to plan the characters' arcs but leave the actions (where, when, and how the characters play out their conflicts) to whoever writes the scripts.

When I was a beginner, I wrote for *A Year in the Life*, which began as a beautiful limited series that followed a Seattle family in the aftermath of the mother's death. The short run proved so successful the family drama was picked up for a full season. The showrunners, Joshua Brand and John Falsey (who now write for *The Americans*), had planned complete character arcs for the season, and since this was very much a serial, all episodes were like puzzle pieces that had to fit a larger picture.

The first outline Brand and Falsey handed me was unlike anything I'd encountered at the time. It followed the psychological and emotional progress in the hour but suggested only a little that could be termed "plot" or even incidents. Yet, it was an important point in the season. In the "A" story, the family patriarch, widowed for less than a year, proposes marriage to an independent woman who has a fulfilling life as a doctor and no need to marry. The "B" story dealt with the teenage granddaughter who is arrested for driving without a license. In the "C," The newly married daughter-in-law tries to get a first job; and she and her husband have a fight. So it's not as if the hour was devoid of contents, but the outline I was presented had hardly any guidance about how to relay these stories.

For instance, one beat said something like: "Coming into the kitchen after arguing with his wife, the son wants to confide in his father, but can't. The father's proposal has just been turned down, and he'd like to tell his son, but he can't confide either. During the scene neither man ever says what is on his mind, though they comfort each other." That was all.

I loved the challenge, but before I could write that scene I had to create a mini-outline for myself. In this case, the scene was set in the family kitchen late at night, each man surprised to find the other there, not wanting to show vulnerability. I kept the dialogue entirely "off the nose" (indirect), each man emphasizing his strength for the other, while they comforted themselves with food. No chase scenes or car crashes or anything larger than two people at a table, but the delicate moment did have tension because the audience knew what was being withheld. I tell you, this is the most difficult kind of scene to write because you have no external jeopardy to lean on; the conflict comes entirely from character, and much of the opposition is internal.

Because it was so difficult, I made notes for the turning points within this tiny scene — the optimal place to enter, when to take the milk from the fridge, exactly when the son would ask what happened with the proposal, the moment he'd let his dad off the hook by mentioning football tickets, the spot where the father would sigh and pointedly reveal nothing, and so forth. It helped me to have that map even though no one else saw it.

Many writers use outlines somewhere between the specific, detailed "cheat sheet" and the loose emotional agenda from *A Year in the Life*. On *ER*, for example, the outlines didn't tend to have numbers but each step was a fully realized scene with dramatic structure. Here is a fragment of an actual *ER* outline of the Emmy-winning episode "Love's Labor Lost" written by Lance Gentile. I'm grateful to Warner Brothers, executive producer John Wells, and writer-producer Lance Gentile for permission to print it here.

Episode 18

TEASER 7:00 AM

— ROSS and GREENE toss a football outside the ambulance bay. An ambulance races past, a familiar face in the window. "Was that Benton?" Ross goes long for a pass as a car careens down the street and a bloody gang member is tossed out into the street.

— Ross, Greene, and HATHAWAY race the gang member down the trauma hallway, passing HALEH, who takes us into Trauma One, where she finds a distraught BENTON. The old lady with the broken hip is MAE BENTON, his mother.

— In Trauma Two, CARTER and JARVIK join the heroic resuscitation of the trauma victim. Carter witnesses Greene at the top of his game, impressed.

— Mae is shy about her son seeing her naked, exposed and in pain. Haleh reassures him that she'll give her special attention. Benton wants to write out the orders as Haleh has been insisting. She lightens up on him: "Don't worry — I'll take care of it. Go see if Greene needs any help."

— Benton enters Trauma One as Greene is prepping for a thoracotomy. As Benton pulls on a trauma gown to do the procedure, Greene says he doesn't need any help — go be with your mother.

— When orthopedic resident JANET BLAIR arrives to admit Mae, Benton insists that the chief of orthopedics be called in.

— Greene and Hathaway escort an OR team out of Trauma Two. As Hathaway heads home from the night shift, she passes DR. GREGORY NELSON, chief of orthopedics, steaming into Trauma One.

— Nelson, none too happy about being pulled from his department meeting by Benton's persistent calls, does agree to do the case. Benton tries to get him to say that he, not the resident, will actually do the case. Nelson flatly refuses, and he and Blair take her off to OR. When Benton tries to get on the elevator, Nelson flatly forbids him to go anywhere near the OR.

All that occurs in the first several minutes, so you can see how fast television storytelling needs to move, how packed it is with dramatic stakes, and why you'd need to be at the top of your craft to write a show like that. The episode you're writing might not be as intense, but you can learn a lot from observing the skillful blending of arcs and the way an outline can blast each story out of the opening like cannonballs.

For example, in the very first beat, a peaceful "status quo" is immediately broken by the inception of the "A" story when Benton arrives in an ambulance, but rapidly diverts attention to the urgent "B" story when the gang member is tossed onto the street. Talk about grabbing attention!

Reread your own outline and read it to friends until it's as powerful and clear as you can make it.

SONNY'S LIST

One of my former MFA students, Sonny Calderon, told me he taped reminders around his computer, mostly tips that came from my response to someone's work in class. He thought these four might be useful as you begin your first draft.

- Every beat is an action. A character "realizing" something is not a scene. Each scene involves a character who wants something but faces resistance.

- The antagonist must be as strong and motivated as the protagonist. The more equal the sides, the more suspense. See the world from your antagonist's viewpoint also.

- Aim at the turning point where the protagonist must make a difficult choice, a moral equation that is nearly balanced.

- Anchor your story with the worst-case scenario three-fourths through. This is where the protagonist seems to fail and must overcome his internal problem to deal with the opposition.

YOUR FIRST DRAFT

How close should you stay to your outline? That depends how close your outline is to what works on screen. If you're on an assignment from a show, you will have vetted your outline with the head writer (and maybe the whole staff), so you're sent off to your first draft with an implied contract to deliver what they expect. Sometimes an outline is considered "locked," which means you're committed to the beats on the page and you'd better stick to them. In hasty or ultra-low budget productions, some companies have been known to start prepping (preproduction) based on the outline. (That may mean scouting locations and rough scheduling, for example.)

But what if you come upon something you want to fix? Say, in the outline, a beat exists to reveal a character's secret, but while writing you realize the secret is already apparent from a previous scene, so you need to cut the extra beat. Or you might want to make a larger change: The guest cast pops out, speaking in a way that's more interesting than appeared in the outline, and the "voice" of the character demands that certain scenes be angled differently.

If you're doing a spec, absolutely go for the revisions if you're sure of them. You don't get points for sticking doggedly to an outline that doesn't make sense! But if this script is for a producer, it's better not to make large changes without asking. I made that mistake once. I was doing a script for a show and had thoroughly worked out my outline with the showrunner. But as I approached Act Four, I was inspired by what I thought was a more clever resolution, so I went ahead and wrote it.

Well, one day after I delivered the script, the producer was on the phone complaining I hadn't given him the ending we'd discussed. Surprised by the emotional tenor of his reaction, I listened silently as he went on about this single point before I appreciated what he was really saying. The original ending had been his idea. Whether or not my version was better, his feelings were hurt — not just because I hadn't used his suggestion, but because he felt I'd disregarded him. This was about respect. Aha, I made a mental note: In the future, pick up the phone and ask. If you get the boss on board, he'll probably say okay to write what you think is best.

Now, how do you actually do the script? You've written screenplays before or you wouldn't have reached this point, and this one is not so different. Once you get past the structural requirements of the hour format, and you've told your stories via the show's continuing cast, the next special factor is speed. Episodes may be due two weeks after the outline is approved, and that feels fast if you're used to mulling over a feature for months. Of course, if you're speculating, no one will know how long you took to write, but a concentrated schedule is a habit you'll need if you're going to work in television.

In streaming shows when the entire season is completed before the first episode hits the screens, you may have more luxury. Even in that case, though, episodes build on each other so if you're slow, the writer after you (and the production staff) may be jammed up, and that's no way to make friends, or get hired again.

I'll show you how easy it is to deliver in 14 days. Let's say you have a long outline with 28 beats for a full hour episode. I like to follow my outline exactly, so I write just two scenes each day. Voila! 14 x 2 = 28. When I'm writing at home (not on staff), I begin each morning reading over what I wrote the day before, fine-tuning it. Then I take a breath and get ready for the first scene of the day. I approach it as if these next pages are the single most important piece of writing I'll ever do. I want to bring to this screen moment the richest experience, full of subtext and nuance, while delivering the action in the tightest way I can. I might imagine the whole scene before writing a word, or take a walk and jot down ideas, or close my eyes and wait for the characters' voices. Whatever it takes. Then I write two or three pages. And stop.

I find that pushing on diminishes quality, and I want to come to the next scene fresh. So I'll take a break. Lunch, errands, gym, emails — I try to take my mind off it, though when I'm most relaxed, not even trying, I'll have ideas for a way into the next scene or a perspective on one I wrote. Much later in the day, in the afternoon or night, I'll reread the morning's scene and revise it. Then I repeat the process of finding, forming, and writing the second scene of the day. And stop.

I've found that by the time I reach the end of the script, my first draft has already been edited because I refine my work each day. Of course, not everyone works like this, nor should they. I have a writer friend who starts work at 4:00 AM and smashes through as many pages as she can before she runs out of steam, hardly looking back. She tells me she'd never let anyone see that "mess" that rambles, repeats, and wanders into tangents. She regards it as raw material that she edits away after she arrives at the end. You could think of it as the difference between painting and carving a sculpture: The painter pays attention to each brush stroke, adding one after another until the picture is formed. The sculptor begins with a hunk of material, and cuts away "everything that isn't the statue," to paraphrase Michelangelo. One method isn't better than another — whatever works for you is right.

If you're frightened by a blank page, put something on it — anything. A painting teacher once taught me that as I stood staring at a blank canvas. He walked over and threw ink on my pristine surface, and that got me moving, even if only to clean up the ink. Some writers break the emptiness with automatic writing or anything a character might say, even if it's not the way to open the scene. Some people write by hand for the visceral feel of words flowing from the mind onto paper. Others talk into a recorder.

Aaron Sorkin commented to the Writers Guild Foundation Seminar: "When I try using a recording device, I freeze up immediately. It's walking around and talking to myself; it's driving and talking to myself. Ultimately, it's about typing."

So do whatever spins your wheels. But stick with professional form when you turn in your draft. You already know you need specialized screen-writing software, and you ought to be up on how scripts look. It might help to refer to the sample from *Breaking Bad* in Chapter Three. And in case you need a quick refresher, here's a "cheat sheet" on standard form.

Remember, you're writing a "selling script," not a "shooting script." You want to entice a reader, especially if this is a spec, so write what will keep someone interested. Mr. Sorkin shared this insight at the seminar:

". . . The selling script is the most important right now. I'm not writing a script right now for a line producer to sit and budget, for a DP [Director of Photography] to work at. I'm writing a script for you to read, to sit there at night — you can't stop turning the pages, this is so much fun. Even now in the scripts that I write, I only, frankly, describe what's important for you to get that moment. It's possible that I'm going to describe, 'and the camera pushes in and pushes in and pushes in' and I'm probably going to write it like that because I'm building tension for the reader at that point. . . . Mostly I write for dialogue, and dialogue is what you read fastest when you're reading a screenplay. Description just slows it down . . ."

For broadcast and basic-cable series with commercials, aim towards page 17 to end your first act (including the teaser if you have one), page 25 to 30 to end Act Two, around 35 to 40 to end Act Three, and somewhere between 45 and 55 at the end of Act Four. Those are approximate guides, not rules, though. A produced episode might run anywhere from 42 to 52 minutes (before commercials), depending on the outlet, but you won't know the actual length of your script until several drafts from now when a shooting script is read through by the cast and timed with a stopwatch. I gave you that page count only so you can check yourself. If you're way off — for example, an hour script that's thirty pages or ninety — it's time to trouble-shoot. Here are some quick diagnostics:

ACT TWO

FADE IN:

EXT. LOCATION - TIME OF DAY

The action is in a paragraph at the outside margin and goes
all across the page, single-spaced.

When you introduce a character for the first time, use
capitals. Example: CHARACTER ONE enters. But when Character
One is mentioned again, that name will not be upper case
(except when heading dialogue, of course).

                    CHARACTER ONE
               Dialogue. Try to keep this to under
               5 lines per speech, and always
               condense to minimum.

                    CHARACTER TWO
               Responses can include pauses, often
               indicated by...
                    (beat)
               And then the dialogue continues
               after the parenthetical.

                    CHARACTER ONE
                    (parenthetical)
               The parenthetical above should
               modify or describe how a line is
               said, but not give a large action.

If you want Character One to go across the room and do
something, that belongs here in action, not in a
parenthetical.

                    CHARACTER ONE (CONT'D)
               When the same character continues
               speaking after an action, indicate
               it with (CONT'D) after the name.

INT. LOCATION - TIME OF DAY

Give only enough description to build dramatic tension or
reveal an essential insight into character or plot. Do not
indulge in set decoration.

                    CHARACTER ONE
               Notice that after a new slug line,
               you don't need to write "CONT'D"
               though the same character is
               speaking.
                    (MORE)

2.

                    CHARACTER ONE(cont'd)
              When dialogue goes on long like
              this and breaks in the middle of
              the page, use "more" and "cont'd"
              as illustrated. Do not write long
              dialogue speeches like this though!

SECONDARY SLUG LINE

A secondary slug line might include ANGLE ON A DETAIL, or one
specific room or part of a scene, such as CLOSET.

In spec scripts and all first drafts, do not put numbers on
the scenes nor "continued" on the tops and bottoms of pages.
That happens only in the final shooting script.

And when you reach the end of each Act and the end of the
script...

                                        FADE OUT.

If you're running long:

- Are the speeches overwritten, explanatory, or redundant? Tighten the dialogue.

- Have you indulged in set decoration, directing on the page, or overblown description? Take a sharp knife to these.

- Are certain acts long, though the script is the right length? Move the act breaks by enhancing a different cliffhanger or reordering scenes.

- Have you indulged in backstory, expository speeches, or tangents? Return to your original outline and stick to a clean, clear telling.

- Have you engaged the scenes as close as possible to the conflict? Have you ended scenes immediately after the climax or goal? If you have written prologues or epilogues to your scenes, get rid of them.

- Is there too much story? If your outline was accurate, this shouldn't be a problem, but you might have fooled yourself in the outline by counting sequences of scenes as one beat. If so, you need to rethink the stories themselves, or delete an entire arc. This is major work, not editing (see the discussion of "second draft").

If you're running short:

- Have you fleshed out your scenes? A script is not merely an outline with dialogue. It requires reimagining each dramatic moment as an experience. Make sure you've fully told your story, including reactions as well as actions.

- Do you have enough story? If your outline only seemed to be complete, but actually contained mostly a premise or the circumstances in which a story would occur, you'll need to go back to the outline stage and create more events, more real turns — more of a plot. Rewrite the outline before you rewrite the script in this case.

AT THE END OF IT ALL...

Sorry, there isn't an end, at least not anytime soon. This process will go on for as many more drafts as you can stand, and if your episode is produced, you might want to revise all through post-production and only quit fixing things when you're forced to because the thing is on the air! As a beginner on a staff, once you hand it off, you'll be onto the next assignment anyway. In television, obsessive script tinkering is limited, because shows get on the air very quickly.

If this is an assigned script, you probably have to deliver it to the head writer now. But if you're ahead of schedule by a day or so, don't hand it in early. Take that day to let the script "cool," then reread it with as much distance as you can muster and refine what you can, but deliver on time. TV schedules don't have much slack, and slackers don't get much work in TV.

If this is your own spec with no deadline, now is an opportunity for feedback. Have your draft read by everyone, not just other writers or your grandma who thinks everything you do is perfect. Sometimes an outside reader will ask what you need to hear: "Why would she do that?" "I don't get why they don't just make up." Or you might hear awful reactions: "Is this supposed to be a parody of *Buffy*?" Don't be crushed by one misguided reader. On the other hand, the reader might be on to something. It's a gift to have the chance to reconsider.

If readers are too polite, or don't know how to give feedback, ask them three simple questions:

— Do you care about the people in the stories?

— Were you rooting for something to happen?

— What do you think this script is all about?

After all the input, I suggest setting the draft aside for a couple of weeks, if you can manage that. With enough distance, you might see what you need to change by yourself. You'll also see typos that your eyes glazed over no matter how well you spell-checked and proofread. My favorite was a student script for the series *Boston Public* innocently handed in with the "l" missing on the first page.

YOUR SECOND DRAFT

You need to understand the difference between revising and rewriting. The kind of editing you do every day — fixing spelling and punctuation, tightening lines, omitting a speech, clarifying an action, lopping off the heads or tails of overlong scenes — all those corrections are parts of normal writing. Rewriting is a whole other job.

A rewrite means rethinking the structure and sometimes characters as well. You're still dealing with the same general story, but you want a fresh way to tell it. You can't do that by crossing out lines or replacing words. Go back to the drawing board.

Start by putting aside the script. I mean it. As long as you cling to the precious moments you've written, you'll be tied to your first draft. Take a breath and let go. Maybe you'll be able to use many of the pages you've written; and certain scenes, even sequences, might survive intact. But when you begin a rewrite, everything is on the table or you'll turn into a pretzel trying to fit a structure around scenes that don't belong.

Depending on the notes you got from the producer or readers, your episode may require a new outline. Can you work with your existing outline as a reference to reorganize the beats, or do you have to start over? Either way, boldly get rid of what hasn't worked and add completely new elements, even a new arc, if necessary.

Then begin the second draft using the new outline, though, again, you might be able to keep much of your first draft. Now, I'm not saying to throw out the story the show bought (if indeed it was bought). On that point — being told to do a second draft on an assignment is terrific news. The alternate is being cut off after the first draft and having your script given to another writer. Don't imagine for a minute that anyone's first draft is shot exactly as first written, not even when the showrunner writes it himself! And if you're on assignment, the second draft generates a payment.

I had a funny experience with a rewrite. I'd handed in a first draft (this was actually a TV movie) and the network called for an in-person meeting at their office. That didn't bode well because if notes are minor they're often given on the phone or in an email. So, in we went — the producer, a company executive, and me — anticipating a high-level effort to save the project. As it happened, this particular network exec wasn't experienced, and she sat there going page by page through the script. Two hours. And at the end of it, she'd asked for changes in five lines. Five lines! The producer was so steamed that he told my agent to bill the network for a full second draft, which amounted to something like a thousand dollars per word. Don't count on that kind of waste in episodes, though. Showrunners mean it when they want a rewrite.

If you're speculating, draft numbers make no sense. Every selling script is "First Draft," even if you've written this thing eleven times. To keep track for yourself, you could put the date of the draft in the lower right corner of the title page. Or you might run a header showing the revision dates of specific pages (some screenwriting programs have this application). But submit your script with no draft numbers or dates. And no colored pages — that's for production revisions after the shooting script. Remember, the sample you send to a producer is always shiny new, hot off your printer.

YOUR POLISH

Technically, a "polish" means what you'd think — a small revision, like polishing a surface, fine-tuning. Frequently the term is used for a dialogue polish where a writer goes through a script and sharpens the speeches. Polishes do not include restructuring or creating new characters or story arcs.

For you, if you're working on a series, a polish may or may not appear in your contract, and if it does, the payment is slight. That shouldn't matter. If you're fortunate enough to be kept on an episode after your second draft, cling with your teeth and fingernails and polish anything including the boss's chair. Scripts keep changing, and the more you're willing to do, the more the final product will be yours. Of course, if you're on a staff, you'll be polishing other people's scripts routinely, sometimes because the original writer is busy with something larger. It's a normal stage in preparing a script for production.

As for your spec script: Polish until it gleams.

WRITING YOUR PILOT

This chapter has focused on writing scripts for existing series because that's what you do when you work in this business. But pilots make good writing samples to get those staff jobs. In Chapter Three, we discussed a great pilot written by Vince Gilligan. Now it's your turn, and here's how.

When you write a pilot script, you're the creator of a universe that includes places, people, churning and contradictory desires, threatening situations, even day jobs. And always at the core are secrets: mysteries so deep and intricate they will take 13 or even 100 hours to discover. But some writers don't start with those specific revelations, or even with the cast.

CREATE THE "WORLD"

Many pilot writers begin with total mental immersion in a location where they will dwell virtually for years. David Simon, creator of HBO's searing and insightful urban dramas, *The Wire*, *Treme*, and *The Deuce*, are intensely tied to their locations. But the source is deeper. I asked him for advice to new writers. This is what he told me:

"It's very hard when you haven't experienced a lot of life to comment on life. I had the benefit of spending the first part of my career as a newspaper reporter for about fifteen years from the time I was in college until I left the [*Baltimore*] *Sun*. Those fifteen years grounded me in lives other than my own. A lot of beginner's literature tends to be singular and onanistic because people don't know much of the world when they start writing. They might become a craftsman as a writer and people could do it at a young age because they're smart. They read and learn other writers and they get the dynamic. But that doesn't answer the question whether they have anything to say about the world.

"To speak to something serious about life or about society it helps to have lived awhile, endured a bit of loss and tragedy and the things that happen to you when you get older. Not to mention, as you get older you see the cycle of political behavior and you're better able to parse things for what they are rather than what they claim to be. What I look for are writers in their forties and fifties who have seen a little bit of life, and if they've been in situations or places in the world where they can bring something to bear on the subject at hand that's even more important.

"But if you want to be current, maybe you have to go and research dialogue, do reportage. If I want to write something about New Orleans in 2007, it matters that I was paying attention, that I was down there in 2007. We sold the pilot idea for *Treme* to HBO in 2005 right after the storm. I needed to get down there while *The Wire* and *Generation Kill* were both still in production. I needed to start doing reportage. We took about two and a half years before we tried a first draft. We also needed time to see what was going to happen with New Orleans. How can you know how to arc the thing until you know what you're trying to say?"

I asked Mr. Simon about creating characters as he plans each new show. He replied:

"Your characters are your tools to tell a story. They have to stay sharp. You can't build a house with a bad toolbox. Everything — the characters, the actors, the directors — you want to have the best possible toolbox. But if all you're doing is writing characters, what's the difference between what you're doing and a soap opera except that you're executing on a better level. What do you have to say about the world? What do you have to say that hasn't been said already?"

Sometimes a show's "world" is tied to a quest or special character rather than a place. No one would mistake *Grey's Anatomy* for a show about Seattle. Instead *Grey's* world is a hospital; and within that, the internal landscape of relationships. And no one would mistake *Grey's* world for the one in *The Killing*, though it was also in Seattle. Think of how these worlds differ from each other in similar locations: *Transparent*, *American Crime* and *Glow* are all set in California. In New York we find *Luke Cage* and *Mr. Robot*. *Empire* and *Stranger Things* are both set in the Midwest. Clearly, "world" is not limited to geography.

Damon Lindelof, co-creator of *Lost*, began his world with a place: a mysterious island where a plane has crashed. But he advises that the starting point for most shows is usually not as challenging. "When you talk about television shows, there is a franchise element, and the franchise is the world. A hospital, a law firm, or a precinct — those are the easiest worlds for a television series. You know what kinds of stories inhabit those worlds. The harder worlds are a spaceship that is being pursued across the galaxy or you're on an island in the middle of nowhere that the audience knows you cannot leave.

"The question is who's going to be interacting with that world? That's what separates a good cop show from a bad cop show and a good medical show from a bad medical show. They both deal with the same patients, but the issue is: who are the doctors who are tending to those patients?"

FIND THE STORY SPRINGBOARDS

Okay, let's say you've fully moved into your new mental home — the world of your series. What's next? Not writing — not quite yet, though you should be jotting notes all along. Now you need to fully imagine what makes stories happen in your world. That's not limited to the pilot episode, but requires figuring out the "motor" of the show. Do people come in with cases to solve? If so, that doesn't necessarily mean a legal or crime case, or a disease. In a sense, a case could be a relationship issue, or coping with extra-terrestrials or extra-dimensionals (as in *Stranger Things*), or your internal demons (as in *Mr. Robot* and *House of Cards*). As long as characters have long-range quests that incur conflict, and their stories present both internal and external jeopardy, you can discover the "springboards" for stories within your world. This potential for future stories is the essential that differentiates writing a pilot from writing anything else on screen.

POPULATE THE "WORLD"

Once you know how your show "works" within a rich world, your next step is probably to draw out the main cast. I use that phrase "draw out" as opposed to introduce or even create, because if your world is fully enough imagined, these people already live there. In fact, if you have a problem knowing the three or four or five people who your show is about, you should go back to step one and delve deeper into your world. That's not to say you'll know everyone in a large ensemble cast, or that characters you didn't see at first won't step out and greet you as you write. Actually, as a writer it's wonderful to be surprised like that. But beginners shouldn't tackle a big ensemble anyway. It's difficult enough to write a few people well!

Some writers do thorough bios of their characters at this point. Some sketch out moments, phrases, or images that "pop" a character. I once wrote a pilot where I needed a way to tag a character (express her) in order to pitch the show. I saw her speeding into the outskirts of Los Angeles at dawn in a beat-up convertible, bare feet pressing the pedals to the metal while her butt danced on the car seat to the sound of "Mustang Sally." In another glimpse, close and tight, she took her time licking the remnants of Kentucky Fried Chicken off a paper wrapper while a motel proprietor banged on her door. Only one of those moments actually appeared in the script, but both helped me visualize her at an early stage.

I spoke with Ron Moore, who runs *Outlander*, and asked about his process creating his previous show, the great dramatic allegory *Battlestar Galactica* on Syfy. He described how he arrived at the characters. Initially, he wasn't interested in the project because the original 1970s show by the same name lacked depth. "But," he said, "when I watched it again I was struck by the dark premise at the heart: an apocalyptic attack destroyed humanity. The show was about the survivors and the Cylons chasing them forever. I thought that was a really interesting format because the core was this disturbing notion of death and being lost in the cosmos. So I thought, what if you took the premise and really did the show and asked yourself in those circumstances what would happen to real people? If you took normal, screwed-up people who just happened to be the ones that made it, what would that show be like?

"I knew I wanted to maintain the premise: the show was about the survivors who were on this last battleship. Then I decided the old show was about a family. I looked at the family tree and decided to make some changes. The daughter in the old show didn't serve any purpose so I just lost her. Then I made Starbuck a woman immediately, and decided she's the surrogate daughter to the father figure. The father figure of Adama had no counterpart, neither a mother nor any counterpart in the civilian world. I didn't want it to be just a military show. Okay, the premise was that the remnants of human civilization were in these fleets. So how do they govern themselves? Are they going to try to maintain their democracy as they move forward? Is the president to be a real player in this show, unlike the old one? And I decided that should be a woman, and that sort of completes the family, and that's who the show is really about. Those are the general parameters I thought that show was about and how I was going to translate it to this show."

MAKE A PLAN

Let's say you have your world, your springboards, and your main cast. Yes, you're creeping up on writing the thing. Remember that you must grab readers even before this pilot ever gets to viewers, so your first ten pages (or less) are critical. Don't lay back and wait for episode 5, or 13 to reel in your audience with a revelation. Get a sense of anticipation started now.

What do you need to generate anticipation? Answer the basic dramatic questions: Do we care about (or are we intrigued by) your main character? What does the character want urgently? Why does she need it so desperately? Who and what opposes her? Are the chances of succeeding and failing nearly equal? Then you rev up the action until we expect her to reach the goal . . . at which point you twist it, pulling out the rug, so we discover this quest will have way more ramifications, to be continued in later episodes.

Of course, that's oversimplifying. The point is that in the early pages you need to set your series in motion by rooting us in at least one of your main cast and establishing the series franchise. As for writing the world, I recommend that you don't write text to describe it. As vital as is creating the world for your series — so important that we began with it — it has to "breathe" through your script, not ever feel "made." That is, the world of your show *is* the show; it's where your people live. If you have to explain it, something's not alive here.

After all that, you're ready to plan your pilot as you would any ongoing episode of your show. Does it have four acts? Five? None? A teaser? Think about the broadcast grid as well as the character-driven chart without acts and the discussion of structure earlier in this chapter. Since you're the creator of this show you get to make those choices (at least until some network tells you otherwise — but you should be so lucky as to have a network!). Then move right along to outline, first draft, and all the revising and polishing that follows.

Once upon a time, spec pilots were indulgences in a fantasy of running a series of your own. Now, agents and producers want to read them as writing samples. And, yes, sometimes they even get made.

WHAT'S NEXT?

Do it again! If you're speculating, write another spec for a series that demonstrates you can work in a different genre. If you're writing on assignment, you'll have the thrill (really) of seeing your creation on screen. And if it's well received, you'll get another assignment in the future. If your spec script is a pilot, write another on a different subject.

No matter how this script turns out, the best way to write better is to write more. If this is your first dramatic episode, you've taken a great leap. Just think how much you learned. And next time it will be easier. Just kidding. If it's easy, you're not stretching. So don't expect easy, but once you're comfortable with the basics, next time will be more fun.

Finally, when you have a few writing samples in your portfolio, you're ready for the next step: joining a staff.

CHAPTER FIVE

IT'S WHO YOU KNOW: WORKING ON STAFF

Recently, a student on the verge of graduating asked me what was the single most important lesson I'd learned in writing for television. Her question started me thinking. Of course, I'd acquired writing skills, some insights into what works on screen, and a few experiences negotiating the system. But that's not what she meant. She was looking for career advice gleaned from what I might have done better.

I fast-forwarded through mistakes I'd made, like the time I turned down a staff position on a series because three better opportunities were around the corner. Well, one show wasn't picked up; on a second, the producer decided to write the pilot himself; and for job three, another writer was chosen. I found myself out of work as a writer for more than six months. Fortunately, I've had a "day job" teaching screenwriting at USC throughout my writing career, but it's not unusual for writers to be "between assignments" for months at a time. I'm telling you this at the start of the chapter on staff work where the pay is consistent and you may feel lulled into a sense of security. Here's my advice: Until you're receiving big bucks as a writer-producer or you have an "overall deal" that gives you a salary all year to develop new shows — Get yourself some other survival resource, whether that's an alternate writing venue (like journalism or web content), or a non-writing job, or a partner who helps carry expenses. But was that the most important lesson I wanted to pass on to the student?

I also thought about scripts I might have written better. When you see your work on screen, sometimes you're grateful — really — to the actors and directors who bring a moment to life. But once in a while you cringe. "I did not write that clunky line . . . did I?" Or, "Does this seem as slow to you as it does to me? Why didn't I tighten that beat? No, it was the director's fault . . . or was it my fault?" But all that's really fleeting.

The more I considered what mattered in building a writing career I came to a single lesson: Make friends. No doubt, you've heard the line, "It's who you know, not what you know"; or, put another way, "This town is all about relationships." Those glib sayings fit certain agents, managers, and producers. But I suggest you think about it somewhat differently as a writer.

Especially on TV series staffs, the act of creating is not private, though you certainly bring your unique talents. Writers tend to want to work with other writers who enable them to do their own best work. That often means choosing collaborators who make them comfortable enough to take creative risks, and who can be trusted to deliver quality dialogue or story twists or humor or tales of life. Much of this rests on what's on the page. But no producer-writer has the time to comb every writing sample. Producers hire whom they know.

Now, that doesn't mean you have to party with powerful people or suck up to their families. It means forming networks of professional trust. You do that through good work followed by staying in touch. Students just out of film school often form workshops that meet at each other's apartments, not only for continuing feedback on writing, and commiseration, but also for the connections. One of my writing students formed an alliance with a producing student who wanted to be an agent. On graduating, the junior agent got a job as, well, a junior agent, and brought along the writer as a first client. In time, they rose together.

If you're not in film school, you might make similar connections at seminars, workshops, extension classes, social networks, and blogs. Or maybe you'll land a beginning assignment on a small show. The people in the cubicles next to you aren't always going to be in those cubicles. Someone's going to move on to a better series, someone's going to become a producer, someone's going to be asked to recommend a writer, maybe with qualifications just like yours. Join professional groups, and when you're eligible, become active in the Writers Guild. Even if you're shy or a hermit (or so focused on the characters you're creating you don't want to be bothered with actual humans), push yourself out of your shell. That's the one thing I wish I'd done more, and I offer it to you as the career lesson I learned.

If it wasn't for my history with one particular network executive, I wouldn't have been able to tell a story that meant a lot to me. A teenage friend of my daughter was visiting one day and mentioned, all too casually, that her mother had been diagnosed with breast cancer. The girl blew it off as if it didn't affect her. I realized she was in deep denial, utterly unprepared to face the reality of the upcoming surgery. Thinking about her, it occurred to me that dramas had been done about breast cancer — and the last thing I wanted to do was a disease-of-the-week movie — but no one had dealt with this serious subject from the daughter's point of view. What interested me was not the illness but the relationship and how such an event would affect a teenager's sense of what it means to be a woman, and what would happen if she lost her mother.

Had I set out to write a script, or even a treatment, or even a pitch, and asked my agent to arrange meetings with potential producers, followed by waiting for their responses, followed by scheduling network meetings, and rescheduling them after they're postponed, followed by who-knows-how-many network pitches, followed by who-knows-how-long-I'd-wait for an answer that might be no . . . half a year might go by before I could write this, if ever.

Instead, I picked up the phone. I had some credits at a particular network — four were on series and a couple of others on original dramas — and a year earlier I'd shared a table with one of the vice presidents. We were at the ceremony for the prestigious Humanitas Prize that gives awards for writing in film and television, and I was a finalist for a script that she'd greenlighted. When I didn't win, she leaned over and whispered something like, "Let's try again," or "let's do something else." I don't think I actually heard her words over the applause for my competitor.

But that was enough of a "relationship" for her to take my phone call. I did a minimal pitch, like, "Let's do something about breast cancer, but from the teenage daughter's point of view." She said, "Sure. Who do you want to produce?" I chose a company I'd worked with before because I liked their attitude of respecting the script and I believed I could trust the taste of a particular producer there. Also, I knew they'd be approved because they were a frequent vendor. The network VP said fine. One quick call to the producer's office, and the deal was done. A year later, that project, *Between Mother and Daughter*, did win the Humanitas Prize. My point isn't about winning awards, of course. I'm showing you how wheels turn based on relationships — not personal ones, but through mutual respect.

At other times, I've lost out on being considered for staffs of shows because I wasn't part of a social circle — the showrunners simply didn't know me. I understand how frustrated you may feel on the outside looking in. So in the spirit of learning from my mistakes, here's a tale of:

THE STAFF FROM HELL

(Cue howling wolves and lightning)

Anyone who has been on staff has a war story. That's because the proximity of staff writing resembles a trench during a battle. You make close buddies, or have to watch your back, or both. When I entered my own staff hell, I already had a number of produced credits and had spent time on staffs before, though they were either outside the mainstream or short-lived because the series were quickly cancelled. So this was my first experience on a staff of a major network show, and I made every mistake in the book — only there wasn't any book at the time. I wish I'd had this book because I might have avoided:

• MISTAKE 1: DON'T SEPARATE FROM THE STAFF.

Since the series was new, it was allotted a floor of empty offices on a studio lot. The showrunner walked the whole staff over and let each of us claim the office we wanted. I thought the quality of my writing was what mattered so I grabbed the quietest spot waaaay off in a distant corner. Meanwhile, the savvy guys nabbed offices that hugged the showrunner's. Every time he walked out of his office he saw them, and they'd be at hand for quick rewrites — the staff members he'd come to rely on. And they'd be first to overhear gossip — actors in or out of favor, network pressures, production, or story glitches — and nudge their drafts accordingly.

This principle of staying in the mix infuses all the situations below, though it applies mostly to beginning staffers. At higher echelons, producer-writers can't be in the office all the time because they're on the set or away on location shoots. And on many shows, "creative consultants" aren't around at all unless they're called. But these lessons are meant for you.

• MISTAKE 2: DON'T MIX PERSONAL AND WORK ISSUES.

Every staff becomes a family, dysfunctional or mellow. Now imagine your family members locked in one room together all day, every day for six months. Got the picture? A degree of intimacy is unavoidable at the writing table when the staff is delving the feelings and motives of characters, pulling from their own experiences. "When a guy stood me up, this is what I did . . ." That sort of insight can inform the realness of storytelling — a good thing.

But honesty can rise awfully quickly to TMI (too much information). You'll know you slipped over the edge between confessions in group therapy and story beats by the discomfort in the room or the head writer saying, "Let's move on." Remember, this is collaboration on shared character arcs that involves "catching the voice" of existing characters. One day, if you're the series creator it may also be a more personal expression; now, you're on a team.

Even if you're cool at the writer's table, watch out to maintain "friendly professionalism" at lunch, at the water cooler, everywhere at work. The other writers may be competing with you. On the staff-from-hell, I stopped by the office of my "new friend," whom I'll call Mr. Horns. Like me, he was a lower-level staffer trying to get a toehold on the career ladder. Two tiny pink booties from his baby daughter hung from his desk lamp.

I related immediately — I also had a young child. Ruefully, he said he left in the morning before she was awake and came home after she was asleep and was too busy writing on the weekend to spend time with her. "I'll see her in six months when we're on hiatus," he shrugged. I commiserated and confided that juggling my schedule was an issue. He shook his head — his wife didn't work, so she took care of everything at home. "You're not going to be able to do this job," he said flatly, as I noticed the protrusions on the sides of his head. And he was sure to relay my problem to the boss.

• MISTAKE 3: DON'T HAVE OTHER PLANS.

Unfortunately, Mr. Horns was partly right. Working on a series staff consumes most of your time and all your energy. It's great for people who have few outside obligations, but balancing a home life is tricky. I did work on one show where the entire staff had kids, and it was so well organized that we almost always arrived at ten and left at five. The supervising producer had the clout to negotiate a deal to arrive at 8:30 so she could leave at four, most days, and be around when her kids came home from school. That's rare, though.

This is not about women's issues or family versus career. When you agree to join a series staff, your life has to change. You can't take much of a lunch break with friends. Chances are you're catching lunch in the studio commissary or at your desk. You may have only an hour between the morning staff meetings and an afternoon screening, or between casting and dailies, or between a quick, urgent script polish and breaking a story for the next episode. If you drive off the lot to lunch, you'll be late for your afternoon meeting. As for your other screenplays, making YouTube videos of your cat, dating, or answering long emails — hey, that's what hiatus is for.

• MISTAKE 4: DON'T WORK AT HOME INSTEAD.

Each staff member writes individual episodes in addition to workshopping everyone else's scripts and rewriting other people's drafts. In a series of 13 episodes, you can usually count on episodes, but depending on the size of the staff, how much the boss likes your work, and how clever you are at pitching stories, you might write more.

Maybe you're used to working in bedroom slippers at 4:00 AM, or blasting a CD in your private room, or shutting your door and hovering over the computer in silence for hours, then going to the gym before returning to your computer. Sorry, folks, none of that's likely on staff. Personally, I find it difficult to concentrate in a public office off a noisy corridor with interruptions every half hour, having to break for screenings and meetings. But some writers tune out the world so well they can write in the office all day. And headphones may help.

On the staff from the netherworld, I wanted to prove myself by bringing in a wonderful draft of the first episode assigned to me, and deliver it ahead of schedule, certainly within two weeks. So I asked Mr. Horns if he thought it would be okay to write at home. "Absolutely" he grinned widely. "Do whatever it takes to write what you want to write. Just go. And if it takes three weeks, that's cool too. Don't waste your time coming in." I asked the showrunner for permission, and he shrugged "Sure," though he was busy with something else.

So I went home. For two weeks. Let me tell you, in that two weeks the script slated to run before mine killed off the character I needed to twist my story, a pivotal location was ruled out by the network, two actors in the cast were having an affair, and an intern took over my office because "no one was in it." By the time I emailed my draft to the writer's PA for distributing, it was out of touch with the series. And so was I.

Learn from my experience: Stay connected, even if you get virtually nothing written all day and have to work all night at home.

• MISTAKE 5: DON'T BE PRECIOUS ABOUT YOUR SCRIPT.

You become attached, of course. Look how wonderful your script is: The shape of a certain scene builds to a climax then twists unexpectedly and turns the story just in time; a precise detail reveals passion felt but hidden; in a nuance of character, the backstory is deftly sensed; a phrase came so perfectly as if the character was writing instead of you. It's everything a writer would want from a script, or so you believe as you type "End of Episode." So it's difficult to bring your script to the table, no matter how supportive the staff, and no matter how often you've been through the process.

But the day arrives when your script has been distributed to the staff by email and everyone is carrying laptops into the writers' room, assembling for the meeting at which it will be discussed. I said discussed, not deleted. Let's not be paranoid. Somehow, you'll need to distance yourself from it now. Try to think what's good for the show, not what bolsters your ego. It really doesn't matter how hard you worked, or how you arrived at the reasoning under a speech or action, or how much you don't want to lose a certain moment.

If the consensus of the staff — or simply the opinion of the head writer/ showrunner — is that something isn't clear or doesn't tell the story well or is not credible or steps on something in a different episode, or any other criticism, I advise you not to argue. Of course, you may clarify your intention, but then let it go. If you're a good enough writer to be on the staff, you're skilled enough to rewrite and come up with a revised draft that's even better than this.

If you don't, someone else will.

• MISTAKE 6: DON'T "DIS" THE CULTURE OF THE STAFF.

Skilled professional writers fill the staffs of television shows, but that's a little like saying most human families consist of people — it's a minimum requirement but doesn't tell much about what goes on. Each staff develops a kind of culture, just as families do. This comes from shared interests, experiences, memories, and (in the best cases) shared goals. If you think you and your dog begin to seem alike after a while, consider a room full of writers melding their minds to tell stories about the same characters.

Often the showrunner sets the tone — formal, laid back, brooding, artistic, intellectual, homespun, sex-tinged, political, romantic, drugged-out, pious . . . and so forth. Sometimes the culture fits the nature of the series, but not always. In the case of the staff from hell, the prevailing ethos had nothing to do with the subject of the series. It was blatant misogyny.

Every staff meeting began the same way: A half hour of sports talk, football, basketball, or baseball, recapping the plays from a game in detail, arguing over which man is better. And there I sat, the only woman in the room, irrelevant because I didn't know about guys doing things with balls.

Even when the sports-talk gave way to writing, the sense of the room remained. And one day, when we were working on an outline for an important episode, and it was time for a break, the entire staff (except me) convened to the men's room, where they stayed for twenty minutes, finishing the outline.

I wracked my mind to figure out how to function with this staff since watching sports and shooting hoops in the parking lot seemed more important than anything I could write. The frustration mounted until one day I erupted: "Are you finished with the male bonding yet?" Mr. Horns couldn't contain his smile that I'd finally sunk myself, so my future episodes would be his; he'd get the promotion, the raise, the credits, and acclaim — or so he calculated. If I'd been wiser and more confident, I wouldn't have tried to join on their terms, but might have discovered other interests in common with at least one of the staff and created an ally. "Dissing" the culture of the show — putting it down — alienated me further and made it more difficult to work.

Think about high school. Everyone is in cliques and you're the new kid who just transferred. How do you begin fitting in? Probably you start with one interest, and someone else is interested in it, a first friend. An important lesson.

• MISTAKE 7: DON'T WORK ON A SERIES THAT'S WRONG FOR YOU.

The staff from down below was probably a wrong fit, no matter what I'd done. Lots of TV series are out there and even though you (understandably) need to start somewhere, misery is not an essential rung on the ladder. You need references as well as good work to move ahead. A show that you have to omit from your resume can hurt you more than having had no job at all. When you apply for your next staff, the new producer will certainly phone the former one, and may ask the other writers how it was to work with you.

I stayed through my entire contracted season with this show, but in retrospect it would have been better to leave sooner and get on with my writing and career. I'm not advising you to quit when the going gets rough; if the quality of the show is worth it, and you can write well despite bad vibes, stay with it and amass those credits. But if the quality of your writing is suffering, go ahead and bail after speaking with the showrunner, especially if you can negotiate a non-damaging reference from him. With all you've learned, you can go on to another, better staff. You're not alone. Almost every TV writer has had a difficult experience at least once, and everyone omits the rubble of their history from their resume. You'll survive it too.

THE GOOD STAFF

Emmy Magazine, the publication of the Television Academy, asked several showrunners, "What does it take to make a creative ensemble run smoothly?" J.J. Abrams (who wrote *Star Wars: The Force Continues* and was writer/producer on many TV series including *Lost* and *Alias*) said, "The key is having collaborative, smart writers who keep the room running. Whether it's the official showrunner or someone else saying, 'We have to get past this and keep going.' It's crucial to get to the act breaks and the end quickly, so you can reverse and make it better. You need people who share the same vision and are collaborative and mutually respectful."

Abrams continued, "You want to make sure the show isn't repetitive, but you want to keep doing certain reveals. How do you keep doing that so that the show isn't contrived? A show like *Alias* can be preposterous — how do you keep it real? As a viewer, I'd be furious if I invested in a show that ultimately went nowhere."

For Abrams, the best thing about working on a staff is "being in the trenches with people you admire, respect, and who bring to the group ideas that make you smile. That's fantastic. When things are working, you celebrate with them, and you despair with them when things don't work. Whether you're celebrating or commiserating, you're doing it together."

A SLICE OF LIFE

For a well-run staff, let's peek in on John Wells, who headed *Shameless*, *ER*, *The West Wing*, *Southland*, and many other shows.

Picture a long dark wood conference table dominating a conference room. Ten chairs surround the table for four senior writers, four staff writers, one full-time researcher, and Mr. Wells. At the back of the room, more chairs and a few couches for full-time researchers on the staff, and production personnel as needed. All chairs face a monitor where dailies are screened.

The walls are hung with large whiteboards covered with plot points and story breakdowns for the twelve episodes to be completed for the season. On a sideboard, colored markers list ideas for possible scenes under the headings of Big, Serious, Humorous, and Other.

The staff begins laying out the season the first week in June. Working as a group for six weeks, they come up with the entire season's episodes — ideas for them and specific storylines, and the group "pounds them out." That means the team figures out all the major turning points of the stories, where the act breaks fall, and how many episodes an arc may cover, structuring the episodes.

Then an individual writer is assigned to go off and do a story treatment. When that writer returns, he gets notes from the staff. The writer does a revision. Another notes session. Then he's sent off to write the script. When the script comes in, there's a notes session. He does a second draft. If that works, the episode is ready to film. In all, the process for one script takes about eight weeks.

On a visit to *ER* several years ago, *Written By*, the magazine of the Writers Guild, described the scene on a day a first draft has come in, so this is the first notes session on the finished script. The writers file out of their offices and head for the conference room, each holding a copy of the script. Wells is in position at the head of the table, and the room is full. Coffees are brought, but this staff gets right to business going page by page through every beat of the script.

In this episode, a teenager has cystic fibrosis and his mother is afraid her son will die. The twist is that the son doesn't want to be saved, which puts Dr. Ross in an awkward position between mother, son, and his Hippocratic Oath. Someone asks about the kid's girlfriend, another about Ross's choice whether to save the kid. A debate breaks out over whether the writer is showing traits of Ross that the audience has already seen. While the staff throws out suggestions, the writer is busy taking notes.

However, I recommend you use a recorder. This experienced writer was able to get what he needed, but you might not. Three problems: First, you're not likely to be quick enough to catch every point, or distinguish what's worth noting among contradictory remarks. Second, under pressure what you type on your laptop will have all the nuance and detail of a tweet. Third, by keeping your head in your screen, you're absent from the discussion, and constantly behind. Unless the showrunner objects, record the session so you can pay attention in the room, and deal with exactly what was said later, when you can concentrate. Of course, you might also be writing directly on the script if you have a hard copy and suggestions relate to specific lines.

Back at the meeting, Wells says the story is almost there, but it's missing a pivotal action that will define the emotional rhythm for the sequence. That propels a debate about another character's developing depression. Then Wells cues a new discussion about comic relief scenes. And on the meeting goes for four more hours as they move from scene to scene to the end of the script.

This kind of meeting happens again every Monday, Wednesday, and Friday afternoon. But don't misunderstand; it's not all about logistics and group-think. Writing on a staff still emanates from each writer's art. As Wells told *Written By*:

"Writers have a responsibility, and it's sort of a particular responsibility that all artists share. You have to find a way to return yourself to that place from which you work, and not allow it to . . . float off of it into this pop-referential world in which we're only writing about or talking about things that we've seen or know from television and movies.

"I think that you, as a writer, you fight that and at whatever point you lose it, you're in big trouble. And your work suffers mightily from it, and then you'll have to find some way, if you're going to write again, to get back to it. And that's beyond all the dealings with success and all of those things that have their own problems, which . . . you certainly don't want to complain about because you don't want it to go away, but . . . artistically, it has an impact on what you're doing. And that balance is very difficult to strike.

"I look at writing as a craft and as a gift. As a craft you have to work on it all of the time, and as a gift you have to protect it. And one of the things you do to protect it is to make certain that your world doesn't become too insular. And, particularly, that your points of reference don't become too insular, because then you find yourself writing exactly the same things because you have nothing new to say about the subject. That's when shows become uninteresting to people, because they feel that they've already heard what you've had to say, and they're not interested in hearing it again. So there's a constant need to be looking. Not to see your name again on another show or anything like that, but just creatively, to protect that place from which you write."

THE STAFF LADDER

John Wells stands at a pinnacle of success shared by very few creators of hour series including Vince Gilligan, Jenji Kohan, Ron Moore, Melissa Rosenberg, and Shonda Rhimes.

Each showrunner was a writer first, and though the top rung involves as much skill in management as writing, the entire television ladder is built on writing titles. This differs from theatrical movies where creative power resides in the director, and financiers can buy their way to a credit or even an empire as film producers.

Beginning at the bottom, here's every step:

• 1. WRITER'S ASSISTANT

Long ago, writers got a foot on the bottom rung by pitching and winning an assignment to write one episode as a "freelancer." Most shows don't use outside writers any more, and the few audition scripts are given to the assistants as rewards for their hard (and underpaid) efforts. But a few smaller shows still hire freelancers, and for context, here's how that works:

A freelancer is responsible only for writing a script and is not on the staff. If you freelance, you won't participate in story meetings or screenings or have an office at the show, or share in any of the inner workings of the series. You might not even meet the staff, except for the producer who hires you and whoever supervises your episode.

But you do have an opportunity to demonstrate your skill and talent. This teleplay — especially if you receive sole screen credit — can lead to a staff offer on this series or open doors at other shows. If it wins any acclaim, and a buzz begins about you, this one break could leverage a career.

Today, the most likely start is being a writer's assistant. Don't be fooled by the word "assistant." Writers who have recent MFA degrees in screenwriting and may have won some awards compete for this job, though it doesn't involve any writing . . . yet. Nor are sample scripts used to qualify the beginners who have the best potential to be promoted to the staff later. If you intern at a show while you're still in school (working part time for free), that may lead to being hired at this level. What if you can't intern? Well, honestly, knowing someone at the show helps or being recommended by a person or program the boss respects. Yeah, it's back to whom you know. If you don't know anyone yet, apply directly to the show and see if you can get an interview. That's key, because the upper-level staff is seeing if you're a fit and willing to learn. In a way, this position is like a hospital residency after med school for a new doctor. In addition to helping the flow of script revisions (and anything else that enables the staff), a writer's assistant may be invited to observe the work of the writers' room, and that's a first step to being ready to write for this show. If an episode assignment opens, it's usually given to the writer's assistant who understands the tone and style of the show because of being there all season.

Since the script is a one-off, and not part of the job contract, compensation follows Writers Guild minimums. Whether the job is a rare freelance assignment or in effect "freelanced" to the assistant, here's what you might expect in compensation.

Minimum compensation for a primetime network series under the Writers Guild Basic Agreement covering 2018/19 is more than $39,000 for "story & teleplay." (All figures are approximate because the WGA schedule of minimums is revised periodically.) For comparison, that's similar to the first draft of a two-hour theatrical screenplay for a movie whose budget is under $5 million. Since networks license two runs of any episode, and successful series usually rerun, you will soon receive approximately the same initial payment a second time in residuals. Later, payments from ancillary markets that may include online streaming begin, and that can continue for many years, though the amount declines to pennies after a while. In addition, you'll receive foreign royalties because successful American-made television series are sold overseas. On a series that syndicates to cable and online platforms, you could see well over $60,000 for a single hour you've written as a freelancer.

But not all freelancing is top tier, and not all contracts guarantee the full ride. Network, premium cable, and streaming rates might not apply if you write for smaller outlets where prices may dip to around $28,000 for "story & teleplay" (around $10,000 less than on premium outlets). Figuring out how to calculate residuals in an era of streaming was one of the goals of the 2017 WGA contract negotiations.

And you might not be allowed to write the episode to its finished draft. Inexperienced writers are usually offered a "step" deal with "cutoffs." That means you are given a chance to write the outline ("story"), and if it doesn't work, or it seems that you would not be capable of a quality teleplay, the deal goes no further — you are cut off. Someone else (often a staff member) takes over the project and writes the script from your outline, or even writes a new outline.

In those cases your credit will be arbitrated by the Writers Guild; you might keep credit for the story if it remains essentially what you wrote; or you might share credit on the story if more than 50% of what you wrote is in the final script; or you might lose credit altogether if the new writer had to start over and changed more than 50%. If someone else wrote the script, of course, you'll have no credit on the teleplay even if the underlying story was yours.

The next cut-off comes after the first draft. If the head writer/showrunner believes you failed to catch the voices of the characters, or didn't convey the sense of the show, or the writing is just not excellent (for example flat or expository dialogue, unfocused scenes, lack of tension), the script will be given to a writer on the staff. Just as happened with the "story by" credit, the teleplay credit will be arbitrated and the second writer might be awarded some or all the screen credit, depending on how much is changed.

In a step deal, you are paid separately for each stage. Using network rates, the story alone is above $15,000, the first draft is around $26,000, and the second draft is the balance of whatever has been negotiated. This adds to more than the "story & teleplay" contract, and that's intentional. It's a kind of reward if a writer is asked to go to the next step of the project (if "the option is picked up") though the contract did not guarantee continuing.

As with the "story & teleplay" model, you'll receive residuals for reruns in proportion to what you've actually done (when you're cut off after the story, clearly you don't get the full residual for the episode).

Before I describe the rest of the staff ladder, here's one more writing possibility that can go with the Assistant position: rewrites rather than original scripts. Throughout your season, if the boss has been hearing your insights into the show and is interested in what you bring to the creative party, the showrunner may give you a story the staff has already developed that needs to be rethought from the outline up, or a teleplay that needs to be rewritten though the story basically works, or even a pretty good teleplay that just needs a "dialogue polish" (that means revising some of the speeches but not touching the structure). In that case, you probably won't get screen credit or extra pay. Say yes. Think of it as dues.

• 2. STAFF WRITER

If you succeed as a writer's assistant, you may be invited to become a staff writer, sometimes called a "baby writer," someone who's never been on a staff before. A lot is at stake: you're up or out by the end of the season.

Let your expectations be to learn, grow, form relationships, and write every assignment exactly as needed. If you're given one scene to tighten, don't think you'll grease any wheels by restructuring the entire script, or rewriting scenes on both sides unless the boss says okay. Depending on the size of the staff, during a season you might be given one script to write, especially if a senior writer is available to "supervise." That means the senior writer will advise you at every stage; but that person is also standing by to write the script if you can't. No one has time to wait while you figure it out. If the staff is small, and you're on top of your craft, you might even write two episodes that are credited to you.

Staff writers receive regular salaries according to Writers Guild minimums. A writer on a primetime network show is paid more than $4,000 per week ($16,000 per month). But your contract might be limited to 10 weeks (or less), with an "option" to renew you for the rest of the season. Off network, some beginning salaries are much lower. And if you write a script, the fees will be credited against your salary, so you won't see additional payments until you go to the next step:

• 3. STORY EDITOR/EXECUTIVE STORY EDITOR

Once you get past staff writers, it's tricky to guess what any job title means on a particular show because those ranks may be honorary. You see, as a writer advances in a series, his agent negotiates a new title every season. "Story editor" is for people who are beyond staff writer, but how far beyond depends on the size of the staff and the showrunner's style. For example, a story editor may be a virtual beginner, or one of several seasoned writers on a staff where everyone except the executive producer is a story editor, or the puzzling title "executive story editor" may even indicate the head writer.

In any case, story editor doesn't mean someone who sits and edits stories all day. Like all the other rungs on the ladder, it indicates a writer who does all the stages of an episode from breaking stories, through outlines, through first drafts, and rewrites. Generally, a story editor would expect to write two original episodes in a season, and might be asked to polish or re-dialogue scenes in other people's scripts.

If you're first trying to break in and your pitch meeting is scheduled with a story editor, though, see if you can change to someone higher. A story editor usually doesn't have the power to hire anyone, and, worse, wouldn't have much personal incentive to make your pitch sound usable to the showrunner. On the other hand, if the story editor is a buddy who recommends you, that might have some weight. In a way, we're back again to whom you know.

Story editors are salaried employees on contract for a defined number of weeks, just like staff writers. They're paid more, though — between around $7,000 and $9,000 per week (depending on the length of their contract), and that's boosted by payments for writing. The minimums under "freelancing" apply to anyone above staff writer, so if you're receiving approximately $32,000 per month as a salary, and you are also assigned an outline ("story") for an episode at the same time, you might earn around $11,000 on top of the salary, for a total of something like $43,000 that month.

Now, before you're carried away with visions of paying off your student loans, I warn you: You'll only see a fraction. Your agent takes 10%, federal, state, and local taxes may add to 40% or more, guild dues are around 3%, and you'll have other mandatory reductions (disability, social security, and so forth). If you have an attorney, he'll take 5%, and if you also have a manager (though you don't need both an agent and a manager at this level), that might be another 15%. All of that comes out of the gross (off the top) before you see a dime. In fact, you won't even see the original check. That goes to your agency that takes out their share and mails you an agency check. And remember, shows get cancelled; writers are frequently out of work for months at a time. As they used to say on a cop show, "be careful out there."

• 4. PRODUCER

If you watch screen credits before or after a show, you'll see lots of names called producer, but they don't all do the same job. Some are like line producers on theatrical movies, dealing with equipment, schedules, budgets, crew personnel. Others are writers who have risen to the producer title but have nothing to do with physical production. Their job is to write and rewrite, much like a story editor. And some are hybrids — mainly writers, though they interact with production (especially casting, and in creative sessions with the director and editor) and have a presence on the set.

Typically, producers are invested in forming the season and are responsible for the quality of the episodes, along with the showrunner. So if an episode needs to shoot tomorrow and a script has last-minute problems (no matter who wrote it), a producer may be the one up all night rewriting, though the credit would likely remain with the original writer. Not taking screen credit is one of the courtesies that higher-level staff members traditionally give lower staffers.

Producers on a set are also expected to rewrite on the spot if a scene isn't working or the director or actors have a problem with a speech or action. Sometimes this involves staying out with the crew past midnight in the freezing rain. Offsetting the long hours is not only the satisfaction of having influence over the shape of the series, but, frankly, good money.

Producers normally are not salaried in the same way as story editors. They may have "points" (a partial ownership expressed as a percent of profits), and producing fees for episodes that air. This results in a bookkeeping oddity in which producers might work all summer without compensation to put a show on the air in the fall, but then pull in hefty sums each week an episode airs.

At this level, the studio may begin looking at you to create an original series while you continue up to:

• 5. SUPERVISING PRODUCER

The distance from story editor to producer to supervising producer is in increments of responsibility, but all are writers. Some supervising producers actually run the writing staff, or even virtually run the show, while others spend the entire season writing and rewriting episodes like everyone else.

If you're breaking in, you're likely to pitch to someone with this title. Though your deal will need approval from the executive producer, this office usually has the power to give you an assignment and guide your script.

• 6. CREATIVE CONSULTANT

Now here's a mystifying title. On theatrical features, it might refer to the person a movie is about, or the original writer who was totally rewritten, a famous writer who polished the final draft, an expert specialist, the financier's nephew, or the director's yoga teacher. On TV series, it may be a specific job, though the status depends on the situation. Normally, the title goes to a highly regarded writer who comments on drafts of scripts but is not expected to keep regular hours in the office. This person may or may not actually write any episodes or attend meetings.

At one time, I was working on a show where the neighboring bungalow housed an action series that seemed to be staffed solely by four executive producers. They were all good writers in their thirties who had been writer-producers on other shows, now promoted to the top title. Writing their series was no problem, but as for managing it, each of the four was lost. Any visitor could quickly figure out what was going on — in the shadows was a semi-retired éminence grise with the obscure title "creative consultant." His credits were so eminent indeed that he didn't want to be known for this little action show, and anyway all the executive producer titles were taken. I think he educated the "executive producers" as quickly as he could and got out of there, but when I knew that staff, the creative consultant was actually the showrunner.

On another show, the "creative consultant" was a famous movie producer-director. I soon learned his interest in our success was mainly financial — one of his companies owned the show. As a "baby writer," one of my jobs was to send each script to him before it shot, and to my surprise, he sometimes read them and even made suggestions. He never visited in person, but seeing his name on screen was a kick.

My only other experience with a so-called "creative consultant" was someone experienced on the art festival circuit but clueless as a television writer. Since he had never been on a series staff, and had no writing credits (apart from the auteur films he directed) he was qualified to be a beginning staff writer, at best. But his prestige from industry connections made that inappropriate. On the other hand, he couldn't have a high writing title because he wouldn't have known how to run a writers' room or rewrite an episode (or even break an episode). So the showrunner gave him this non-title, hoping the writing staff would be inspired by an outsider's perspective.

• 7. EXECUTIVE PRODUCER/SHOWRUNNER

Executive producers come in all sizes, and it's not unusual for title promotions to create a glut at the top of a series that's been around for years. Most of those executive producers are (as you've guessed by now) simply writers. But two other categories share this title, and you want to know who's who when you go to a show, especially if you're making a first contact.

Some shows have two tracks at the very top — one is the executive producer in charge of physical production: technology, crew, schedules, location planning, construction, equipment, and so forth. The other executive producer is the head writer, in charge of content, which means all artistic aspects of creating and executing the scripts, including directing, editing, and casting. These two people work as a team, a useful division of labor on some shows. Occasionally you'll also see an executive-producer credit for a star with the clout to be called The Ultra-Grand Exalted Pooh-Bah, but don't expect that person in the writers' room.

Among all the executive producers, only one is the showrunner. Often, that's the person who created the series from its original conception, and may have written the pilot, though that's not always the case.

If I could bless your early career, I'd say: Be part of a staff where the showrunner is a great writer, because you'll want to honor that experience in your craft anywhere you work ever after.

CHAPTER SIX

HOW TO BREAK IN

I want to tell you a fairy tale that really happened, or so I've been told.

A long time ago in a galaxy far, far away — actually the mid-1980s — a young woman fell in love, not with a man but a television series whose main character seemed just like her. Each week at 9 pm on the day of her show, she would sit on her couch facing the screen, wouldn't answer her phone or flip a channel. Often, she found herself thinking about the motives and dilemmas of the characters and talking to her friends about stories that might happen. She noticed the speech patterns of each character, how conflicts were set up and resolved, and how the plots were interwoven. And then she made the leap: I could write this.

Gamely, she sat at her electric typewriter, knocked out a sixty-page "spec," and mailed it to the show. A "spec" is a speculated script — no one asked you to write it, no one's going to pay, but it would be her ticket to ride. Except that the script was returned unread with a form letter that they don't accept unsolicited manuscripts. But she was in love, so she tried again.

Script two — somewhat better than the first simply because it wasn't her first — went off to the show. And back it came. Now, this woman had no film school degree, no relatives in the business, no screen credits, no agent. And where she lived no one else had a clue how to break in either. But she was in love.

So here came script three. By now she'd read books on screenwriting and researched the series to find hints where the stories were heading. She aimed this third script at what she thought was a gap in the series, and she included a short cover letter that showed she had something unique. So she sold this one, right?

No. But this time the envelope held something amazing: a note if she was ever in Los Angeles, come visit the office. You know how fast she bought that air ticket.

Luck, fate, or curiosity, who knows, she managed to get an appointment. And what did she have in her hands? Ah, you thought it was script four. Nope, she got smart. She brought pitches, short summaries of ten stories that were perfect for the series — twice as many as writers normally bring to pitch meetings. And she told those stories with wit and insight in five minutes each. So she sold one!

Just kidding. She sold nothing but left with an armful of sample scripts, a log of what they had in development, and suggestions for areas of interest. The producer said he'd be willing to hear her pitch again.

Next time, she finally heard the winning sentence, "have your representatives call business affairs." Does that mean she sold a script or was invited onto the staff? No way. But she'd nabbed an assignment to write an outline, which you know from the previous chapter is the first paid writing step. The producer's assistant showed her their "beat sheet" style, and she managed a workable story that — hooray! — was sent to first draft . . . to be written by someone else. She was too inexperienced to write, though she would receive "story by" credit. With that, she relocated to Los Angeles to watch closely as the episode developed.

And then she pitched another episode. It was good. They let her write the first draft. It wasn't so good. But she learned as the script was revised, moving through the writing staff, production, and postproduction. She pitched, outlined, and wrote another episode — better. She made allies among the writing team. And finally, when the series was renewed for the next year, she was invited onto the staff.

And she rose through all the writing ranks, staff writer, story editor, producer, supervising producer. And three years later, in the last season of the series, she became the executive producer, running the show she loved. The End.

That fairy tale can't happen anymore because the industry has changed, but within it are tips for breaking in. It all comes down to these rules:

WRITE WHAT YOU LOVE.

This is not self-indulgence; it's the way to write well. What separates you from everyone else trying to break in? For our fairytale heroine, passionate identification with the main character in the series, understanding the struggles and feelings that protagonist would face, gave her stories the force of reality. You might find your break-in angle from experience in a field like medicine, law, or police work, absorption in a genre like sci-fi, or even in your family background. Your passion will lead you to authentic stories.

So when you choose a show to spec, pick one you watch often. Sounds obvious, but I've encountered would-be writers who think they're playing the system by speculating shows they would never watch, thinking they're easy to break into. Doesn't happen that way. First, all shows want to hire the most gifted writers they can attract, not reluctant pragmatists. Second, never write down — it hurts you as an artist and damages your reputation. Third, it's not going to succeed. It's obvious if you don't really have a feel for the show. And finally, what you are creating in a spec is a showpiece, not an actual episode, and this brings me to the next point:

DON'T SPEC THE SERIES YOU PLAN TO PITCH.

Okay, that's opposite the lesson in the fairy tale. A few series will read specs for their own show, but most won't, and you don't want them to. Think about it — the producers know their show's minefields. Outsiders wouldn't know the producer is going to scream if he hears one more pitch about the dog, or another swimming pool corpse, or a romance between two actors who (you couldn't know) had a fight yesterday. But producers on a different show will be able to see your script for the great writing it is without the encumbrances.

So go ahead and speculate for a series you know well — then develop pitches for a different show within the same genre, or of a comparable quality.

For example, producers of shows ranging from procedurals to sci-fi to family dramas may read specs of *This Is Us*, though it has nothing to do with the subjects of their shows — they're reading for ability with characters. You might also stay within the same general universe — writing an episode of *Jessica Jones* for *Luke Cage* (or vice versa), if you're interested in Marvel shows. Or you might look towards attitude, writing something from Jenji Kohan's shop, such as *Orange Is the New Black* or *Glow* for something associated with Jill Soloway such as *Transparent* or *I Love Dick*.

Ability is what you're demonstrating — talent plus skill. So choose to study and write for the highest quality series that interests you. Look for one that's been on long enough to be recognized and maybe won some writing awards. (You can find a list of award winning series through the Writers Guild of America and the Academy of Television Arts and Sciences, both listed among resources at the end of the book.) You'll sharpen your screenwriting; and the show's multi-faceted characters may pump up your dialogue.

Quality of writing is the immutable rule. And that brings me back to our fairy tale, and the next principle:

ASK THE RIGHT QUESTIONS ABOUT A SERIES.

Notice what the woman considered when she first tried the show: the motives and dilemmas of the characters, stories that might happen to them, speech patterns of each character, how conflicts were set up and resolved, and how the plots were interwoven. All these can be discovered in the episodes. Once you delve into the underlying motives by asking why the characters behave as they do, you'll uncover the roots of future stories and also subtext that will color the way you write these characters. It is this more subtle layer of characterization that producers want to see in a writing sample because it suggests a source for further writing, as opposed to flat characters or "types" pushed around to serve a plot.

What stories might happen to the characters? Don't answer by using plot lines already set in the show. Those story arcs will be complete before your script is done, and big changes that turn the series are made by executive decision, not by outsiders. Instead, ask what urges or issues come from the characters at a point of stasis — that is, when they behave normally, rather than guessing how the narrative will evolve over the year.

Or come up with an angle of your own for the main cast. For example, if you speculate *The Walking Dead*, where the characters are often in the woods, and in your real life you work as an entomologist, what do you know about insects that might provide a storyline for the continuing cast? When *Friday Night Lights* was still running, the most interesting spec scripts I saw were from writers who'd lived in Texas and had experienced the lore of rattlesnakes and dust storms. You could smell the authenticity in the pages.

Ideally, every character's dialogue is specific and expresses background, education, attitude, intelligence, and personality. Listen well, and ask yourself how Jimmy's choices of words and his phrasing differs from Chuck's on *Better Call Saul*, or how Piper differs from Taystee on *Orange Is the New Black*. A critical hurdle for an outside writer is to catch the "voices." You may begin with the actors, but don't let that fool you. The differences are on the page.

Conflicts and plot structures are somewhat determined by the hour format and, in network television and basic cable, by act breaks, as you saw in Chapter Three, but don't let that hang you up. Do what it takes to keep readers turning pages. Production companies and agents will read only a few pages and if they're not hooked, the script gets tossed. The tension has to stay high and the reader needs to be surprised often — not by a gimmick but by a turn in the story that is true to these people. Be unpredictable within the world of the show. For example, in a story about breast cancer, give the disease to a guy because men can get it too. Be fresh, creative, unexpected.

You see, it's all about good writing, the same qualities you'd apply to writing a feature or other dramas. That's not to say you shouldn't investigate the shows you're speculating or pitching. Do your research. Unlike our woman of the 1980s, you have the Internet. Virtually all series have websites, as do all networks, and many have fan sites too. The official site will assure you basics like spelling the characters' names and a history of the series. Some include statements by the producers with hints to their taste or sources of inspiration. Watch out for the fan sites because they might not be accurate, but the best include summaries, and some list every episode that's been aired, which will save you from writing or pitching what's been done.

The right questions are always about stories and characters, not special effects, costumes, budgets, casting, gossip, or marketing gimmicks, so stay focused.

HAVE THE RIGHT TOOLS.

Our lady of the 1980s toiled on an electric typewriter; of course no one does that any more. For your computer you must have — must have — a professional screenwriting program. If in doubt, "Final Draft" is popular. "Celtx" is a free program available online. Each series adopts specific software that their writers must use, but for speculating, any program that creates a standard screenplay form is fine. As you can see in the sample in Chapter Three, the hour drama looks the same as a feature screenplay (though sitcoms are formatted differently). To be considered at all, your scripts must appear perfect and professional.

HAVE REPRESENTATION.

Easier said than done. Our heroine was out in the cold, sending scripts that were returned unread until her extreme tenacity caught a producer's attention. You could try that, but it took her years in easier times, and she got lucky. So let's talk about agents — why you need them, how to get one, and what to do if you can't.

TV series give the illusion of being so accessible, even friendly, that fans sometimes imagine they can join in. From the outside, series writing seems easier than it is, and television appears less formidable than features, so shows would be inundated with amateur scripts if they didn't have filters. Also, production companies won't risk a lawsuit from a stranger who might claim a show stole his story. That's why companies rarely read scripts that arrive "over the transom" (unsolicited and unrepresented).

You need an agent because that's who gets you read, knows where the jobs are, and puts you in the room. Without, it's difficult to know which show is looking for new writers (or at least, willing to consider one). The agency also negotiates your deal, generates your contract, and collects your pay, deducting their 10%.

While feature film companies may buy an original screenplay, television runs on assignments. The agent may know of an opportunity on a staff, or that an open episode is looking for a writer with a particular background, viewpoint, or style. The agent sends over samples from several clients who meet the criteria. After reading the samples, the producer may invite you in for a meeting. If the producer likes your work enough, he or she might invite you in to pitch.

But a lot of good those systems do you if you don't have an agent anyway. Here's what you need in your writing portfolio before you begin your agent search:

- A pilot for an original series that demonstrates your unique viewpoint (or experience) and your skill to deliver a television hour with "legs."

- At least one hour-long TV drama script for a current series in a genre similar to your target.

- At least one more TV drama in a different "franchise" that demonstrates another tone.

- Original stories ready to pitch to series.

Now you're ready to begin. A long list of agents is available from the Writers Guild. The Guild asterisks the ones willing to consider new writers but don't take those asterisks too seriously. Some "open" agencies turn out to be filled; others who didn't offer may nevertheless be interested in a client with something they want.

How do you make your way through all those names? Try to identify those who represent the kind of writing you do. Some agencies aim mainly at Hollywood features or sitcoms, so check if their client list includes writers with credits in television drama. You'll also have to choose between the "packaging" and "boutique" agencies. Big packaging agencies supply all the talent — actors, directors, producers as well as writers. That can be a powerful asset if you're included in a package led by experienced showrunners. On the other hand, a boutique will give you the personal attention a new writer needs.

Begin on the phone. If you don't have personal referrals, cold call each likely agency. Don't ask for an agent but focus on whomever answers, or one of the assistants, and say you're looking for representation for writing dramatic TV series. You may extract the names of agents who specialize in this or the new guy in the agency who's building his list. Get the names spelled. Out of a hundred calls, ten may be interested. Okay, you only need one.

Next step is a short email to a specific agent emphasizing your strengths — screenwriting awards, a film school degree, well-reviewed plays, published fiction or journalism. If you don't have those, hook the reader with some specialty like having crime stories to tell from your years as a cop. Move on quickly to what's in your portfolio — at least one pilot and spec scripts for Emmy-winning current shows. Your aim is to be invited to send one script.

Now comes the wait. You can probably call once every couple of weeks to remind the assistant; just don't bug people. Meanwhile, your email is at other agencies you've contacted, and in six to eight weeks someone may ask to see your writing.

Even though you're aiming at episodic series, the first script the agent will want is an original. This is to separate your talent from the style of the series you're speculating. Later, when the agent is ready to judge your skill in series writing, the spec episodes will be useful.

Let's say you've jumped through those hoops and you're meeting with agents. Good agents are looking for clients with the talent and perseverance to grow, as interested in where you'll be in five years as whether they can place you on a staff this season. In fact, an agent who only wants a quick sale is likely to drop you if you don't make him money in the first few months. You deserve better.

You're building a relationship, you hope, so you want someone who understands your goals, can guide you to a show where you start building a career, and has the clout to push open that door. The choice is personal — the hungry young agent, the empathetic one, or the seasoned vet with a long client list? High-class problems, of course.

What if you don't get a bite? Next stop is managers. The main difference is agencies are regulated by the state and have agreements with the guilds that define how much they can charge and their responsibilities. Managers are unregulated, so watch out. Professional management companies function very like agencies except they charge 15% of your earnings or more, compared with 10%. Justifying the bigger bite, managers may cover more than agents, sometimes all of an artist's business life.

For you, a manager may be available when agents are out of reach, and they can open most of the same doors. They're not listed with the guilds, but you'll find managers by searching online. So take the same steps: call, send an email, send a script, and interview as with an agent.

If you zero-out with managers too, entertainment attorneys sometimes have connections to producers and may pass along your work or make an introduction. If you retain an attorney for this, the customary charge is 5% of all your screen work in lieu of an hourly rate.

Still too tough? Here are some end-runs around the representation problem.

- Get a job on the show. Any job. The top choice is writer's assistant because you'll interface directly with the staff and might even observe in the writers' room. Production assistant or even secretary are fine. The point isn't a career in photocopying but relationships with the writers. Once they know you, they won't be able to avoid reading your work. And when you're around the series, you learn the inside tips.

- Go to film school for a screenwriting degree. The best schools promote their graduating students to the industry, and friends you meet there help each other.

- Write for an actor. Many actors have small production companies to find them material. You might get into a show by writing a compelling role for one of the less-served cast who will fight for your script. You'll need to figure how to get the script through to him or her, but it's not impossible.

- Start with new and alternative outlets. Apart from network, premium streaming, and national cable primetime programming, dramatic writing jobs may be available in niche cable outlets, in off-hours, and increasingly on the web. Those markets don't tend to work with agents anyway (not enough money), so you apply directly to the producers where your enthusiasm may be welcome.

BE IN LOS ANGELES.

Our heroine flew to an L.A. motel the minute she thought a producer would see her. She was lucky he kept the appointment. But a showrunner juggles delivery deadlines, last-minute rewrites, and emergencies on the set, so appointments are rescheduled once, twice, three times. How long can you sit in that motel?

Some people relocate and work a day-job while poring over the "trades." You know Hollywood is crowded with would-be writers, actors, and directors who followed a dream and were still working as waiters — literally and metaphorically — a decade later. But as a writer you can work wherever you are, so don't leave home until your portfolio is strong, you have a bite, or you're coming to film school. The woman in our tale moved after her first assignment. Then she glued herself to the production, and that led to her next assignment.

Whether you move sooner or later, you do need to live in L.A. to write series television. A few mainstream American shows are based in other cities — New York, Miami, Vancouver, Toronto. But most staffs are on the studio lots. As you read in Chapter Three, TV writers work collaboratively, so there's no way to avoid the palm trees.

THE SECRET OF SUCCESS:

My USC students sometimes ask how likely it is they'll make it — what are their chances of breaking in? The first year or two out of school are usually rough, but I've discovered which ones succeed five years later. They're not necessarily the most gifted, the brightest, or the best connected, though talent, smarts, and relationships do help. No, the ones who succeed have a single trait in common: they didn't give up.

Tales from my recent MFA graduates reflect 21st century realities both better and worse than I'd experienced a decade earlier. Worse is that freelance assignments are rare. Now shows depend on staff writers for most episodes, so the few freelance gigs are really auditions for staff.

But so much is better, more open. Okay, each show has a smaller staff partly because seasons are shorter, but the number of series has multiplied in a world with around a thousand channels — broadcast, cable, and streaming networks all do original programming, plus emerging markets on the web. When I was first breaking in, I had to pitch to guys (yes, guys only), an old guard who held a lid on traditional network formats and the kinds of plot-driven stories that had proved reliable. Too many of their shows seemed alike — mind-numbing for a creative person. Some of them are still around, but in an era when shows compete with the Internet and new venues to attract viewers, those showrunners are becoming dinosaurs.

Among new trends:

- Some shows will read non-episodic samples (features or even stage plays) in an effort to identify original talent, along with TV specs;

- Hybrid forms include dramedy, reality/drama, and music/drama;

- More flexible act structures and no apparent act breaks;

- Content that features nontraditional lifestyles, cutting-edge issues, honest relationships, gutsy language, and fantasy;

- Computer generated imagery (CGI) that enables locations and effects formerly impossible.

ADVICE FROM SOME EXPERTS

I spoke with Carole Kirschner, a former CBS executive and author of *Hollywood Game Plan*, who also heads the CBS Television Writers Program and runs a consulting service called "Park on the Lot." She advised:

"First you write incredible material and you make sure it's incredible by having someone in the business read it. Then, if you qualify, you get into one of the network programs. That's the fastest way to get representation. You apply in the spring. For CBS they need an original piece of material such as a pilot, plus a spec episode. NBC and ABC both require specs, and ABC also wants other things. Warners requires a spec and backup material. Also Fox. They need to know you have a body of work, so you wouldn't even apply until you have a whole body of work. To get that body of work people should take classes. It's presumptuous to say, 'I've never written anything but I watch television so I should be able to write television.' It's just not true. They should learn how to write and then practice writing.

"Another way to go is do everything you can to get a job as a writer's P.A., not a writer's assistant because that's five steps up. Writer's assistant is the entry point; it used to be staff writer, but now it's writer's assistant. Find somebody who knows somebody who knows somebody who knows somebody who will take your application to be a writer's P.A. Sometimes you can do it cold, though, by asking if you can apply — 'May I send my resume?' If they say no, you ask 'May I call you back in a few weeks?' It always helps to have someone recommend you.

"And absolutely enter every writing contest you can. Win the first or second prize, but don't put down that you're a quarterfinalist because no one cares.

"There are different kinds of showrunners. Some are willing to take people with talent and bring them up. But there are far smaller writing staffs, so when they hire somebody they do need that person to perform well. Still, I'm hearing we don't look for baby writers to be writing drafts; we just expect them to sit and learn. There's more room for that in cable — the staffs may be smaller but there's more time to make the show, so there's more time to work on the scripts."

I also found practical advice for you from Jennifer Grisanti, who runs NBCs "Writers on the Verge" development program. Author of *Change Your Story, Change Your Life*, Grisanti also runs a private consultancy.

"When clients sell pilots it's a village coming into play. People come to story consultants to learn about how to develop stories in the strongest way possible. It's never an overnight thing, as much as people want to believe that. It's working together to get a script to the best place possible and then utilizing a manager or agent to get it to the network or studio. And then it's a matter of the script deal. Out of the 20 pilots my clients have sold, only two have gone to series. It's just a step toward that process.

"I love when people have had another career and then come to me because they have something to write about. For a new writer it's all about creating a portfolio. It's also about managing expectations. If they imagine they're going to write one pilot and make it I help them understand how our business works. This could be a five to ten year journey before anything happens. A manager once said if you're not going to give it five years, don't give it five minutes.

"Being a writer is like being on a roller coaster. When you get that first staff job, that isn't the end. It's the beginning. You may need to learn social skills because you're going to be working in a writers' room with the same people ten hours a day.

"I tell writers to plan to have three original scripts in their portfolio and current spec scripts. I believe they should have current spec scripts. I've staffed 15 shows and I've had showrunners who would not read pilots; I also had showrunners who would read pilots but after they read the pilots they wanted to read a spec script to understand if the writer knew how to mimic somebody else's voice. That hasn't gone away. I wouldn't recommend having only original material. You're hurting yourself if someone asks for a spec script and you don't have one.

"The writers I work with who have the most success have a number of scripts. They send their submissions to programs and hope they do well in a competition or get into a program and that leads to getting an agent or manager and that leads to staffing."

NON-TRADITIONAL WAYS

Nowadays, the ways to get into traditional television are no longer limited to tradition.

Carole Kirschner observes, "There are lots of 22-year-old agents' assistants who spend their lives going on the web looking for the next new voice. So someone could potentially get 'discovered' by having his or her work on line. The way people get representation or find their way in is still writing contests, which have been going on for a long time. But having an on-line component is what's new."

Some broadcast outlets are creating their own "minor leagues" of new series online. For instance, the CW launched CW Seed as a sub-site on CWTV.com, with the tagline "What's Next." "I think this is a kind of a unique thing for a broadcast network to do, to have an incubator to really look at and get feedback from the fans," said Rick Haskins, CW Executive VP of marketing and digital programs. We can test out new talent, test out new ideas, test out new ways for finding exciting new opportunities for advertisers and moving [the successful shows] to the mainstream CW."

Can you really tweet or blog your way to a show? For a legacy network, these sources can be seen as ways of keeping up with the times . . . or acts of desperation. The test is if the blogs and tweets are able to work as storytelling over enough hours. That is, can 140 characters embody enough narrative potential to roll out even one season, even a limited series of 8 episodes? How about a Tumblr blog consisting mostly of hand-drawn musings about being 20-something?

A few years ago, NBC put in development *F*ck! I'm In My Twenties* as a half-hour comedy series based on Emma Koenig's Tumblr blog about just that. Here's a sample of one of Koenig's entries, handwritten: "When anything VERY GOOD happens to me, I can only enjoy it for so long before I think: COUNTDOWN TO PEOPLE RESENTING ME: 5! 4! 3! 2! 1!"

Okay, students, here's your assignment: from that raw material find the inciting moment that will drive action in the pilot. Delineate the antagonist and his or her goals and internal conflict. Develop the "worst case" break in the story that will culminate the rising conflict. Create a twist in the resolution of the pilot that leverages the next episodes. Then suggest how those potentials play out over an arc of a season with emphasis on arcs for supporting cast in addition to the protagonist. Then, after all that is done, demonstrate opportunities for humor and clarify the kind of humor (satire, farce, situational, and so forth) that completes this as a comedy series. Can you describe hilarious moments or write jokes drawn from this premise?

No doubt NBC was on top of all that and more by giving Koenig experienced cowriters and top executive producers. Since Koenig herself was not going to run the show, or write it, that makes me wonder what it is they bought, and whether they were really after the imprint of someone in a desired demographic as opposed to actual television writing.

Nor is that the only Tumblr blog to get a TV adaptation. Earlier, Lauren Bachelis's *Hollywood Assistants Blog* was set up as a comedy at CBS. The show titled *20-Nothings* has a similar profile of attaching experienced talent to run it. And the same question arises: apart from the sourcing, how much is this kind of deal actually development from a non-traditional venue, and how much is it a very traditional development from an idea, similar to the way shows have been developed from pitches for decades?

Are tweets, blogs, and Internet sites just a new form of pitching to traditional networks? And do they work? You need more than a tweet, but in a previous chapter we heard from Michael Ajakwe, founder of the L.A. WebFest, who believes YouTube series do have potential to move onto larger platforms. Here's a case study of one entrepreneur who tried.

KICKSTARTER

Many writer-producers have ventured to the web looking for aesthetic freedom by escaping from a money-driven culture. But unless they were personally wealthy, they found themselves even more involved in chasing money. Ironically, the trail to personal expression turned into a hard road to being entrepreneurs that left them little time for being artists.

I introduce you to an amazingly aggressive entrepreneur, Matt King, whose career as an actor allowed him to make the pilot for his web series *World of Steam* without needing a financial return for himself. Coming at his subject through analyzing a large, specialized "steampunk" fan base, every step was thoroughly researched. I asked him to share what he discovered about how to succeed with a Kickstarter campaign.

"If you have an idea that's on the outskirts, that's more genre, something that hasn't been developed yet, and you don't have a 'Medici' that's willing to invest in you, then where do you go? That's why I decided to go to Kickstarter and create a whole new environment where I could find a million Medicis who would help me out.

"Kickstarter is a crowd-funding website that allows people to state they have an idea within a single forum — whether it's technology or entertainment or design — and tell people about their idea in the Kickstarter format. People can choose to endorse or not endorse that idea.

"You incentivize, much like a public-radio fund drive or backers. You say if you endorse me in this moment, I will give you a DVD or a piece of swag or the product itself. Now Kickstarter is turning into pre-sales in a way. You're giving them a portion of the production and turning them into the smallest producer possible. You're using people in aggregate to support your production. Kickstarter is the way I want to promote my show.

"I realized Kickstarter lives or dies on three things — it's a triangle: it's star-driven, or the newest coolest thing nobody has heard about, or it's something sentimental. So Zac Braff does his movie and it makes a million dollars. The Dell ice cream scoop invents itself and decides to come out, or GoldieBlox engineering for girls says this is what we want to do. Or the sentimental route — my friend has a disease and wants to walk the Appalachian Trail. If you can hit two of those, you're guaranteed success on Kickstarter.

"Now, how do you do that with a television show that nobody's heard about? In order to create a grassroots movement to put me through Kickstarter I had to have a set of fans going into it. So I decided to channel social media to that purpose. Social media, like an agent or manager, is a way to have your name said in certain circles. We don't know who the people are going to be for our movement. We don't know who controls the right circles. All we can do is get our words out to the greatest number of people as possible, and if we can find the tipping points, we can move the ball.

"I needed at least 6,000 people on Facebook saying my name over and over again. I decided to go to individuals within social media and use them to drive the bus. Facebook is largely about connectivity over an image. I started driving images of what I wanted to create onto Facebook.

"I went around to everybody who could be within this small niche of Steampunk-ism and said look, this is what I'm doing. Then I went to Pinterest and Tumblr and Twitter and Instagram and YouTube, hitting each with individual content tailored for each of those social media. Every day, every hour, depending on the peak times of those social media . . . Every Thursday, from 1 to 4 PM if you're not putting out content on Facebook, you're dying. Every Saturday, make sure you're putting out content from 2 to 3. . . . I made sure I was in front of their eyes when people took their lunch breaks. I made sure our content just drove and drove and drove and drove.

"My goal was 6,000 'likes' on Facebook. I was lucky enough that some amazingly talented people within the social media sphere caught onto the idea and we sold it through. By the time we walked into Kickstarter, we had 20,000 'likes' on Facebook. Now, each 'like' correlates to a certain number of eyes. Each 'like' is a person who has a certain number of friends. Facebook takes each of those into account and keeps track of them. So I would know week-to-week how many people were actively talking about my show. Maybe I was getting out to 800,000 eyes that week, and then I could use those eyes to drive into different formats. At its essence, it was really marketing.

"With that in place we went to Kickstarter. I hit two out of three on the triangle. I tried to hit three out of three by saying: Here's me. I'm a small, independent filmmaker. I'm just like you, but I'm doing something you're not doing. I want to make something that I love.

"I did my research. I went to the Kickstarter Machine. I went to Kick-track. I tracked everything that was possibly like my piece and I did a month of research into why did these things fail and why did these others succeed. Who do you need at what day at what time to make them get more money? I drove it. Every day for 30 days I made sure we had new content on every bit of social media.

"People like being saviors. They like to come in at the very last minute to save the project. Once we had Kickstarter in place and we had people excited about our concept, we told Kickstarter, you can help us get over the edge with this, and then you could take us even further. We had asked for $70,000. We ended up with $130,000. All that went into creating this production.

"$130,000 is a lot for a web series. But it's not a lot if you're trying to pay a major composer and other people who work for a living. All of them donated their time, working after their 60-hour weeks, and worked for parts, materials, and hard drives. And that still was choking our budget.

"We also had to get out a great deal of swag. We had to put in the budget that we had to become exporters. For the first half of this year I was an exporter. I was dealing with manufacturing and making sure all the T-shirts and all the necklaces were done on top of doing all the preproduction for the show.

'I still think what I'm doing is traditional television. I'm just doing it all myself. What the Internet has provided me is the tools to do it all myself. I'm following the same rules of disseminating things out to people. I'm doing the same rules in marketing and creating content. The only difference is I'm not going to someone who has laid those channels in place, CBS, ABC, NBC, Warner Brothers, or whoever. They have a lot more facility in being able to get things out to people. But what the Internet has let me do is be directly in people's laps. My goal next is how do we take this show, now that we have it, and turn our channel into ABC, NBC, or CBS? That's the next goal."

The *World of Steam* pilot did get made on the budget that was raised and it ran on YouTube. In the end, though, not enough people followed it to warrant a series. The failure wasn't caused by any lack of marketing or energy on the creator's part or the originality of his concept. The question was whether viewers cared about enough about the characters and their relationships to root for them and want to see more episodes. It was essentially a matter of the script. The writing just wasn't there, no matter how hard it was promoted or where it aired.

ENTER THE EXECUTIVE PRODUCERS

Creators of digital series form a spectrum of experience, a continuum, rather than dividing into sharp categories. But executive producers who have run network shows have been migrating online for a while, and they really are different from the do-it-yourself pioneers. The EP's don't need Kickstarter. They arrive with funding, or are financed through one of the larger YouTube channels.

Geek and Sundry is a commercial YouTube channel and multimedia production company. Launched in 2012 by actress Felicia Day, it was part of YouTube's $100 million initiative, funded by Google to bring original content onto YouTube, meant to kick start Google TV. At the time, *Forbes Magazine* suggested that "if successful, it could help blaze a trail for the future of network television."

Since then, so many trails have been blazed the whole frontier is on fire. The explosion can be overwhelming, so I'll focus now on one creator: Amy Berg. Formerly on *Leverage* (TNT), *Person of Interest* (CBS), *Eureka* (Syfy), *Da Vinci's Demons* (Starz), and many other shows, Berg was in a position to negotiate a new model of ownership. Her company, Bergopolis, is a co-owner (with Geek and Sundry) of her original series *Caper*. She told me "I had to hire lawyers to create a contract from scratch because this model does not exist anywhere yet. I'm coming in with a level of experience and the attitude I'm going to make this thing — do you want to be the distributor?"

Berg said, "This is the new frontier now. I'm still a television writer and I will always be a television writer. I don't know how to make web series. I only know how to make television series. So that's what I made. I'd been friends with Felicia Day [owner of Geek and Sundry] for years since I hired her as an actress for a guest spot on *Eureka*. I'd been a fan of *The Guild*, which was the first web series that existed. So I had huge respect for her as a producer who could get stuff done. Over the course of years whenever we had lunch we said one of these days we should get together and do a web series. I was always working. I just didn't have time.

"Earlier this year I shot a pilot for TNT, and that reinvigorated my passion to make things that are my own. It did not get a green light, though we'd been under the impression it was going to go. So I had not made a backup plan for staffing. Suddenly I was presented with time in spring 2013.

"I had a lunch planned with Felicia . . . and I started talking about my passion for doing something that was mine after spending so many years writing other people's ideas. Felicia said this is good timing because we're in development season for Geek and Sundry on YouTube. We pitched it to her over the lunch and by the end of the lunch, we had a show.

"In traditional outlets nothing happens that quickly, and it never feels like two creative entities coming together to decide to make things. It always feels like you're coming into what you know is going to be a long, arduous process. You come up with an idea for something. You go and pitch it. They may not like it. If they like it, it goes to a next step, writing the script. Then there's a whole set of notes. If they like the script, they make the pilot, and then there's a whole other process. They have to decide whether or not they want to air the pilot. It takes a long time and the odds of actually making the thing, at the end of all this, are very slim.

"The Internet is a whole new frontier. It's the future. I wanted to get a foothold on the web as a creator and it all came together at the right time. It happened the way it's supposed to happen — people come together, they think it's a great idea, and they do it."

So, in a way, we've come full circle from our fairy tale. Television shows are still all about a writer's passion and her ability to write. If you write well enough, you can find a way in, and that's where I advise you to put your energy.

CHAPTER SEVEN

PROFILES IN PROGRESS

This chapter introduces you to five working writers at different stages of their careers. Often, writers who are on the outside looking in ask me how to start and what it's like, day to day, working on a television series. In past editions, I've presented interviews with celebrity writer-producers and executives — and their interesting quotations still appear throughout. But for this edition, I thought hearing from an array of "real people" might be more practical for you.

Yasemin Yilmaz had just started her first week as a staff writer when we spoke; it was her first paid job in television soon after school. Joe Peracchio has written on a number of shows that were cancelled after a season, like many other writers who move from staff to staff sometimes with months between jobs. Taylor Martin was an assistant for several years before being promoted to the writing staff on the same show where she is now a story editor. Akela Cooper, 11 years out of school, has climbed the ladder working on both network and streaming series, steadily improving her title. In 2018, she became the showrunner of an original series on Netflix. Finally, David McMillan, 14 years since his MFA, is executive story editor of a Hulu show, and has sold pilots, while writing feature scripts.

They come from different places and have different life stories. Yasemin's family emigrated from Turkey when she was a child, a Muslim family arriving in the U.S. right before the 9/11 attacks. Joe previously had a 15-year career as an actor and ran a theater company that toured the world. Taylor grew up in a suburb of Chicago and taught in Teach for America. Akela grew up in a small town called Hayti, Missouri, and won an NAACP scholarship. David was a drama major at Yale and worked for YouTube/Google before launching his television career.

All are former students of mine, alumni of the USC School of Cinematic Arts with MFA degrees in screenwriting. That may seem exclusive to those who are not able to attend a great film school, and certainly the craft and connections they got at USC have mattered. As I've advised earlier in this book, I recommend that everyone take classes or workshops somewhere. But each of these five writers has drive and talent, and I believe they would have found other ways to succeed if they hadn't gotten MFAs.

I will step back now and let the writers speak for themselves

YASEMIN YILMAZ

Yasemin is a staff writer on The Exorcist *at Fox Network. She spoke about her first week on staff in her first year out of school.*

Today was a good day. Some days we get stuck on problems and the next day we solve them. So yesterday was difficult and today we resolved a lot of the problems so today was a better day.

It's different from the workshop we had in school because you're working on one story and it's not yours.

After graduating, I went home to Turkey for a few weeks and was writing while I was there. I had applied to fellowships before finishing school and I didn't hear back from any of them. But Fox Labs has a different process in which you have to be nominated by somebody in the business. One of my professors was also running a show and he nominated me. They asked me to send a pilot script and that's what got me into the Writers Lab.

The Lab's approach to the writing was a little different from our workshop in school because the Lab was not so concerned with the quality of the writing and character depth as much as what would sell and emphasizing the crunchier scenes. Over four months, we had some of the executives from the studio coming in to talk. One of the highlights was Glen Mazzara who came in one evening and ran a mock writers' room. We ended up reading a script he had written and the task was to break the second episode. We had a chance to see how a showrunner's mind works. One thing he said that stuck with me is that when you're in the room you're not there to push your own idea but what you can do to support the showrunner's vision.

Over six weeks at the end of the program, we each wrote a pilot. After that I had no real plans. I was taking as many meetings as possible and writing. Then the people from the Lab came back and asked if I wanted to shadow a writers' room. It was supposed to be a two- to three-week gig, and in the middle of the second week they said they wanted to bring me on as a staff writer.

What was different about my first week on staff was when I was shadowing if I ever had an idea I wouldn't venture to speak in the room, but once I became a staff writer I started to speak in the room maybe once an hour.

Our writing staff has four women and six men. But it's interesting — recently the other women had to be out so I was the only woman in the room; you sense the dynamic shift. With more women in the room, more attention is paid to certain things.

I get there at 7:30 AM. The second person in after me is the showrunner. That's the highlight for me because I get a chance to talk to him before he starts getting calls. I've had advice that you have to be the first one in and the last one out. It's true. In the morning, it allows more time to talk about the show and outside interests too.

At 10 AM, everyone is in and we start the room. We go from 10 to 6 with an hour lunch break and a couple of 10- or 15-minute breaks throughout the day.

In cases when the showrunner and creator aren't in the room, the room seems to run itself. Whoever wrote the episode tends to lead the room.

All the episodes were assigned before I joined the staff so I won't have a writing credit this season. But I think I have a voice that would help with the third season storyline, so I hope they will bring me on.

Coming out of USC, graduates will have the education needed for the writing. I wish I had been better prepared to say what I could bring to the table, though. I would have liked more experience answering the questions "Who am I?" and "Why should you care to work with me?" I'd advise recent graduates to focus on your own brand as much as the writing.

We all feel like outsiders in the room sometimes, but if you're in the room *know you belong*. I have to remind myself of that day in and day out.

JOE PERACCHIO

Joe is on the staff of Deception, *a Warner Bros. show with ABC network.*

After I graduated from USC in 2013 I was lucky enough to get into the Warner Bros. program, and I did that for six months and wrote a spec and a pilot for them. That went really well. I got my first job out of the Warner Bros. program as a staff writer on *The Messengers* on CW.

When *The Messengers* was done, I was lucky to immediately get hired on *The Flash* on CW. I watched the premiere of *The Messengers* after I already had a job on *The Flash*. It was super cool. It's too bad *The Messengers* didn't last because the quality of the staff was amazing and the showrunner, Trey Callaway, was great to work for. The atmosphere was wonderful.

The year I did on *The Flash* was the hardest year of my life working on anything. It was the number one show on that channel but the showrunner was not the best to work with. I went from a wonderful atmosphere to a difficult atmosphere. Every year, people were let go midseason. Every year the room is scrubbed and they get a new staff. My year was not an exception, and it happened again the following year on that show. I learned a great deal. I rode out the 22 episodes so by then I had done 36 episodes as a staff writer. I wrote three on *The Flash* and I wrote one on *The Messenger*, so by then I had four episodes of TV on, which was great for residuals.

Whether a staff works well comes down to management. This is something showrunners are talented at or they're not. The vast majority of showrunners are good writers who sold something but many don't know how to manage people, or how to collaborate kindly, efficiently to get the best out of people. To be a good showrunner you have to be a good writer but also a good manager and a good teacher. If you're not all those things, it can make the staff not work well.

I've been on two shows with great showrunners, and one show with someone who didn't value us. When a staff works best the showrunner is attentive to the writers in the morning; is clear about what the group should be working on and what he or she wants to see by a certain time; puts someone in charge who is a listener, a collaborator, a builder; and then the showrunner comes back when they said they were going to come back and hears the pitch from the day, gives notes on it, sends everyone off with a clear objective, values people's opinions, and listens. That way we end up with something we built together even when the showrunner isn't in the room.

When it doesn't work well, what happens is a showrunner either dictates to everyone what the episode should be with a lot of moving targets within it, doesn't give clear expectations, belittles ideas, disappears and doesn't come back for days and days. You're working in darkness because you don't know what they're interested in. An ineffective showrunner might bring the problems from the notes calls and the cuts and problems from the set into the writers' room and take it out on writers. When those kinds of things happen, writers feel like scared children of alcoholic fathers. It's like if Dad comes in and his regular behavior is to slap you, or punch you, or hug you — you don't know which one it's going to be but two of them are bad, so you're scared.

When the writers' room is a safe place to express your personal history, your anecdotes, your ideas, your wild notion, sometimes you might have an idea and say, maybe this isn't a good pitch, and the showrunner can say, "but there's a nugget there that's great, or I see the impetus for why you're suggesting that, there's an urge for the character to have that desire, so let's go with that." If a writer on the staff says, "I think this character wouldn't do that," the showrunner's response might be "I think she would, but why do you think that? As a viewer, tell me why you think that's out of character." You have to be comfortable with ideas and not be threatened by them.

If everything the writers offer is not considered valid people stop contributing and they become yes men. And when the staff becomes yes men, the ego of the showrunner is inflated and he's happy but he's not getting the best out of the staff. You get the grumbling, the factions, the staff that feels *Why would I bother coming up with anything? I'm just going to validate the boss and get through this day.* Then sometimes you end up with a script that is a hundred percent the showrunner's idea and it works or a hundred percent the showrunner's idea and it doesn't work and he blames the staff for not having better ideas. It becomes a cyclical problem that's a result of narcissistic behavior. When it doesn't work, it comes down to management — listening and truly knowing how to collaborate with artistic people. When you think you have all the ideas, you're not getting the best out of your staff, and that's what gets people in trouble.

After that show, I couldn't get staffed. I was out of work for a year. One reason is that I missed the network window for staffing. The second reason is something I'm totally behind, even though it's affecting me. It's new in the industry: the diversity initiative. At the lowest level of a writing staff, being a white male can be tricky in this new era. When a show is greenlit it has a budget and they start hiring the most experienced people first, so they go with their co-EPs and their consulting producers who have 15 years of experience, people with high-flashing credits that they trust. I get it. The showrunners want to have a success. That's most of the budget. Those were people who have been rising through the ranks, and they're mostly white men. And then the producers get to the bottom levels. They've filled up their staffs with white men and the studio and everyone goes "Whoa! We need some diversity — women, gay people, people of color." And then they have four dollars left and they start looking at staff writers and they can't hire another white guy.

There are a lot of diversity studio programs where they can hire people for free. A show might have enough left in the budget to pay for only one staff writer. So at the low levels they might fill those remaining slots with an Asian writer, a Latino, and a woman, for example. The programs pay the salaries for those beginning writers so those positions don't come out of the show's budget. The studio says now we have diversity, and they sign off on the show.

Back when *The Messengers* was breaking up, I heard that it's harder to get a second job than a first. It might come down to budget — with a second year, you have to pay me more. And the second job is not free because the writer is not coming out of a studio program, and you might be competing with people who are free coming out of programs. Even if you have experience, they don't need experience anymore because they just staffed seven people who they're paying a million dollars each. Now they need diversity and maybe a young fresh voice.

I got a second job right away, but that turned out to be the one that fires the staff every year. Still, when I was on *The Flash* I made a point to meet everybody on every show in the same building. I like people. I made friends and I went over to a different show for beers every Friday. That's how I met Chris Spivak, who had created *Chuck* and was the co-EP on one of the other shows. We became friends. Luckily, this show *Deception* comes along created by Chris Spivak. My agent, my manager, and I made a run at that show.

Meanwhile, Chris wants his show to be a success so he does what I told you — he starts staffing the highest levels. Then it gets down to money again for the lower levels. He needs diversity but also he likes me. Everyone started talking. They made a call to the Warner Bros. program and asked if they could help and the program found some alumni money to give me a boost. It was super nice.

Being a good writer is about 25% important. If you don't have the other 75% you'd better be Aaron Sorkin on the page. The job to me is 25% writing. 25% is how good you are in a room — can you pitch and pitch, are you a supportive player (is it "yes, and . . .")? Another 25% is do I want to spend time with you all day as a human; do I like you as a person? Another 25% is can you handle yourself on a set. They're all connected because if I like you as a person and you're good in the room you'll probably be good on a set, which involves problem solving. Are you willing to travel? Do you know how to talk to actors? Are you good managing people as a surrogate for the showrunner who is not there? If you're good at all four but great at two, I think you'll keep working. But if you're bad at three and only good at one, you're not going to work again.

The showrunner on *Deception* brought me in and said, "I just want you to know, I love my family. I want to see my family. I want to be out of there by 6 o'clock every day." He knew that was a concern I might have as a guy with kids. That goes back to what makes a good showrunner. Knowing your staff and caring about their quality of life is a huge part of helping a staff be the best they can be.

Now that I've been through the ups and downs of staffing for three years, seeing how things go, I have a big urge in the spring when I'm off to be pitching ideas for original pilots. I have three pilots that I've written so I have enough samples. I asked my agent to set up meetings to pitch. I haven't really done that yet — develop a 20-minute pitch for an original show. I've gone into meetings and pitched myself for a job, but now I want to start developing. One day before this is all over I'd like to be a showrunner. I think I see what makes them good and I could do it.

Someday I want to write a social justice show, something my kids can look at and say, "He tried to make a difference in the world." I'd like to contribute through television to helping people be good citizens in some way. I'd like to create a show that makes you think about our life and the possibilities for the human condition.

TAYLOR MARTIN

Taylor is story editor on The Blacklist *on NBC.*

Right after graduated I got really lucky because I knew a writer on *Nashville*, where I'd interned. With his recommendation, I got the writer's PA position on *The Blacklist* and simultaneously found out that my script that I wrote in your class won the Humanitas Award. As part of the award, I was given a freelance episode of a 20th Century Fox show that was a big launching pad.

As a writer's PA, we get lunches and groceries, organize the office, and help the writers with anything they need. If the writers were in the writers' room, it was okay to go sit in there. We would also assist specific writers with any research they might need or if they wanted us to write something on their board. You can use some silly small tricks to get people to like you. For example, I have particularly nice handwriting that is nice for the board.

In bringing people their food, you could chat with them about how they got to where they are. We had several nice writers who were willing to read something. Since they knew about the one script that won the Humanitas, they were curious to read that. The best thing about being a writer's PA is networking.

The second season of *The Blacklist* I was promoted to the Showrunner's Assistant. The position had opened up and they interviewed me along with some other people. That was when I wrote the freelance episode of *Bones* that I'd won through the Humanitas Award. The showrunner let someone cover for me during the 6 weeks I wrote the *Bones* episode. Knowing I had written an episode and it went well, people at *The Blacklist* saw me in a different light.

Being the showrunner's assistant let me see the show on a macro level that you don't get in the writers' room. USC taught us so much about the craft of writing and crafting and constructing a story, so I felt well equipped on the writing side. For me it was eye-opening to see what goes into the show in a more holistic way. I also learned about the financial aspect of the show. I also saw how much people make and found out men ask for more than women, and that was interesting to see.

In Season Three, I stayed the showrunner's assistant but I asked for a free-lance episode. In every job you have to read how their hierarchy works, and at that point I felt comfortable throwing it into the universe. They said, "We'll consider it." And then a few months later it came to fruition. My boss sent an article to a few writers and I thought I could make the inspiration for that article into an episode. So I wrote an episode in Season Three and they liked it. By the middle of that season, I knew they were seriously considering staffing me. They staffed me for Season Four and I became a staff writer. Now in the fifth season I'm a Story Editor.

On our show, regardless of title, whoever pitches the best episode wins. They want you to pitch in broad strokes at first. If they don't like it, they're happy to throw it in the trashcan and you think of something new. One difference from being a staff writer is that as a story editor I feel more confident to pitch more frequently and not be afraid to bring things to them if I feel they might be helpful. They have a higher expectation of you contributing to the more serialized part of the show the longer you stay.

The Blacklist is a network show in the traditional sense, with a 22-episode season. We work 42 weeks a year, starting June 1st and ending April 20th. I have the most stable job of any of my friends.

Typically people arrive around 10 AM but we're not in the room all day. Whatever episode is being broken next, the showrunner and two of our EPs are up with that writer and maybe one other writer because a room of 13 is rather large and not the most productive.

We'll have a smaller room breaking the next episode. One or two people are off on their script or outline. The rest of the staff will be working on broad stroke pitches for upcoming episodes.

In a typical week, after we come in at 10 we might have an hour and a half with our showrunner and writers pitching new ideas and seeing what sticks and what doesn't. By that time, you're at lunch. The rest of the afternoon is spent with a smaller room continuing to flesh out each other's pitches, but not necessarily breaking episode beats.

When I say broad strokes, there are a lot of twists required in the structure of a procedural show. So we decide who is our bad guy of the week, who we call our "blacklister." What is a cool teaser? What is the act out of One that is sort of a reversal of our investigation? What is the huge twist in Act Three? *Oh, my God, we thought it was a bomb, but it's really this other thing.* And finally, what's the race in Five? What are we racing to stop?

The show is sort of a combination of procedural that tends to ramp up into an action kind of show in the last few acts. We're always racing actively to stop something rather than finding the killer or solving a crime that already happened. It's more that a new crime is about to happen.

Episodes are written in six acts. But Act Six is the calm after the storm, wrapping up the serialized aspect of the story or understanding why the criminal was doing what he was doing. Really, by the end of Five we're wrapping up the case.

Each episode runs 42 minutes on the air, and we aim for 49 pages per script. We have a lot of action sequences so even if they take a quarter of a page they could take a day to film.

Our showrunners have pretty heavy involvement in each episode, and for the final pass on a script, they might stay late and work together. But after the writer has done a few revisions, they like to work on their own and adjust the script's vibe.

When I'm on script, I like to get a first draft done so I'll work around the clock as soon as I'm assigned it. If it's my episode, I might be thinking about it in the evenings and on weekends, but otherwise I pretty much do a usual workday 10 to 6.

There are three female writers out of 12 or 13. The show has a somewhat masculine energy to it. Industrywide a lot of rooms tend to be predominantly male, though I know a lot of talented female writers. Generally, I feel respected at work, but just because of the number of men working on the show, the tone, the vibe, the point of view feels male to me as a viewer and as a writer.

For a long time I was reluctant to ask for an episode on this show because I thought I don't know if I could write this. I don't write action. I like female-centric stories. I tried to see it as a challenge to acquire these new writing skills.

I might like a slower cable drama. On *Blacklist*, we have to get through so much plot that often an interesting emotional story has to get cut just for time to make sure everyone understands the structure of the main case. I'd like to write a family drama or a teen soap where you can get into the characters more and the plot is not so complex.

The first step in breaking a *Blacklist* episode is like a huge puzzle, making sure it works, and it's an incredibly complicated puzzle. The emotional stuff I'm interested in comes second.

For someone beginning a career I think it's important to keep writing new samples. And it's important to write pilots for a show you'd be excited to work on. Showrunners don't have a lot of time to decide who they're going to choose for a project. When you see how accelerated that process really is, it's kind of upsetting because you might have worked so hard on a pilot and they'll only read about 10 pages. Those pages have to make sense for the show they're trying to create.

Writing new samples can also serve you well on a different kind of show than where you might be working. You hope your pilot blows the showrunner away at your dream show. Personality is another part of it. You could get an interview for your dream show and realize I don't really understand this person. My bosses have met with people and I think, I can't imagine being in a room with them too long.

I think relationships are important and if you find people who work on a show you work on who have similar interests . . . If you like someone on a personal level or if you like their sensibility that's another way to future jobs. People staff people they know and people they've worked with who they trust. That's why getting those first few jobs is incredibly challenging.

There are plenty of people who've worked on *The Blacklist* that I'd love to work with or for again. In that case, I might not care so much about the show if it's a person I really like because you can always bring something from yourself to any show.

For someone trying to break in, my advice is two-fold:

1. Have one or two original samples that are in a PDF so the minute someone asks you to send a script you don't have to need two more weeks to revise it. The scripts need to be ready to go that are a good reflection of what you can do. Often where assistants get stuck is when someone asks them for a piece of material and they say well, it's not good enough or it's not ready. I've always thought it's better to have one A+ sample than five B- samples.

2. Try to network your way to working in a writers' room in any position, like writer's PA, writer's assistant, or showrunner's assistant as soon as you can. That's where your jobs will come from.

If you're not in Los Angeles that's a problem because around 90% of those jobs are here. Getting on a show you'll build relationships that will get you into the system and build your skills.

What's cool right now is that so much TV writing is so excellent. I have almost a "to do" list of all these series. My agent told me there are 525 scripted shows right now. And there are also ways to do niche subjects. There are specific places and audiences for you and you don't have to hit every audience or pander to the lowest common denominator. There are so many opportunities that no matter the story you want to tell, there's a place for you in TV . . . though it's still hard to get jobs.

AKELA COOPER

Akela was supervising producer on Luke Cage *at the time of this interview.*

I graduated from USC in the spring of '06. In my final semester, I was taking your pilot writing class, and at the same time I got into the CBS writing program. CBS had just partnered with NAACP and I became the first recipient of the scholarship. So in that final semester I was doing the CBS workshop and writing a spec script for them and taking other classes at the same time as writing my thesis.

In the CBS program I had a mentor who was developing a show called *Jericho*. At the time they needed a research assistant and two or three weeks after graduating I was working. It was a great experience seeing how a show was made from conception through casting and editing. I was involved in every stage.

When *Jericho* was cancelled, I got recommended to be a writer's assistant on *Dexter*. They let us pitch ideas. A lot of shows don't allow assistants to pitch ideas but *Dexter* did. As a writer's assistant you sit in the room and take notes as the writers are pitching. At the end of the day, you clean it up so you have a record of which ideas were confirmed so the writers know the next day.

Then we had the writers' strike, so no one was working. From there I wasn't employed for a year.

During that time, I applied to Warner Bros workshop and had a great experience there. The main difference from CBS was that Warner Brothers was creating a "farm system." The studio was covering the salary of the staff writers who graduated from their program, so it was an incentive to bring us on — we were free.

From there I got my first staff writing job on the remake of *V*. Finally I got to be at the table, breaking stories though unfortunately my name didn't get on any episode.

After that I was unemployed again for another year. It was hard to get meetings. In hindsight, my agent at the time [was distracted] and I ended up getting a new agent at ICM, where I am now. That agent got me staffed on *Grimm*. That was the big break. I was a staff writer again and did two seasons of *Grimm*.

What makes effective sci-fi writing is the same across writing in any other genre. All good writing comes down to characters you care about as opposed to spectacle and plot. That's what people related to on *Grimm*. For example, the character of Silas was a werewolf but the actor brought so much fun to the role. People were showing up for him every week, and then we fleshed out more of the other characters. For me, everything always comes down to character and whether or not you care about them.

From *Grimm* I moved to *The 100* on CW. And each time I was promoted, so by then I was executive story editor on *The 100* and kept working my way up. We didn't know if the show was coming back so while we were writing my agent busted his ass and got me staffed on *Witches of Eastwick* on Lifetime. That was a great experience. But *The 100* came back so I was yanked to go back. But I had three years of solid work by then so I really can't complain.

I grew up as a geek living in a small town. Around the time *The 100* was ending, Marvel partnered with Netflix and they were creating all these superhero shows that I love. I was able to move over to *Luke Cage* on Netflix.

The way Netflix works is you write all the episodes first and they film them and it doesn't air until the next year. So I had a year off. My agent once again busted his ass and got me a "second position" job, so I did Season 6 of *American Horror Story* in between seasons of *Luke Cage*.

I went from writing act breaks to writing no act breaks. For *Luke Cage*, they're like mini movies now. We're making a 13-hour movie. I do sometimes miss the episodic nature of storytelling, but Netflix is designed to keep you watching. They want you to click on the next episode and never go to sleep. In episodic television, you have breaks and people can say, ok I'm done with this, I'll pick it up another day. Instead of act breaks, you're writing cliffhangers at the end of each show so the viewer will keep watching the next hour.

Sometimes I wish I could break this up so I know how to structure everything. Instead of breaking everything in acts, we do everything by character. So we have our A, B, C, and possibly D stories, and we break everything by character. And then we weave everything together to make the episode. So that's been different.

You might weave A, B, C, and then you see that scene doesn't go there and then you start moving things around. Now you take a step back and ask: *What's our timeline here?* Over how many days does this take place? You move everything around like puzzle pieces.

I'm going back to a network pilot now, so I'm going back to act breaks. It's like learning to be ambidextrous. That's one of the transitional things in TV. People are transitioning out of the act-break way of thinking because the hot thing is to have a show on Netflix or Amazon that don't do act breaks.

I think traditional networks might be forced to cycle back around to taking chances. Everyone has moved over to premium cable or the digital streaming sites. To get eyeballs back networks are going to have to do something besides churning out doctor-cop-lawyer. I don't think networks are going anywhere anytime soon but if they don't adapt they will die. We're not going backwards.

Now I'm in development. Development means that at a certain point in your career people start coming to you for your ideas to turn into possible TV shows. Or they have intellectual properties that they want to develop as TV shows and they're trying to find the right writer.

My awesome agent got me a "blind script deal" with a company called ABC Signature, which is a subsidiary of ABC, which is a subsidiary of Disney. That means the executives of ABC Signature and I develop a show together, whether that's an original idea of mine or, in this case, a book they got the rights to that they wanted to develop. I read it, I liked it, I gave them my thoughts on how to do it. They liked my ideas. So we moved forward and I write the pilot and they take it out and try to sell it. If someone buys it and turns it into a series, great! I am a showrunner and I will have a show on the air somewhere. If it doesn't, I still get paid for the work I've done. A lot of time, that's not necessarily the case. Many writers put in a lot of hours and brainpower, and you try your best, and you still end up with nothing. This is a way my agent saw to get me paid during my development season.

I'd tell someone who wants to be on a staff: *First of all, you need to be writing.* You'd be amazed how many people say I want to be a writer and then don't write, or start something and never finish it. A great piece of advice I'd heard when I was beginning is: If you start something then finish it. Even if it's bad, finishing is an accomplishment in and of itself. Do whatever you need to not have distractions and to focus — just do the work and write.

You can't do anything with something that doesn't exist. Sometimes I have an idea that's been rattling around in my brain for years and I think, *I have to put this down on paper.* I can't do anything with it if it's in my head. You can't submit yourself to be writing for a show if you don't have a spec. You can't submit yourself to a showrunner if you don't have the materials. You need to be writing — something.

I get this question all the time — how did you get your start? Everyone's path is different. I am a kid who came out to California to go to USC, and that's how I broke in. I know people who moved out here and took a job in the mailroom at an agency and worked their way up, working on their writing in their spare time. You have to find the opportunities to get your foot in the door. Everything is worth trying. The writing programs at CBS and Warner Bros helped me immensely. Starting from the bottom helped me immensely. Know your goal and try to figure out what the path is. Everyone's different.

My final advice is: Write. If this is really what you want to do, know that you are going to have downs and then some ups, and then probably downs again and don't let that discourage you.

DAVID McMILLAN

David is an executive story editor on Locke and Key *for Hulu while writing features.*

Right now I'm in the writers' room on *Locke and Key* which has been greenlit to pilot. Hulu is treating it like a show that has been picked up to series and hiring writers who have experience to figure out the first season. Basically, what a lot of nontraditional

networks like Amazon, Hulu, AMC do is, they'll greenlight the pilot for production, but before they've greenlit the season they put together these writers' rooms to figure out what the show is. We'll generate an entire season of scripts and based on those Hulu will make a decision by the end of the year whether to do a full season pickup or not. These newer companies are making the investment in advance, which is different from the traditional model.

There are a lot of shows now but they have shorter orders, so it's not as if you're working on a show for 22 episodes. A lot of the formats are 10 or 13 episodes, so that means writers who would traditionally be on one show for most of the year have to find multiple shows to work on to make their living.

This is how I got to where I am now. I went to Yale for undergrad and I was a big drama nerd. I did plays, but then I decided I really wanted to write and direct films. So after undergrad I came back to L.A. (which is where I'm from) and enrolled in film school at USC in the production program, thinking I wanted to focus on making movies. I thought I was going to become the next Spike Lee or Federico Fellini. That was the dream at least.

In the middle of the program, I took your class on writing the TV drama in 2001–2002. It was the best time to take it because television was beginning to come into its own. It was the start of the new golden age with shows like *The West Wing*, *The Sopranos*, *24* . . . You couldn't do shows like that within the feature space. I thought there was so much opportunity for creative storytelling from a narrative and character perspective. So I wrote a *West Wing* spec in your class and when I graduated, I worked as a PA on a Fox show called *Tru Calling* for a season. While I was working there, I got accepted into the CBS Diversity Program. That was in 2003, the very first year of the program.

From the CBS program I was put on *Judging Amy*, a CBS show, as a writer's assistant. That show was where I got my first freelance episode. I thought, "Wow, this is great — my first year out of film school and I'm on a show where hopefully I'll be bumped up to staff writer in the next season."

Well, it didn't quite work out that way. Two things happened — One: The show got cancelled. Two: We had a writers' strike, which threw me and the whole town out of the loop. It took a lot of people a long time to find their footing after that.

After the writers' strike, my agency at the time dropped me. A lot of clients got dropped. I wasn't working, so I was part of the "excess baggage." Funny thing is, I had written a spec *Dexter* and just turned it into my agent. I got a call from him and in the same call he said, "David, this is the best spec you've ever written. But unfortunately we have to let you go." Lesson of the story: if you stick around in this business long enough, you learn the hard knocks. And it's important to know your first agent may not be your last.

Needless to say, I had to make ends meet, so I went back to my old high school and taught film and worked in the admissions office. Meanwhile I kept writing.

And on the side, I started making political satire videos and posting them on YouTube, which was brand new at the time. The people who worked at YouTube found them and said, "Hey, would you like to be a news and politics correspondent for us?" It was during the first Obama campaign in 2007–2008. It was the wild west of Internet video and they were looking for content creators and people with different points of view. So I got hired as a news-and-politics editor during the 2008 presidential race. It was exciting, exhilarating. I went to all the conventions; I went to the inauguration in D.C. And eventually I ended up moving to San Francisco and working out of the Google-YouTube headquarters. It was a great life . . . but at a certain point I wondered — "Okay, I can keep going down this track, work at Google, have a cushy position that doesn't really speak to my passion. Or I could take the plunge and go back to L.A. and try to pursue my dream."

So after about a year in San Francisco, I did the hard thing and moved back to L.A. I took a job in the marketing department at a tech start-up to make ends meet. I would wake up at 5 in the morning to write, go to my start-up job, write a little before bed, go to sleep, and repeat.

During all this I kept up with all my industry contacts that I'd established over the years — and one of them happened to be screenwriter/producer Alex Kurtzman. He'd gone to my high school and graduated several years before me, and we'd taken some of the same film classes, so we had that in common. We met for breakfast one day and he said he was about to make his directorial debut [*People Like Us*]. He said it's going to be super low budget, but if I wanted to get back in the business, he'd find me a job. I said absolutely! So I left my start-up gig for a few months and worked as a P.A. on Alex's film. It was so much fun. I loved being back with film people, and I knew that, the perks of the tech industry aside, working in TV and movies was where I belonged.

Later, a few months after the film was done shooting and I'd gone back to the start-up gig, Alex contacted me and said he was promoting his assistant and asked me if I'd like to be his full-time assistant. It was a big decision. I was over 30, and a lot of people thought I shouldn't have to work as an assistant at that age, that I was overqualified. It was a moment when I really had to swallow my pride in the interest of the bigger goal. Ironically, I probably wouldn't have taken the job when I was 25, but I did take it at 30. When you're just out of film school, you may think you're more talented than you actually are or you're more deserving of overnight success. But when you've been kicked around for a few years and you realize how difficult this business is, you take every opportunity that comes your way and you get through the door any way you can, no matter what.

So pride and age aside, I took the job with Alex. It was an amazing desk to be on because he was working on *Star Trek II* at the time and he and his writing/producing partner Bob Orci were in development on a ton of movies and TV series. One of those was *Sleepy Hollow*. I was there from the beginning of that development process until about a year and a half later when it finally got picked up to series. The day it got greenlit, Alex brought me outside and said, "You're going on that show as a writer's assistant." To this day, I really credit Alex with giving me my Big Break.

True, it wasn't a staff writer job, as perhaps I'd initially hoped. But I actually came to appreciate that because I do think there's merit in working one's way up the ladder — not in the sense of the nobility of it, but you learn a lot. You learn what everyone's role is. I probably learned more the two seasons I was a writer's assistant on *Sleepy* than in a lot of the classes I took in film school. Especially on that show, where the research was so mythology heavy. As a writer's assistant, you're the memory, the brain trust of the writers' room. You have to take down every single pitch and recall every pitch, and the writers lean on you a lot when they're writing their episodes. So it's a very intense way to learn how the television machine operates.

During *Sleepy*, I was workshopping a play I'd written called *Watching O.J.* I didn't think writing a play would be the smartest thing for my career. But at the time when I started writing it, I was briefly unemployed and thought, *Heck, I needed to write something*. So I went back to my theater roots and wrote a play. We eventually did a full production of it in 2015. That play, by far, has gotten me most of my work so far as a TV writer. It's what the producers read before they hired me for *American Crime Story: Katrina*, and what the *Locke and Key* producers read first before they later read my genre TV scripts.

I think people understand that the most important thing a writer has to bring is his or her understanding of character. You can learn the tropes of a genre — and admittedly some writers are better at genre or a particular kind of show than others are — but showrunners need to know "Does he understand character? Does she know how to relay depth and emotion in a non-cliché way?" Of course, the flip side is that you also need writers on staff who understand television, and when you're a writer who doesn't have that experience, who perhaps comes from features or theater, your first writers' room experience can be a bit of a shock. Which is why you need a really good showrunner who can wrangle those different forces. So while a play can definitely get you noticed, it's important to know that playwriting and TV writing, while they share similarities, are definitely different.

While I was a writer's assistant on *Sleepy*, I got a freelance script, but I ended up leaving *Sleepy* and made the jump to staff writer on the first season of *Lucifer*, which was an awesome experience. And even though I'm no longer there, I'm still close with the EPs on that show [Joe Henderson and Ildy Modrovich]. It was not only great to finally be a staff writer — at long last! — but it was also nice to be on a show where you were reminded that, yes, this is hard work, but it can also be fun and you can work with people who are enthusiastic and who make your work better, and where you enjoy going into the office and coming up with cool, crazy stuff all day long. It was great to have that experience right after *Sleepy* — which, by the end of my time there, had become a pretty tumultuous place to work.

Crazily, around the same time I was on *Lucifer*, I sold a pilot to NBC. A producer [Will Packer] had read one of my spec pilots and we developed a pitch together and sold it to NBC. So I was juggling both jobs at once. Now, *Lucifer* had an intense writers' room that usually met from 10 AM to 6 PM, with few breaks. So what I would do is, after *Lucifer* broke for the day, I'd take a nap in my office, wake up, and then work on the pilot till midnight or 1 AM. It was a pretty crazy time, but as a struggling artist you never want to say no to anything, and that mindset never really goes away. When opportunities happen, you just have to suck it up and seize the moment.

Spec pilots are useful even if they don't get made because what people are really looking for is a voice. It's much more important to demonstrate your point of view than to think, "I'm writing the next *Empire* or another show that the marketplace wants." The marketplace doesn't know what it wants until it sees it. What you have to do is find your place within it and your own distinct voice. Granted you have to build up your abilities as a writer and storyteller and understand the mechanics of solid TV writing, but if you have a point of view, someone, eventually, will gravitate to your voice.

I decided to leave *Lucifer* to be a story editor on the second season of *American Crime Story* on FX. The first season was *The People v. O.J. Simpson.* The second season was initially going to be about Hurricane Katrina, but things shuffled around and the second season is now going to focus on the murder of Gianni Versace, and the Katrina season will come later. I loved working with Ryan [Murphy], and it was amazing watching him oversee four or five shows at the same time, at various stages. The man's a force of nature. I also learned from him the importance of creative vision — and that without it, you really can't make a successful TV show.

At one point while I was on *Katrina*, I was asked to run the writers' room for a week. I was terrified, but I found that I really liked it. It's a skillset one has to learn and grow into, but some people take to it better than others.

TV writing, unlike feature writing, involves a lot of communicating with other people and wrangling ideas. I come from a theater background so I don't have a problem interfacing with people. I love the writers' room because it's collaborative. People are always spitballing. And I enjoyed the role of playing the referee — "That works, that doesn't work." That was the week I realized that this is the job I eventually want to grow into — even though it's a pretty insane job!

During all of this, I was also writing features. One of my features got optioned. We attached a major actor to it and recently just attached a director, and it's set to go into production in 2018. We're cobbling together the financing right now. The feature world is unpredictable, though, and you never know what's going to happen, or when. Besides that project, I also have another feature project in active development, as well as my job on *Locke and Key*. So at the moment at least, I'm happy to say I'm gainfully employed as a writer.

Locke and Key (the Hulu show) is only a 20-week job. After that's up — depending if the show gets picked up and I go back for season 2 — I might take a short break from TV to focus on features. But who knows what the future holds — it's impossible to predict things in this business!

This is a war of attrition. There are a lot of people who come to Hollywood with ambition and talent and big dreams, but what you learn is the reality is much more difficult, and the road a lot more winding. You have to ask yourself how important this is. There's nothing wrong with deciding, "I want a stable life. I don't want the constant uncertainty that comes with this industry." That's totally fine. But if you do want it, it requires a high degree of sacrifice and commitment and perseverance, as well as being comfortable with uncertainty — no matter what level you're at.

INTERNATIONAL TELEVISION

OVERVIEW

"As I was translating my Brazilian friends' quotes to send you, I was just thinking that the younger generation that's part of the middle class in Brazil watches American TV drama series a lot more than they watch telenovelas. If we consider TV as a communicator of culture, then watching mainly products from a different country can have a serious impact on a country's identity. I felt that very strongly when I was writing in Brazil. Since I grew up watching American TV, I've always identified with the culture from here a lot more than I did with my own. Even though I was writing in Portuguese, my cultural references always pointed towards the U.S. It was through film, TV, and music that I became fluent in English, and the more exposed I was to this foreign language being used in drama, the more natural it became for me to write in it.

"Nowadays, my writing flows better in English than it does in my own native language. So it's a weird feeling. It's hard to write something that feels like it's genuinely from there when all of our major reference points are from here. It's also hard to write something that takes place here and sound grounded, unless you can draw from the experience of living here for a while to infuse the writing with emotional heat. And that is why I believe the young middle class with access to online products and foreign-language courses in Brazil is stuck in a kind of cultural limbo, because we don't feel like we really belong anywhere. This might just be my own experience, but I suspect it might be part of a larger scenario as well, so I wanted to share it with you."

That was written by Anna dos Santos Israel who did most of the underlying research for this chapter. By the time you read this, Anna will have an MFA in screenwriting from the USC School of Cinematic Arts and will be on her way to a successful career. Thank you, Anna!

* * *

This book is being read all over the world. I know you are there because earlier editions have been published in translation in Spain, Germany, Italy, France, China, and elsewhere, and I hear from you by email. I've taken that audience to heart in considering this fourth edition. *Writing the TV Drama Series* has been America-centric, and to an extent that's useful because American shows are known worldwide. But many countries are making drama series now. Increasingly, the global marketplace influences what shows are produced and — of special significance to writers — how they're written and the kinds of characters and stories they contain. Though tensions may rise between nations, universal human feelings and relationships travel across time and space, and television is our way to connect.

As I meet writers, producers, and executives from many countries, one question often arises: Why are American television shows so successful? Usually it's asked as if the causes are ineffable, as if creating television drama that speaks to cultures everywhere is too complex or simply unknowable. Actually, I can tell you why.

It's not that Americans are smarter or more talented than people in other places are. Gifted storytellers exist everywhere, and always have. It's not that the United States has more money. Plenty of countries have strong economies. It's not that creating television requires a rarified technology available only here. Some countries are even more advanced in certain ways, and anyway a pencil and paper is all you need to start. And it's not that Americans are more driven to make good television dramas. Really, everywhere I travel people are clamoring for the chance.

The solution is structural, and any place can achieve quality series if they're willing to adopt the system. It's all about showrunners who are *writers*. Those writers have trained in their craft and climbed a ladder, writing episodes and being promoted to writer-producers. American television series — both drama and comedy — are steered by one (or maybe two) guardians of the show's vision. A person, usually the creator who wrote the pilot, oversees the characters and the central questions (the spine), often passionately. That person has a staff of experienced writers whose only job is collaborating in a writers' room and writing scripts for episodes on this show, and, one day, they may be showrunners themselves. But the top writer/showrunner is the decision-maker for everything. That's it.

If that sounds easy, consider the blowback. Cultures where director "auteurs" are revered have difficulty with this approach, and those systems debilitate their own success to the degree they debilitate their writers. In our tour of the world throughout this chapter, we'll visit both successes and frustrations, and time and again the countries struggling most with making quality international serialized dramas are the ones who disempower their writers.

Some places also disrespect television generally and then wonder why their products aren't faring well across the globe. American TV invests in quality. Countries that don't make a financial commitment on par with how they value their own feature films shouldn't be surprised if their TV shows are second rate. It doesn't have to be that way — it's a choice.

Surveying the globe, in addition to the United States, countries making original television dramas seem to fall into three general categories: First are the major transnational successes — creative hubs that make series that are sold elsewhere, often adapted, creating a next-generation hit series. The U.K., Israel, Denmark, and Turkey are among the sources of important television, and others offer remarkable series that uniquely express their origins while being accessible elsewhere. China is a special case in its dedication to cultural influence throughout Africa via television series, a position of strength that is growing.

Second are the countries that certainly have the resources for great television drama, but whose old ways of filmmaking, rigid viewpoints, and bureaucracy have stood in the way. I recommend a hilarious documentary from several years ago, *Exporting Raymond*, about the creator of the U.S. hit comedy *Everybody Loves Raymond* trying to adapt his show in Russia. The film is available on various Internet and streaming platforms — watch it! Immediately you'll see how hard it is to translate humor between cultures, but more than that, you'll see how quality is diminished when bureaucrats control art, when writers are undermined by impossible schedules and lack of influence, and how pinched resources and schedules that could only produce low quality do in fact result in low quality. *Exporting Raymond* is a cautionary tale and a manual for what not to do.

Like Russia's magnificent history of literature and cinema, French films and novels are respected worldwide. You'd think countries like Russia (where the technology that became television was invented) and France, with its venerable arts, would put together literary mastery with film mastery and come up with television writers. Unfortunately, it seems that a kind of snobbery towards the medium, probably based on the limitations of television programming in an earlier era, has gotten some European countries stuck in the past.

Several years ago, a delegation of French television writers visited the professors in the screenwriting division at the USC School of Cinematic

Arts. They were looking for help. They told us that hundreds and hundreds of scripts from the American series *Law & Order* that ran for 20 seasons on NBC (1990–2010) had been dumped on them with an order to translate them into French. But the French legal system is different and a translation wouldn't make sense to a French audience, they said. According to one of the writers, they pleaded with the executives to allow them to do their work as writers, perhaps basing episodes in some story ideas from *L & O* and adjusting characters to fit real detectives and lawyers in France, but creating their own episodes as screenwriters. According to our visitor, the executive responded, "There are no screenwriters in France."

They turned to us to understand how writers here have attained power. We spoke to them about the Writers Guild of America (our influential union), but they said the comparable organization in France had no authority. We shared some strategies and supported their struggle, but they left as sad as they'd arrived. Now, years later, France has embarked on a few original series, and when we visit that country in our tour we'll look at a show that was the first to use a writers' room and became successful, receiving international notice. There is hope for French television writers in the future.

I had a similar experience when I gave a workshop for writers in Cologne (Köln), Germany, where the sophisticated attendees already worked in their industry. They were frustrated because they all watched American drama series (often in English with English subtitles) and were well aware of the potentials. But they told me German television shows consisted mostly of action procedurals that closed with each episode, and the few television dramas that aspired to being character-driven were 90 minutes long and structured like movies. As happened in France, the "auteur" origin of European filmmaking was limiting their potential. The sticking point was not how to write in general but how to write *serialized* stories that required writers rooms and showrunners who were writers.

A few years later, I'm delighted to see the 10-episode series *Dark*, the first German language original on Netflix. The *New York Times* quipped, "You could argue that *Dark* is the German *Stranger Things*. You could also say . . . it's the show for people who thought *Stranger Things* was just a little too much fun." Like *Stranger Things*, *Dark* is a multi-generational sci-fi tale set in the shadow of a mysterious installation in a small town. But the *Times* analyses that the show's European roots are strong, "In place of the American show's ceaseless adrenaline rush, *Dark* offers a hushed, brittle artiness that will be familiar to fans of the French ghost story *The Returned* or the British-French thriller *The Missing*."

The third category of countries includes those that truly lack the resources to make quality TV drama series. What can a writer do who lives there? When someone reaches out to me because they've read my book, I want to encourage them. But I also have to tell the truth. This is a difficult situation. I know because I had a taste of it myself.

When I was very young I spent time on a small island in the Caribbean. The local television station was essentially a transmitter for broadcasts from anywhere else because its production capacity was limited to local news and weather and an occasional talking head, probably selling something. It's not that the island was so deeply "third world" that we were cut off from more sophisticated pursuits. We could easily go to the Hilton Hotel and find all the technology everyone else had, not to mention air conditioning. But creating a scripted television series wasn't in our universe.

Until it was. One day we kids came up with a story idea that grew into a series of adventure episodes for characters like ourselves. We decided on some supernatural elements that had to take place in our nearby forest. At an age when everything was possible, our "executive producer" — the kid whose family owned a video camera (this was before smartphones) — asked his uncle who worked at the TV station if we could put our (nonexistent) television show on the station. The uncle said possibly in an off time, maybe, sort of, but he wasn't in charge of that. With that definite "yes," off we went into the woods to film the scary part first.

In fact, we saw embers that might (or might not) have been evidence that something really scary had happened deeper in the forest. A rumor started among the "actors" (our friends) that a spirit or something had been released and bloody headless chickens were marauding everywhere, and coming to get us. With that, we all ran out of the woods, and that was the end of our television career.

But what if it had actually worked out? What if we'd made a real television pilot? What if instead of children, this venture was in the hands of adults who had worked hard to learn techniques of storytelling on screen? What if the creator was more like the reader who asked what he could do, coming from his own island?

I might encourage him to go ahead and make his show, put it on the Internet, and see if it could get enough traction on YouTube to interest a real production company. Or he could produce enough of it to show on local, or even regional stations and either be satisfied with that audience, or hope to broaden it through promoting it in other localities by himself. Or he could get rich or partner with some very rich entity and develop an industry on his island.

But, honestly, none of this answers his real question: how do you get here from there? How can someone in a place with no television infrastructure write the kind of television drama he so much admires and develop a career?

I'm sorry. You can't get here from there, at least not directly. I was fortunate to grow up mostly in New York City, attend good schools, move to Los Angeles, and get jobs in the industry. I returned to visit the island, but never worked there. If I was the same person I am, with the very same talents, but had never left, my career could not have happened. That's a tough truth. Not everyone wants to leave home, and the costs and risks may be impossible. So what can you do?

Well, there's something no location or situation can take away from you: your writing. You can't get a job as a staff writer in Los Angeles if you're not in Los Angeles. You might not build a television studio or production company to be noticed by Netflix or the BBC. But all you need is a computer and a screenwriting program to create a world and characters that form a compelling pilot. Find consultants who will work with you online or by Skype. Polish your script, enter it in international contests, and get it read. Let the writing travel for you, and later you might follow and get here from there.

Whatever your circumstances, global television is affecting you, sometimes as an opportunity for show creators and sometimes as an international financial colossus too vast to interact directly with an individual writer, but influencing any show you imagine. No matter where you are, it's smart to have a sense of the big picture. In a *Hollywood Reporter* article from 2016, writer Kayti Burt analyzed four ways that countries interface in making television drama. I used her categories for the discussion below.

FOUR TYPES OF INTERNATIONAL COOPERATION

• 1. Nationally funded productions designed solely for a domestic audience.

If you create a show that is likely to appeal only to an American audience, or any specific regional audience, is that enough? Maybe. Your romcom that depends on comedic winks and nods from your home culture and references only they would understand can delight a niche audience on certain networks, especially those that depend on advertising revenue for a targeted market. A clever show like *Portlandia* that relies on in-jokes about the tastes of a certain American class might be incomprehensible in other parts of the world, but is very much appreciated by the IFC Channel.

You might be surprised what has historically traveled, though. As far back as the 1980s, *The Cosby Show* was enjoyed internationally, and that was long before it could be streamed, so it relied on syndications to specific foreign "territories." Later, *Mad Men*, on AMC, which at the time didn't even have a system in place for foreign sales, was avidly followed as far away as Johannesburg and Lagos. When I spoke to television writers there, they knew exactly who Don Draper was. (They had found a way to access the show via satellite.) Why would someone in contemporary Nigeria be interested in Madison Avenue salesmen from the 1950s and '60s? The characters transcended the subject, and that's the ultimate answer to why anybody cares about any show. To a network, though, those international viewers don't matter. To count towards their profits, domestic viewers are enough.

The studios have a different viewpoint. They want to make back their investment by distributing internationally. They try to guess what will work. This gets into artistic choices: must a writer avoid rather specific or personal subjects, casting, and jokes for fear the show won't "travel?" The question quickly gets tangled by executives who prejudge what people elsewhere might enjoy. In the past, it was thought that shows with black characters would not succeed in Europe, though *The Oprah Winfrey Show* was wildly popular there. So maybe we're talking about bias. In terms of comedy, *Married With Children* remains comprehensible in any culture where people are indeed married with children. Still, from a writer's point of view, if your project is a personal expression that relies on local references you might ask yourself if you care about the studio that decides which TV dramas get made or renewed. Maybe you don't have to care. Maybe the scale of domestic viewership in the U.S. and a few other places is sufficient for your show. And maybe the well-observed specificity about a culture is exactly why it does succeed far away.

• 2. Nationally funded productions with a global audience.

This can be a result of the first category: domestic shows domestically funded that nevertheless attract international audiences. Denmark's *Borgen* is an example (more about that show when we visit Denmark on our tour). More likely, the global intention exists from the moment a writer is assigned to write the pilot and continues down to the level of specific episode scripts. Joe Peracchio, one of the writers you met in the previous chapter, shared his up-close experience of the process:

"Our studio that owns the show and then has the rights to repackage it and sell it all over the world — they love elements that translate internationally.

Those elements are procedurals — police stuff. They love explosions, action. They love magic because magic is universal. They're more critical sometimes of comedy: they say make it less funny because comedy doesn't travel well internationally. Different cultures have different ways of telling jokes or think different things are funny.

"Then we have to address those notes and take the script to the network. But the network is really focused on the domestic audience. They want more comedy. They love the elements where we learn a lot about the characters and their drives and why. For example, the lead had a sister who died from a drug overdose, and that's why she wanted to be an FBI agent. They want more of the serialized character stuff. So it's an interesting balance.

"It's a big deal these days that the studio wants to sell internationally. New shows getting picked up have to involve diverse casts and topics that translate well internationally. Meanwhile the traditional networks are still trying to appeal to the 'fly-over' states that love comedic procedurals. You try to find a middle ground to keep everybody happy."

Later in this chapter when we visit a tiny production in the Czech Republic, we'll see an entirely local project, but the showrunner, Harold Apter, is aware of a possible larger context. Their show is about a lynching in a small town in Eastern Europe. "Every country has small towns with their fears of outsiders," he commented. It wouldn't be the first time a local series gets international attention, as happened in Scandinavia. These days even a small production can dream.

• 3. International co-productions that keep most creative control in the hands of one country's production team.

Showtime entertainment president David Nevins told *Variety* how he decides whether a project might make a good international co-production: "When we have something that we feel is going to have equal relevance in multiple markets because of the show's setting or shared cultural history, that's probably when a co-production makes the most sense. When you are doing a show that's intrinsically American set in an American city, there's no need for a co-production. We only do it when there's some defined financial advantage."

Jeffrey Schlesinger, president of Warner Bros. International Television, reacted just as warily to *Variety*: "We'd rather not participate in co-productions. We'd rather take the risk and own the full reward. Rather than partnering with a bunch of territories to lower our risk profile on the deficit, we would prefer to own and control our programming, take the risks, and bet on success. It takes a lot of money to be in this business. You need to be pretty fiscally powerful. A lot of companies don't have that financial ability so they need to syndicate their risk."

The fact is most European drama series need to be co-productions because other countries don't have the budgets of the U.S. shows. Lee Morris, a producer at the BBC, explained: "In the past, all major dramas, BBC dramas, generally speaking, would have been mostly financed by the channel. I think now it's different from previous times. It's not possible for the BBC to fund a series by themselves, and, actually, they don't need to do that, either, if clearly the project has international appeal."

Downton Abbey and *Sherlock* are examples of British shows where the creative control stayed with the BBC, but were actually co-productions with partial financing coming from America via PBS' *Masterpiece* franchise. Rebecca Eaton, of *Masterpiece* commented on the legacy of British programming, speaking to the *Guardian*: "British accents, the way you talk, the orderliness, appeals to us unruly Americans. You are at a different stage, at the end of your empire, looking back on it. The way you approach British culture, revere writers, literature, that appeals. *Masterpiece* is like the little black dress of British drama: we are always in fashion, elegant in style, reliable. All in all, I think *Masterpiece* has put half a billion dollars into British drama, either via financing it, acquiring rights or publicity, by flying over the casts to meet the American press."

Probably the most famous international co-production fully controlled by its home country is *Game of Thrones* that challenges any definition of international. It films entirely outside of America but is based on books by an American writer, and has an American writing staff and American producers. It is also owned outright by HBO. On the other hand, most of the cast is international, and it is largely filmed in Northern Ireland. Now here's the co-production part: around $15.3 million of the show's budget was paid by Northern Ireland Screen, a government body in charge of encouraging filming in the country. Ireland did well with the deal — they're said to have benefitted by around $108 million of revenue. Does that make it any less an American show? Or is it international because its content and its audience are emphatically global?

• 4. Transnationally funded productions with multiple international markets as defining factors.

With all the tensions in the world, we can be inspired by the cooperation that grew naturally in Sweden and Denmark when they collaborated to make *Bron/Broen*. It asks what happens when a body is found on a border bridge, half in Sweden and half in Denmark. The drama was so popular it has been remade in America as *The Bridge* on FX, set on the U.S./Mexican border, and in U.K./France as *The Tunnel*, set in the Channel Tunnel between the two countries. In all versions, two countries' police must work together despite cultural differences to solve the crime.

Is this a wave of the future? Peace on Earth through television? Well, we're not there yet. Writing in *The Hollywood Reporter*, Kayti Burt suggests both a caution and a hope: "In a global marketplace already dominated by English-language content, especially of the American and British variety, could the potential transition into an era of more international co-productions further homogenize the global market? Or will the fact that American and British production entities are bringing their money to other regions with fewer resources mean more diversity in the stories being told to a wider, global audience? . . .

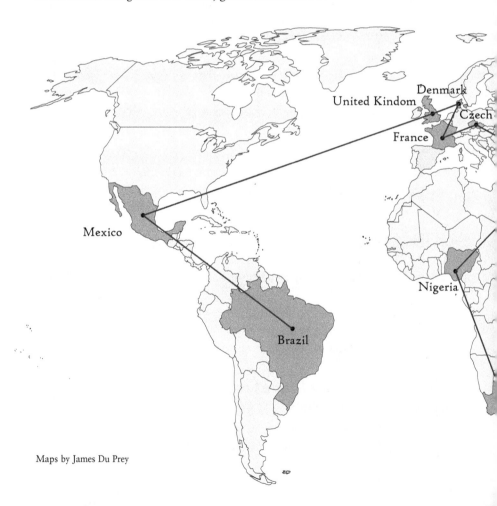

Maps by James Du Prey

"Transnational TV drama co-productions may be a commercial function of a global market, but I still have hope that an increase in more transnational and international stories will be good for the American public. Sure, in a domestic market where more people watch *Dancing With the Stars* than *The Americans*, high-end TV drama is not going to change the hearts and minds of a country with isolationist tendencies in an increasingly interconnected world, but — as an art form that specializes in empathy — it might change a few."

A TOUR OF THE WORLD

The Earth is divided into 194 countries now, and we can't go to all of them, so I've selected 15 that are interesting for discussing television drama series. That doesn't mean good shows aren't produced elsewhere — actually every country has television of some kind. I apologize to Australia, Canada,

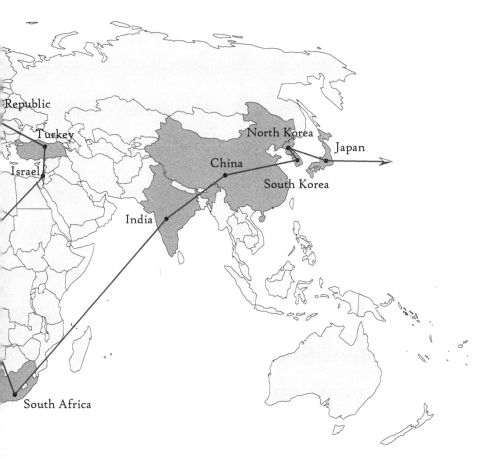

Germany, Russia, Spain, and other countries that have mature industries, but our air miles ran out after this list. My aim is to give you impressions and insights, not a comprehensive survey.

We will begin in Anna's homeland, Brazil, and travel north to visit Mexico. Then we cross the Atlantic and land in the United Kingdom. From there we make three stops in Europe in Denmark, France, and the Czech Republic. Flying south, we'll see what's happening in Turkey, and move on to Israel. Continuing south to Africa, we'll visit Nigeria and South Africa. Zipping north over the Indian Ocean, we'll land in India, and spend time in China. While in Asia, we'll find out what's happening in television in South Korea, North Korea, and Japan, before our final flight across the Pacific back to Los Angeles.

It's whirlwind adventure, which also describes television today, so fasten your seatbelt!

BRAZIL

Brazil

Young writers from Brazil began appearing in my classes at USC's School of Cinematic Arts after 2012 and applications from Brazil for the MFA in television writing have been increasing ever since. Why the sudden surge, I wondered. And what would all those graduates do with the craft they acquired?

Their presence was no coincidence. Brazil had passed a law that mandated more indigenous shows. A nice idea, but it's not as if they had writers ready to fill all the new writers' rooms. Or any writers' rooms. Or experienced writer-producers prepared to run the explosion of original television series. Thus began the pilgrimage to prepare a new generation and turn their industry around.

Brazil's National Telecommunications Agency (ANATEL) released a study in 2016 that said: "It's true that the pay-TV law has been helping the audio-visual sector maintain momentum in spite of the economic crisis that Brazil has been going through. However, the law doesn't protect the consumer from being exposed to low-quality products. Audiovisual production comes mostly from Rio de Janeiro and São Paulo, and even in those cities, very few production companies have the expertise and the experience to come up with quality content. The teaching of film and TV in Brazil is not only rather limited to those cities (which is already a problem, considering that Brazil is a country of continental proportions), but rather limited, period. There are very few film schools and so most people who want to really learn the craft try to go abroad (mostly to the U.S.) to study. That is why a lot of professors are invited to Brazil to speak about the American TV and Film industry so we can learn about what works there so that we can try to adapt it to our reality."

What is this law that attempts to revolutionize television in Brazil? In 2012, *Lei da TV Paga* established quotas for Brazilian content on pay-TV channels that air films and series: at least three and a half hours per week of national productions in prime time (defined as 6 PM to midnight). The law also says that at least 25% of the channels in any package offered to the consumer by a pay-TV operator must be owned by Brazilian program-mers. So for every three channels from a company like HBO, they need one national channel to meet the quota. The goal is to represent Brazil-ians better in a market that offers films and series mostly produced in the United States.

This effort is not unique to Brazil. Canada is overwhelmed by U.S. shows that easily cross the border. On top of that, the many shows that film in Vancouver and Toronto for tax advantages further blur the line between U.S. and Canadian properties. In response, Canada established rules that a certain percent of workers must be Canadian to get the credits, and that has tilted hiring decisions "below the line," though the shows remain created, written, and supervised in Los Angeles. Canada also instituted time limits on U.S. shows that resulted in oddities such as losing the last ten minutes of a U.S. broadcast. This kind of struggle for influence over a country's television programming has become an issue almost everywhere.

It's not difficult to understand how the imbalance arose. Brazil does not have a tradition of producing serialized drama outside of telenovelas. Like in Mexico, they come from radionovelas that could not rely on images to tell the story, and even now telenovelas rely on telling rather than showing. Dialogue is supposed to be "on the nose" to entertain an audience that isn't paying full attention to the screen. Like series in the U.S., telenovelas are a writer's medium rather than a director's. Globo, the powerhouse organization that dominates Brazilian media, keeps the handful of authors who have a successful track records tied to a contract with Globo so they can't write for anyone else.

These Brazilian shows really aren't like U.S. primetime dramas, though. From a U.S. viewpoint, we'd compare them to what we call soap operas that usually run during the day. Daytime soaps in the U.S. are a dying breed, hatched in the 1950s to keep stay-at-home women watching romantic intrigues between ads for household products (thus the nickname "soap opera"). They were cheaply made and written quickly to air every day. Writers on those staffs discovered their scripts weren't respected and they became stuck as soap writers. As women increasingly joined the workforce, and the Internet replaced traditional networks, making quality shows available at any time, American soap operas faded.

But in other countries, telenovelas are their heirs. In Brazil, they are made on an "industrial" scale, since one episode airs every weekday. Each telenovela on Globo is chosen to air at a specific time according to its themes or genres, so that they can appeal to a targeted audience. For instance, a teen drama called *Malhação*, which has been going on forever (but with a different cast every "season"), airs in the afternoon when teens are back home from school.

The formula for telenovelas (essentially melodramas) has been working for free-to-air TV channels since their inception in Brazil, so the companies don't take a chance on something that might not be as successful. Nevertheless, some limited series that are clearly inspired by the storytelling style, genres, and rhythm of American TV shows — more focused on quality than on quantity — have been popping up on Globo and have received critical acclaim. These are considered vanity projects, where a limited number of episodes attract talent that is more associated with film than TV in Brazil. This more sophisticated storytelling appeals to the audiences that watch American drama series on cable, though they maintain Brazilian storylines that can appeal to mass audiences that stay tuned after the main soap opera that airs at around 8 pm.

Breaking into creating original television drama series in Brazil is very different from the path in the U.S. This is how it goes for a production company that doesn't have its own resources: The government opens up a bid about a certain type of project that they would like to fund. Then the production companies, after developing the projects in-house with their staff, enroll the project online and wait for a board to decide which projects are moving forward. Sometimes the selection process involves a pitch to the board. But even after the projects are selected, the money takes a while to come. In a context where no first-look deals can be made with studios (because there are none), it's tough for smaller production companies to build a portfolio and afford the cost of their overhead while they wait for one of their projects to score. Therefore, what usually keeps a new production company afloat in Brazil are freelance jobs like photographing events.

If a production company wins one of these government bids, they are able to maintain the overhead of a writer's room. If they don't win, some production companies use the money from their freelance gigs to invest in a writer's room to develop projects for future bids. And then the clock starts again for government money, and it goes around and around.

Despite the difficulties, original Brazilian dramas are beginning to break through. The first 100% Brazilian show that crossed over to American audiences is Netflix's 3%, which started as an independent project in Brazil. According to Wikipedia: "3% is a Brazilian dystopian thriller series created by Pedro Aguilera. Developed from a 2009 independent pilot episode, it is Netflix's first original Brazilian production and the second produced in Latin America, after Club de Cuervos (the Mexican comedy-drama series). The show is set in a future wherein people are given a chance to go to the 'better side' of a world divided between progress and affluence in the Offshore, and devastation and poverty in the Inland, but only 3% of the candidates succeed." Netflix gave the show an 8-episode order for the first season in 2016 and then picked it up for a second season.

I sometimes hear from my former students who have returned to Brazil to find success. One became the showrunner of a drama series in her first year back home, a position that would have taken years to achieve had she stayed in the U.S., if she could rise to it at all. Another, Luis Gustavo Ferraz, wrote to Anna and me about his experience:

"The law was important for works in which I was involved. I hoped they would gain new viewing windows and, with that, new audiences. The series *Entre Fronteiras* (*Between Borders*), on which I was one of the writers, was licensed to a channel, *Mais Globosat*, which, because it belonged to a Brazilian programmer, became stronger with the Pay TV Law. Around the same time, a web series I wrote, directed, and produced had several episodes licensed for the channel *Curta!* The series had been shown on the website of PIPA Prize, a Brazilian art award, and at the Museum of Modern Art of Rio de Janeiro; with the syndication, it started to have an audience that the project hadn't reached yet, which was amazing. The *Curta!* channel, by the way, is one of the best examples of the law's effects. Founded in November 2012, just two months after the new rules went into effect, this channel has gained space in the packages of many TV operators. Initially, that was driven by the quota for channels from Brazilian programmers. But *Curta!* is much more than that. It airs a type of content that had no place in Brazilian TV before, and it got an extremely loyal audience.

"Now the miniseries of broadcast TV have a lot of aesthetic experimentation and thematic ambition, and I think the new law opens up more possibilities for this. Those series from pay-TV channels would probably have difficulty finding space on broadcast TV because of the way they represent sex and violence and perhaps because of the refined subtext. There is a consensus that broadcast TV, mainly because of telenovelas, offers stories that are too on the nose. But I think Brazilian TV is rich in examples in the most diverse formats, from telenovelas to series, from broadcast TV to pay TV, of stories that are very well told. What I think the new law brings are more windows to tell those stories and, especially, a great stimulus to storytellers who had less or no space on air — and a great stimulus to new storytellers, of course."

MEXICO

If you're a talented writer of Mexican or other Central American heritage and you're fluent in both Spanish and English, a job might be looking for you in American television drama. That's not to diminish working in other countries, but the large Hispanic population of the United States has bred an enthusiastic television audience, and beyond that, shows that are not primarily Latin American in overall content may also have storylines that benefit from your experience and insight. Recently I've taught some students who think they should run away from their backgrounds in the belief that being a colorless "all American" who has no ethnicity would

Mexico

help them get jobs. It's not true. Producers want and need your unique voice. If you've learned the craft of writing television drama, go for it now.

Several years ago, I happened to be in my agent's office when a call came in that created a buzz in all the rooms: *Dexter*, a major Showtime series, was phoning agencies all over town looking for a Spanish-speaking writer to add to their staff. The show was set in Miami, and authenticity demanded characters that were credible in that largely Latino city. It turned out *Dexter* wasn't an exception, and fellowship programs are reaching out to writers that had been underrepresented in the American industry.

Mexico has a special importance to television here. Maybe that's partly because the Mexican-American population of Los Angeles is the largest single ethnic group at almost 50%. Just as likely, the vibrancy of Mexican culture and the availability of its telenovelas have impacted Hollywood storytelling, even when the writers are not conscious of the origin.

I described telenovelas in the previous section on Brazil. This form occurs in countries throughout the world, so you should know what it is. To summarize: Telenovelas come from radionovelas, which could not rely on images to tell the story, and even now telenovelas rely on telling rather than showing. Dialogue is supposed to be "on the nose" to entertain an audience that isn't paying full attention to the screen. Like series in the U.S., telenovelas are a writer's medium rather than a director's. These shows really aren't like premium primetime dramas made in the U.S., though. We'd compare them to what we call daytime soap operas. They are cheaply made in a system that mimics industrial assembly lines, written quickly to air every day. But what they lack in quality they more than make up in quantity, hooking passionate viewers into melodramatic relationships that can string out for decades.

Jane the Virgin is a delightful sendup of the form, created with love and humor. It's a rare example of delivering Mexican television tropes on a traditional U.S. network, and it proves that the cultural mixture can appeal to a wide U.S. audience and even win awards.

For fuller immersion in Latin-American television, we'll visit the two immense Spanish-language networks based in the U.S., beginning with Univision. Based in New York City, with production just outside Miami, Univision is available in 60 U.S. markets. Its logo resembles a three-dimensional heart to represent its slogan, *"El latido del corazón hispano de Estados Unidos"* ("The Hispanic Heartbeat of the United States"). This shape is intended to represent Univision's growth as a "360-degree," multiplatform media company, while its seamless form represents the unity of Hispanic cultures. By 2016, the network reached viewership parity with the five major English language U.S. television networks.

But Univision is really Mexican television if you consider the majority of Univision's programming consists of telenovelas produced by Televisa that originate on the company's flagship network in Mexico, *Las Estrellas*. In fact, the production and distribution of melodramatic telenovelas places Televisa among the top five exporters of television programming in the world; the programs are exported not only to the Americas, but to countries that include China and Russia.

What does that mean for people who want to create content? Media scholar Florence Toussaint says that the soul of Televisa resides in its programming. She's critical of it, and points out that the organization offers an apparent diversity through its channels, but within all these programs, "a singular discourse is being elaborated." Plurality, she suggests, is not its goal, and all the different shows in the various genres are, in fact, similar. This is especially true of the telenovelas, the main programming form of Mexican television. Toussaint says, "This genre can be seen to prescribe the gender roles and the aspirations that the social classes should have. Bourgeois values and symbols are the ideal, the goal, and the measure of failure or success."

Univision's competition is Telemundo, which is actually a U.S. company owned by Comcast through NBC-Universal, with programming syndicated worldwide to more than 100 countries in over 35 languages. Like Univision, its corporate base is near Miami.

Unlike Univision that is sticking to its traditional telenovela formula delivered mainly through free TV, Telemundo is experimenting. For example, it debuted the "social novela" *Secreteando* on Facebook, with comments made on other social media websites. With the debut of *El Señor de los Cielos*, Telemundo also launched the "Super Series" format, a slate of action-oriented telenovelas — which usually air during the final hour of the network's prime time novela block — designed as a reinvention of the genre using the multiple-season continuity model common with English language drama series, shorter episode runs (between 60 and 80 episodes per season, compared to traditional single-season novelas, which produce between 100 and 200 episodes on average) and the incorporation of storylines more relatable to American audiences.

Still, Telemundo shows aren't comparable to mainstream U.S. productions. The average hourly primetime drama on Telemundo costs $70,000 to produce, but an episode at its parent company NBC-Universal would cost three to four times as much. And even if Telemundo shortens its seasons to 60 episodes, shows on NBC used to be 22 episodes (typical for a traditional U.S. network) and are now closer to 12. From a writer's viewpoint, you can see how the time allotted to each script would affect how much attention you can give it.

Despite political remarks about building a wall between Mexico and the United States, in truth the border is entirely porous for television signals that fly back and forth over any wall and bounce off satellites. Nevertheless, the television system in Mexico has its own history. It developed out of the shifting balance between the state, private investors, and outside interests, going way back to 1940 when foreign capital and entrepreneurs were looking for new investment opportunities and a few powerful families came to control Mexican media empires. Whether the situation stays the same, whether the same groups remain in control of media industries in Mexico in the face of new technological developments, remains to be seen.

Now Mexican television is in a state of transition from quasi-monopolies to interact with other companies on a global stage. Meanwhile, Mexico's troubled economy has affected the growth of alternative channels on pay TV. According to Tony Payan, director of Rice University's Baker Institute's Mexico Center, "Moving people from analog to digital TV requires people to buy televisions. Unfortunately for Mexico, many of the sectors and rural areas or many of the different households are not quite ready for this switch." Digital televisions can be expensive — about 5,000 pesos.

"Now think about that," he said. "The minimum wage is 73 pesos a day. That's about $4, which means buying a TV on a minimum wage job would take many days of work." To help, the government has given out about 10 million TVs to the poor.

Limited broadband capacity, poverty, and payment problems mean that audiences for content available through streaming are still limited in Mexico. "There is a danger of public TV networks missing out on premium entertainment, leaving many Mexicans unable to reap the consumer benefits of the drive into upscale TV entertainment," according to financial analyst John Hopewell.

On top of those problems, I can't avoid mentioning the current political tensions with the United States. A report issued by Mexico's Television Committee of the Instituto Nacional de Bellas Artes y Literatura (National Fine Arts Institute and Literature) criticized the commercial model of the American television industry, favoring instead the public television system of the United Kingdom. A Television Committee had been formed that wrote: "Commercial programming is the simple packaging of commodities with no other aspiration." The report also characterized Mexican radio as "spiritual tequila" and television as the "monstrous daughter of the hidden intercourse between radio and cinema."

In a *Guardian* article in 2016, Rupert Neate and Jo Tuckman summarized the debate over the future direction of Mexican TV: "This connection between public and private, government and TV, is still very current. Mexico's largest television network, Grupo Televisa, said President Trump has 'offended the entire Mexico population' and Ora, a TV network owned by Mexico's richest man, Carlos Slim, described the comments as 'racist.'" In 2017, both of the networks cut all ties, taking the number of Mexican TV companies ditching U.S. businesses to four following NBC Universal and Univision.

Writing for Telenovelas

Aside from hostile attitudes and international politics, many nations enjoy telenovelas as their own original dramas. For someone who lives in those countries and wants a career writing fiction on television, these may be your only choice. Writing telenovelas may limit your opportunities elsewhere, and as I said about the hopeful writer who lives on a small island: you can't get here from there. But given the prevalence of telenovelas, working on these might be your way to be paid for writing, so it's worth doing well, especially if you enjoy the stories.

Titles and methods vary somewhat between countries, and even between production entities within a country, but a typical template can guide you to what to expect. Friends on the staffs of telenovelas have described how they work, and I'm passing their advice on to you.

Throughout the earlier chapters, I've used the highest quality American shows as examples, reasoning that you will write the best by learning from the best. I want to inspire new writers to reach towards honesty, depth, and insight in characterization and relationships on screen.

But you also have to be practical. If you can demonstrate your ability to "catch the voices" of characters in a telenovela and write speeches the actors are comfortable saying while also advancing the plot, you could get a job.

Often audition scenes are used to determine your qualifications, especially if your independent scripts are not similar to the shows. An executive will give you the outline of a few scenes (or possibly a whole episode). You'll dialogue them for free, and deliver the script segments very quickly. Speed in turning the sample around is a way of proving you can succeed. Once you start on a show, your writing will occupy almost every day, but you'll get faster as you're more familiar with expectations. And the job can potentially go on forever. In some places, the prospect of steady work is important enough to offset the artistic limitations, and you can earn an adequate living.

The top of the show is usually controlled by a network- or government-broadcasting agency whose main concern is continuity. That means characters and storylines can include dramatic experiences, of course, but the nature of the show has to be reliably what the devoted audiences has always seen and assumes they will continue to see every day. That means writers should not think about character arcs in the sense of characters growing to the point of change. That's one difference. The executives on top will have long-range story goals stated in terms of what characters experience — someone gets married, or sick or richer or poorer — but the arc is not drawn in terms of psychological evolvement.

Writers who may have climbed the staff ladder lay out these overall story-lines. That would be similar to the U.S. system of promotions through quality writing. But it doesn't quite work that way on most telenovelas because nobody writes whole scripts. The top title might be producer or story editor or head writer, which sound like familiar titles, but the work of a telenovela "executive producer" consists of outlining the plot for a week of daily episodes (or more than a week). These outlines can be quite specific, though they include no dialogue, interpretation, or cinematic qualities. Their job is all about building to frequent cliffhangers before the many ads. These outlines, or segments of these outlines, are distributed among several writers on staff. More about that writing job in a moment.

Since the planning is top-down, these shows have no writers' rooms in the American sense. The executives will discuss with each other, but the notion of a writer on the staff pitching a new storyline or a stand-alone episode or a new character doesn't fit in this model.

Another quality of planning telenovela scripts is repetition. As mentioned in the segments on Brazil and Mexico, telenovelas assume a viewer might not be watching the screen, and might have missed some essential story beats, so events must be reestablished in dialogue. For example, an outline beat might say "Carlos" confesses to "Maritza" that he had an affair and she throws a pot at him. In the next episode — sometimes the next beat — Maritza might have to recap "I was thinking about what you told me about having the affair . . ."

Dialogue must carry the story. But the top "writer" who executed the outline doesn't write the dialogue. In a best scenario, one writer is assigned the episode and fills in the dialogue. That way the resulting script might have a kind of writer's sensibility and maybe hint at a "voice." Unfortunately, in many cases, I'm told the dialogue is given out like piecework in a factory. The person who dialogues scene #3 might not dialogue the scenes connected to it, depriving the writer of developing a tone or rhythm. This assembly-line method also deprives the best writers from demonstrating their talent — or having a produced script for their portfolio.

The relationship of characterization and dialogue is misunderstood. A key way we know a person is through what he or she says. Small subtleties in speech can suggest layers of nuance and internal struggle. It's the stuff of good writing. But if you remove character development from speech, you lose the possibility of creating a dimensional human being on screen.

Wait, it gets worse. Writers in some cases are assigned scenes from other shows simultaneously, each one representing fragments of a story. And they're given no time for rewriting. It's a matter of turning in dialogue pages on deadline because two or three episodes have to shoot the next day on two or three shows you're assigned to dialogue.

Now, here's the rainbow: Some of these telenovelas have true emotional power for their viewers. Credit goes partly to passionate acting, especially on long running shows where actors have fully inhabited their personae.

But credit also goes to the beleaguered dialogue writers that manage to shine despite the deprivations. Coming back to the hypothetical scene between Carlos and Maritza, nothing in the outline prevents the dialogue writer from insightful and deeply felt words given to both the betrayed wife and the guilt-ridden husband.

As the assigned writer, you're still stuck with throwing the pot, and repeating what happened, and conveying everything they think in speeches, but if you give up on the potentials, you're giving up on yourself. As for the pot, you don't have the option to replace it or avoid it by dialogue that would make it irrelevant. You can't call the supervisor and say you have a better idea for the character. For all you know, that pot might have some significance in a later episode that you have no way of predicting. But you can be clever and find a way to integrate the pot in a way that is both credible and emotionally satisfying. That's where your writing skill comes in. My advice: always give them better than they deserve.

Telenovelas can be culturally rich. As the writer, all you have to work with are standing sets and few (or no) exterior locations. Special effects are out of the question on the low episode budgets. But think about artifacts that can be meaningful even within the simplest environment. What about that pot? What's in it? Is there a design on it that signifies anything? Did it belong to Maritza's mom? Is there any way your characters can use artifacts within the scene that will resonate with your particular audience, even if they have to narrate their thoughts? You can just smell the stew she's cooking when Carlos enters, and how much love she put into it before he confesses. I'm not suggesting you lengthen the scene beyond the time you're allotted or give in to bouts of poetic monologue that will surely be cut. You really have to play by the rules of this form. But I am recommending that you dig in. Use what you have to get what you want.

Telenovelas are slowly evolving as audiences become used to the premium dramas they can now stream. In many lands across the globe, these "soap operas" occupy all of free TV, along with sports and news. But pay TV offers premium shows made in other countries, and hybridization is inevitable. Go ahead and take the frustrating job. You have to start somewhere. But keep writing your own scripts too. That will help remind you of the quality you can slip into a moment on a well-loved telenovela, and it will keep your writing instincts alive.

UNITED KINGDOM

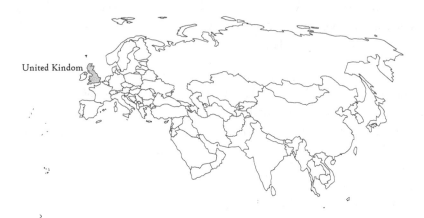

United Kindom

Try this for a head-trip: Find the first episode of original British version of *Shameless*. (It's available several places; I got it on Netflix.) Watch the first few scenes. Then go to the American version of that same pilot episode that ran on Showtime and watch the first scenes. What did you discover? Interesting, isn't it? The words in each scene are identical and the scenes are identical. But the British and American series feel very different. This comparison is instructive because it's not a matter of dismissing changes as translations, or ethnic traditions, as we might find with shows from Denmark or Turkey or Israel. Here are two English-language countries with advanced television industries and a mutual history. So why do the differences exist and how would understanding them be useful to a writer from either place? You'll read some analyses below; meanwhile, think about it yourself.

A blogger writing as "Solitary Muser" posted this insight: "When we watch our favorite television shows, we generally don't realize how much of those shows are informed by our shared cultural identity. It is not until we see shows from other countries (or subcultures) that we do realize it. A show from Spain, for example, relies on knowledge of Spain that a Mexican viewer may not have. We may like these foreign shows, but we cannot necessarily appreciate all their nuances. I may love *Upstairs, Downstairs*, but the British class system is completely alien to me. Similarly *Seinfeld* does not translate well abroad because there is something so American (specifically New York) about it. Thus we get the remake — a way to reinvent the show in a new cultural medium."

The relationship between shows made in the U.S. and the U.K. is complex because a British presence permeates so much of American drama. It's obvious on *Masterpiece Theatre*, and studios know that stories about British royalty draw audiences, as evidenced by the Emmy-nominated series *The Crown* on Netflix. But viewers may not realize that many shows on Starz premium-cable network come from the BBC, as do series elsewhere.

The writers' rooms for these shows are usually in Los Angeles, and production offices are here (even when they are actually filmed overseas). But writer friends have told me their telephone notes sessions include executives in London. Do you hear different kinds of writing pressures from "across the pond"? I asked the friend. Well, in his case, the creative power stayed local, so he says he didn't sense a tug to satisfy British tastes or idiom. But when your bosses are from different countries, the issue might arise. My advice, if you're caught in the middle of competing notes: go with the American showrunner's version. Generally, the U.S. is the larger audience that has to be satisfied. Still, the balance can be tricky.

For decades, American television has co-opted hit British television shows with mixed results. For every show that transcended its British predecessor (e.g., *All in the Family*) or became a hit in its own right (e.g., *The Office*), there are tons of knock-offs that are best forgotten. The U.S./U.K. mash-up doesn't have one easy solution. In Canada's newspaper *The Globe and Mail* critic John Doyle wrote: "Smoking, swearing and drinking to excess. Hey, it happens. People do all three. Mostly, on TV, they do it on British TV shows. For long and many the day, the behaviour of people on British TV series was a thing to behold. People lit cigarettes and knocked back a stiff whisky and, amazingly, nobody stepped forward to tell them they were a) killing themselves and b) setting a bad example. This was one of the key elements that appalled some viewers and entranced others.

"Then along came American cable dramas and comedies featuring people swearing, smoking and drinking to excess. In fact, the raw reality of life is presented with such gusto on cable dramas that Brit TV started to look tame. These days, most British TV looks sedate, sitting glumly in the shadow of what HBO, Showtime, AMC, and other cable channels create and air.

"Still, there is always the temptation on the part of U.S. studios and channels to remake a British hit. It's an ignoble tradition, one with a history of more failures than successes. The explosion of cable channels in the last decade has complicated matters in more ways than one. Why would anyone want to watch an American remake when the original Brit series can be seen on BBC America or some other outlet? It's a complicated matter."

With those thoughts in mind, let's return to the opening questions about how *Shameless* was transformed. Look again at the early scenes from both the U.K. and U.S. pilots and you're quickly reminded that the dialogue is identical but the shows are different. For writers this is edifying for anyone who equates screenwriting with scripting speeches. If the difference is not in words, then where is it found? Of course, the shows have different actors who bring their own interpretations to their roles, and the lighting is darker in the U.K. compared to the U.S. version where the interiors seem "TV-lit." As a producer-writer, those choices may be within your domain. But a lower-level writer doesn't directly influence casting or lighting, so let's look for other aspects. The original and the American remake differ in *intention*, and that does come from the concept that is the purview of writers.

Look at the location choices. The original was set in Manchester public housing; in the remake the Gallagher family is in Chicago, where "the projects" and Section 8 housing certainly does exist. But this impoverished family that surely would have qualified somehow has a big house. A review in *Salon* by Matt Zoller Seitz analyzed: "The show conspicuously avoids any mention of government help — welfare, food stamps, Social Security payouts, anything. Why? Maybe it's because [executive producers] Paul Abbott and John Wells couldn't devise a suitable U.S. equivalent for the English/Irish/Scots fiction tradition of the alkie father who drinks away the dole money. Or maybe it's due to a knee-jerk belief on the part of American film and TV producers that any character on public assistance will be seen as unsympathetic, perhaps innately worthless. So the show has Frank collecting disability from an injury that healed a while ago and being followed by a private investigator trying to prove his fraud — an amusing contrivance that nonetheless lacks the necessary bite."

This reminds me of a discussion I had with a producer on a different network drama some years ago where my script called for an overcrowded apartment in an urban setting. Lo and behold I went to the set and discovered the cast in a pretty suburban-type single family home with a bright (always noon in summertime) window looking out on trees. Why? I bemoaned — these people couldn't afford a place like this. The producer answered that viewers don't want to see ugly; no matter what problems the characters may have the screen needs to be attractive. Of course, American television has moved on — check out where Jessica Jones and Luke Cage live in their Marvel series on Netflix, or anything by David Simon on HBO. But as I consider the American *Shameless*, I wonder how much TV tradition softened this show.

That's the root of it. The British *Shameless* is a provocative social critique, a dive into how the very poor manage to survive. It's a show about class. It won both the "Best Drama Series" award from BAFTA and the "Best TV Comedy Drama" prize at the British Comedy Awards. The American remake keeps the family just as poor but this show competes only as a comedy for Emmys in the U.S.

How does a writer convey this difference of tone if not through dialogue? Especially as the two versions diverge over time, Frank Gallagher is approached with a different attitude, and that can be indicated on the page. The original Frank was a mad, ecstatic drunk, roaring endlessly through the lives of his children. But the new Frank seems self-indulgent, even pitiful. Fiona, the eldest daughter who has taken charge in the role of mother, is beautiful and needy in the U.S. version but tougher and less consciously pretty in the original. What does this say about the American conception of a powerful woman?

In the original, rage is palpable, even as it is tempered by tenderness. In the American version, the struggles to survive sometimes come off as farce. Nevertheless, both versions offer humor, poignancy, affection, and guts, and each is beloved by its separate audience. These comparisons are not intended to disparage the beautifully produced American *Shameless* that has become a huge success under showrunner John Wells. Likely the bleaker British version would not have succeeded here as well. That's an acknowledgement of cultural difference, not blame.

For a writer creating your own original, or pitching episodes for a transplant, awareness of subtle variations in viewpoint can determine how an audience responds to your show and whether the underlying material flourishes in a new environment.

IRELAND

"Ireland could be the new Israel," an industry guru proclaimed at the MIPTV international TV festival in Cannes a few years ago. Israel has become a benchmark for exporting TV drama (*Homeland*, *In Treatment*, and many others), and we'll visit that country later. For Ireland, the comment acknowledged their debut on the international scene with deals in

New Zealand, Poland, Sweden, China, France, and several South American countries at this festival.

What are they producing, and how does this relate to you as writers? *Love/Hate* is one of Ireland's prominent achievements that reviewers compare to *The Wire*. According to the *Guardian*, "The Dublin-set gangster story is heavily influenced by U.S. crime dramas. But its unflinching willingness to explore modern-day Irish culture makes it a powerful and compelling show."

Here's the aspect for you as writers: *Love/Hate* creator Stuart Carolan is one of the first writers on an Irish drama to also have an executive production role. He's a showrunner, so he has the overarching creative vision beyond ratings or taste, the one who keeps the story in focus, modeled on how premium American shows are run. Another Irish series in development, *Acceptable Risk*, brought in an Emmy-award winning L.A.-based screenwriter who was born in Northern Ireland to be showrunner. Keep that in mind: not all shows travel internationally, but experience in an American writers' room can lead to opportunities elsewhere.

Back to *Love/Hate* — With weekly ratings of almost a million viewers (a lot in a country where the total population is only 4.5 million) it is hoping to go where no Irish domestic TV series has ventured previously and break into the U.S. The original has been available on Hulu for a while, but according to *The Independent* (an Irish newspaper), "talks are under way for a full-fledged American remake, which would transpose the action to the U.S. equivalent of one of Dublin's drug-riddled outer suburbs. The news has been hailed as a breakthrough for Irish television and arrives after a period of soul-searching in the industry here, with many wondering why it has been unable to replicate the success of Denmark, another small country on the fringes of Europe, which has exported smash shows such as *The Killing* and *Borgen*."

The Irish television industry is pursuing an international status with the kind of determination the Gallagher family in *Shameless* reveals: Being poor and relatively powerless won't keep them down. Ireland, with little money to spare, has invested in generous tax credits for productions there.

The section 481 tax credit, which incentivizes film and television production, means a production company can claim a tax credit up to 32 per cent on expenditure related to cast and crew working in Ireland, post-production, and other expenses. Amazon Prime's *Ripper Street*, HBO's *Game of Thrones*, the History Channel's *Vikings*, and Showtime/Sky Atlantic's *Penny Dreadful* all shoot in Ireland.

The *Irish Times* concludes: "When big series shoot here, the productions become a training and a breeding ground for Irish crews. So when those shows wrap, you end up with better cinematographers, better hair and make-up artists, better set designers and builders, better camera crews, better sparks and a better overall infrastructure to provide facilities for big productions."

What does this mean to you as a series creator or writer/producer? If you have a show with potential looking for a co-producer partner, consider Ireland. It's an example of broadening your scope in the new world of television.

DENMARK

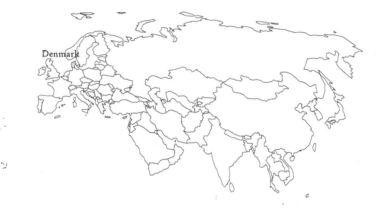

Why is Denmark doing so well? With only 5.75 million people, the whole country has less than half of the population of Los Angeles. For a place that's been called the happiest country on Earth, it has succeeded in making some of the gloomiest-looking television dramas that are hits not only at home, but in critically acclaimed remakes around the world. For American audiences *The Killing* that ran on AMC is probably the most familiar, based on the Danish *Forbrydelsen*, and its other shows have also been influential.

What are they doing right? First, they make the most of where they are. A genre called "Northern Noir" that is familiar throughout Scandinavian countries provides a context. Rainy darkness conveys an instant mood when contrasted with peaceful, unsuspecting characters. In every way, Danish television honors its indigenous materials. But lots of places have interesting, moody environments, so that alone doesn't account for successful dramas.

We can look towards the society itself. Denmark is progressive. More than 70% of women in Denmark work; 97% of young children attend daycare. A former Prime Minister was a woman. Actress Sofie *Gråbøl,* who starred in the original Danish version of *The Killing* and the series *Borgen,* commented on the impact of Denmark's liberalism: "Rather than spawning preachy programs about kids and love life and work, it has obviated the need for them. Television writers are free to plumb the realities, rather than the desirability, of gender equality and women's liberation." Early in the first season of *Borgen,* the star political reporter learns that she is pregnant. She has an abortion. The scene is sad but not grim. The woman meets no comeuppance. And the next time we see her, she's in the newsroom.

In the blog *cinemascandinavia,* Emma Vestrheim commented: "When talking about television drama, one has to pay attention to that fact that all Danish television dramas that became successful belong to so-called Nordic noir, a genre of crime story with a social, psychological, and narrative twist. *The Bridge,* a recent world success, made jointly by Denmark and Sweden, is the best example of Nordic noir drama: the body of a female Swedish politician, which appeared on the bridge after the power was off and on again; cold northern sea; laconic, minimalistic style, which is so typical Scandinavian style. Therefore, we have three main constituents: crime, social issues, and the psychological aspect.

"Another striking example is the killing of several government ministers in *Wallander* who in fact were involved into human trafficking, importing young girls into Sweden. Besides politics, Scandinavian crime drama also plays on such psychological and interpersonal issues as relationships between parents and children, partners, and coworkers.

"To sum up, one can say the combination of highlighted social issues, deep psychology, and 'realistic, simple, and precise' style is what makes Scandinavian television drama so popular outside Nordic countries."

Denmark also benefits from available excellent film education and being willing to learn from what works elsewhere. In Denmark's system, film and television are blended. Nearly all the country's leading directors, cinematographers, and screenwriters are graduates of the state-funded National Film School of Denmark. Eva Novrup Redvall, an assistant professor in the Department of Media, Cognition, and Communication at the University of Copenhagen, has written that the school's screenwriting department fosters a "shared language between professions." DR — Denmark's public service broadcaster — uses the school as a farm system, hiring talented young alumni and pairing them with trusted veterans.

Great education alone doesn't make great television . . . though it's one more rung of the country's climb to the top. What originally revolutionized Danish television was a trip to America. In the mid-1990s, DR sent several of its top executives and producers to Los Angeles, where they visited *NYPD Blue*, *L.A. Law*, and *24*. They returned to Denmark with new concepts: writers' rooms, showrunners, multi-episode series. "From then on, we were consciously trying to professionalize," Piv Bernth, of *The Killing*, said Jeppe Gjervig Gram, writer-producer on *Borgen*, explained, "We said, 'We're going to do it the American way,' but it took some years to find the Danish way to do it the American way."

The first hallmark of the Danish way is a principle DR calls "one vision." This means that the writer is king. A ten-episode season of a show like *Borgen* is made on a relatively small budget of about eight million dollars, but DR lavishes its writers with time and indulgence. An incubation period of several years is customary. "I think it's very important that every one of us stands guard around the author's mission," stage and TV director Morten Hesseldahl said. "It's a romantic impression of how the artist should work."

The structure of the industry itself enables its writers to aim for great television. I already mentioned DR, Denmark's public service broadcaster that made *The Killing*, *Borgen*, and *The Bridge*. Americans might think of it as a mix of PBS with CBS and HBO. Danes pay an annual licensing fee of about four hundred dollars, giving DR a yearly budget of six hundred and sixty million dollars. Because Denmark is small and relatively homogeneous, DR can attempt to appeal to almost everyone. It is both mass-oriented and high-minded. Nadia Kløvedal Reich, DR's head of fiction, said, "We have a huge influence in society. Our main goal is to tell stories about Danish people, in Denmark." Like the BBC in Britain, DR is considered a tent pole of the nation's identity.

When a television series is so close to the heart of a national viewpoint, how can it be remade elsewhere without losing its soul? The issue affects American adaptations especially. Take the case of *Borgen*, the Danish word for castle, which is what Danes call their government building. The show is about Danish coalition politics, and Andrew Romano of *Newsweek* called it "the best political show ever." Here's the problem: HBO put a version into development but once they Americanize *Borgen* they risk converting it right back to its source material, *The West Wing*.

FX has announced plans to remake *The Bridge* in the United States with detectives working on the border of Ciudad Juárez and El Paso. "The Scandinavian version is really dark," John Landgraf, president of FX, remarked. "Not just a little dark. I would say even, at times, perversely dark. I want to be really respectful of it, but I think we're going to try to maybe simplify the plot a little bit."

British television seems to have more affinity with the Scandinavian originals. The *cinemascandinavia* blog observes: "Nordic Noir holds up a somewhat grey mirror to life in Scandinavia and through its fictional drama it examines the true nature of the human condition. This same mirror also effectively reflects back to the British audience the nature of life in Britain today and all the problems that we, like our Northern relatives, face. We are fascinated by our own reflection in this mirror and we seek to look deeper, into the deliciously dark void that lies beyond the glass and into the reflected world that lies beyond as we look into our own national and personal psyches, our present situations and our own shadowy pasts through the medium of Nordic Noir."

Funny thing is that on the path to victory, Denmark decided to try a different direction. "Nordic Noir is over," Piv Bernth, producer of *The Killing*, and now head of drama at Denmark's DR Drama, wrote in a Danish newspaper in 2016. *The Leftovers'* Damon Lindelof, Series Mania jury president, concurred: "We are going to see TV programs that are self-aware of the tropes of the procedural and will reinvent again. Shows like *The Bridge* or *The Killing* were revolutionary when they were made but that is six to ten years ago. It's time to say: 'How do I subvert the idea of *The Bridge*'?"

Variety concluded: "Scandinavia is indeed already moving on. Its biggest show at Series Mania was Adam Price's *Ride Upon the Storm*, a faith-themed family drama. One of the biggest deals announced during Series Mania was Netflix's acquisition of *The Bonus Family*, a Scandinavian drama, yes, but a contemporary relationship comedy-drama. Notable among Series Mania series and pitched projects were Nordic Noir riffs — in their set-ups, violence, or darker take on human character — which tried, however, to bring something extra to the table."

FRANCE

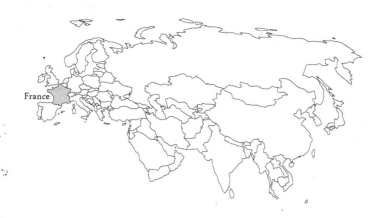

We'll stop over in France only briefly. That's partly because we already considered French television in the Overview, and partly because so little original French television drama is made. We'll try to understand why. As I said earlier, it's puzzling that a country with a history of brilliant literature and cinema has missed out on the "golden age" of TV drama. It's almost the opposite of Denmark, where indigenous Nordic elements create unique character-rich dramas, where television writers are empowered, and an established infrastructure including enlightened education and generous schedules leads to great series. In France, much of television drama is from other countries and dubbed or subtitled in French, and television writers say they feel powerless.

Barbara Nance, one of my screenwriting colleagues at the USC School of Cinematic Arts, who has a solid professional career writing American TV drama, has been developing an original series with a producer who is trying to set it up in France. Prof. Nance told me she was shocked to be told she wouldn't be permitted to pitch her own show to the network, that **the producer does the pitching.** In fact, she was not expected even to be present during pitching sessions between producers and networks. This happened in 2017.

Though the French bureaucracy rejects the American system, French people are ardent fans of the shows that system produces. Netflix reached more than 100,000 subscribers in France by 2017 (probably more now). So

French audiences can access most U.S. shows. If you look at the wish list among entrepreneurial French production companies, you find them trying to imitate American hits. There's even been an outreach to American creators. For writers who are reading this, an opportunity may soon open for you in France. Maybe.

That possibility gave rise to a panel discussion at the Writers Guild of America, West in 2017 where writers anxious to explore the potentials of the French market heard from speakers with experience there. According to the panel, France is still under the influence of *Nouvelle Vague* that describes French cinema of the 1950s in which the director is the "author" of the piece. Today, a typical French television show has two writers, but one of them is the director, who is considered the creative leader. It's a remnant of the "auteurist" ideology from the 20th century.

Writers' rooms and showrunners are just now starting to appear. This is partly because of French television budgets, which range from 700 thousand to one million dollars for an hour episode, compared to several million per hour in American TV. Panelists explained the American model doesn't work in France because their budgets do not allow for big teams of writers.

On top of that hurdle, a law designed to protect the right of the author to own his ideas further restricts French series. Collaborating in a writers' room is the way American shows work, but it disrupts the French sense of personal ownership. It's an unintended consequence of applying well-meaning rules from a time before television to today's media.

The panel compared the landscape of French TV today to the U.S. in its "pre-cable" era. The TV market in France is limited: a couple of network channels and only one cable channel with the ability to make series, which is Canal + (Canal Plus) that is sometimes compared to HBO. But mainstream French networks are limited to predictable procedurals and family-friendly shows. Panelists said the networks are afraid of doing something new, just as traditional American networks were in the 20th century.

But change is coming to France. Writing in *The Hollywood Reporter*, Scott Roxborough observed: "It's no surprise that the French model for high-end television resembles the American one. That's where it comes from. The new French wave in TV originated not as a means to create more national content, but as an attempt to deliver more of the U.S.-style shows the French channels love. Unlike in the U.K., where homemade series have pushed American shows off the main networks, French channels have always been pro-USA. Crime series such as *The Mentalist* and *CSI* are huge hits on free-to-air channel TF1 while subscribers of pay TV network Canal Plus are slavish fans of darker dramas such as *House of Cards*. That French fan base created a market for entrepreneurial French companies to make U.S.-style shows, in English, for the French and U.S. markets."

Bureau, one of the first beneficiaries, applies the American method complete with a writers' room and a showrunner. On the panel, French writer Claude Scasso described it as "the best series being made in France right now."

Meanwhile, Gaumont, the venerable French film company, has leapt into television, staking out the country's international future. Their slate incudes NBC's *Hannibal*, and *Hemlock Grove* and *Narcos* on Netflix — all English language shows that are doing as well as those with completely American origins, though to be clear, those shows all have writing staffs based in Los Angeles.

In adaptations, A&E is in production on *The Returned*, developed by American showrunner Carlton Cuse. It's a U.S. version of the French zombie series *Les Revenants*. Endemol Studios that was behind *Hell on Wheels* (on AMC) has picked up remake rights to the crime drama *Engrenages*. And HBO is developing an English-language version of the French prostitution drama *Maison Close* produced by Marc Wahlberg.

"There's kind of a French wave right now," says Pascal Breton, producer of *Marseille*, a political series billed as the French *House of Cards* that Netflix has commissioned. "French creators are thinking of ideas that will appeal outside of France. And in the U.S. now, there are 50 great channels or services — with Netflix, pay TV, and all the cable and networks — that are looking for great series." Christophe Riandee, Gaumont's vice-CEO added, "Actually, I don't even consider us a French company when it comes to our international television division. We are just like any other American producer, competing with the same U.S. companies as everyone else."

Where does that leave us as writers? Showrunners are discovering France as a ripe frontier, so writing staffs can't be far behind. *X-Files* producer Frank Spotnitz's company Big Light Productions has a first-look distribution deal with StudioCanal's Tandem Communications. He said, "I've long had a love affair with France and French culture. France is never going to be a TV factory like the U.S., and that's fine, but for a certain percentage of shows — and there are going be more of them — the French know how to do them and can deliver the quality."

CZECH REPUBLIC

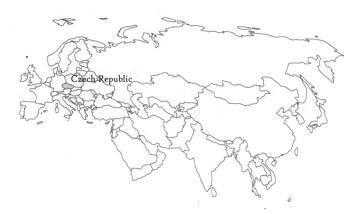

This visit to Eastern Europe is about transformation: how one American television writer traveled to the Czech Republic to create a generation of future Czech showrunners. Harold Apter, a veteran TV writer-producer, was also a professor teaching screenwriting at the USC School of Cinematic Arts before embarking. He described his experience to me:

"I was asked to train writers. I went over there to teach at FAMO, the national film school. While I was there I met the head of development for Czech TV. He said they had a need for trained TV writers. I said let's do a show and that's how we'll train them. I said the way we do it, writers are in control. He said directors wouldn't like that. And I said well, we have to also train directors.

"Their television culture as with most European cultures is very director-centric because they're coming out of the auteur thing. For us, when you have multiple people collaborating in a writer's room, you have the opportunity for discovery. It isn't just the European idea 'you write the scripts and that's it.'

"We started with 10 writers from all the film schools in the Czech Republic, two years ago. I came in for three weeks and set up a writers' room. We ran it the way we would teach a pilot class. We talked about ideas. We broke the pilot stories. We talked about what a pilot is and how to construct a show. All the basics. They pitched their episodes. The students ranged from 20 to 30 years old, evenly divided among women and men. Now the youngest on staff just turned 22. We had a director attached who is also on the writing staff.

"Everything we've done is completely outside the mold of Czech TV. They're producing in Czech language for a Czech audience. They're used to specific kinds of programs, especially procedural cop shows. Normally they have one person or a couple of people write everything. Then the director takes it over and tells everybody what to do. In this case, we set up the writers' room. Everybody pitched. I was the arbiter of what would make a good series. I was showrunner and also their professor.

"One of the pitches was a procedural and the rest were serialized. I explained in a serialized show, the pilot is not really a pilot in the usual sense. It's the first episode that you might think of as the beginning of act one for the series. We ended up with seven projects. After I returned to Los Angeles, I would work with them over Skype. They would send me pages and acts; I would give them notes. They had to understand the difference between screenwriting that they'd all been taught and TV writing. Television writing is much more character driven than most screenplays.

"Finally, we chose the one to produce called *The Lynching*. Now we're making it for Czech TV, their equivalent of PBS. They have a family drama block Sunday night, and a crime block Monday night. Our show is in their drama crime block on Monday nights.

"In the U.S., we produce our shows sequentially. We tend to shoot on a seven-, eight-, ten-day schedule. We're prepping, shooting, and cutting at the same time. This process is alien to them. What they do is shoot like it's a movie. So if they have twelve episodes they'll build a police station on a soundstage and shoot all the police station scenes.

"Also they write all the scripts in advance. We had to write all the episodes ahead to get approval. But we're going to shoot them sequentially. We'll make eight episodes. It's something they're not used to budgeting this way. There are other differences too. Each episode is 52 minutes with no commercials. The budget is around $300,000 per episode, but because it's all in house the budget is just about locations. And there are a limited number of good actors who speak Czech, so we have to schedule around the actors.

"The most difficulty they're having is letting go, understanding this is a collaborative experience. They have to differentiate between somebody's taste and what's working. In television when it's happening so fast and you have a showrunner, everything gets deferred to the showrunner's taste. That's difficult for some writers. If you're good at writing television, you're good in the room and you know to back off when you have to.

"People ask how do you do this. How does America come up with all these great shows that everybody wants to watch? You start to tell them this is what we do, and the answer you always get back is "It's not Czech enough." In storytelling, a note I've gotten is 'she wouldn't go this far in this conversation. She wouldn't express herself to that degree.' So I have to find another way to get the subtext into the scene. In terms of translating the scripts into Czech, there are certain emotional highs and lows that have to be portrayed in slightly different way than I'm used to doing.

"Every human being comes from the same emotional underpinnings. We all want love and we're all afraid of death. We all have a basic set of human desires though culturally we may express them differently, but they're all there. One of the reasons American television works universally is it covers those bases. It's character based. We deal with human emotion all the time. We stress emotional conflicts in our writing. In the Czech culture particularly, the difference goes to how language is spoken and how people think in their language. People can get really emotional but they get there more slowly and they express themselves in the time frame more slowly.

"We want to create showrunners. These writers are going to follow the entire production. They go to editing, casting, everything. The goal is to create television writers who know their craft and can eventually create and run their own shows.

"We want to create shows that can play internationally. The show we're currently making could also be done in America in any small town that has prejudice. That's the other goal — do a show that can also be done in other countries. Part of the ideal is to become more international in terms of product."

TURKEY

Turkey is a behemoth in today's international television. I had no idea until I researched this book. Nearly 150 Turkish television series have been sold to over 100 countries in the Middle East, Eastern Europe, South America (yes, that one's a surprise) and South Asia. I wouldn't have guessed that by 2016 Turkey had surpassed Israel and the U.K. to become the second

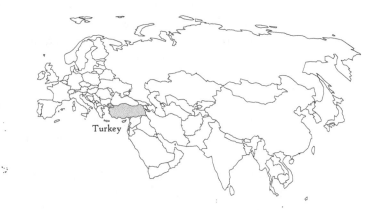

Turkey

highest exporter of TV series after the United States with more than $350 million in volume each year. We don't know much about those shows here because until lately they haven't been available. But now Turkish shows are arriving, and here's a hot tip for any writer fluent in both Turkish and English: adaptations are on the way with jobs for writers.

It's an explosive rise for a country that had no legal private television industry until the 1990s and didn't produce original drama until the 21st century. That's when television series became an intentional political and cultural instrument. According to the *Washington Post* in 2017: "*The Last Emperor* is Turkey's newest television blockbuster, consistently rating among Turkey's top dramas. Every Friday night, viewers tune in to relive the last years of Abdul Hamid II — an absolutist, pan-Islamist Ottoman sultan who resisted the secular-reformist Young Turk movement until it finally overthrew him in 1909. The series, airing on state television in three-hour episodes, promotes a worldview similar to that of Turkish President Erdogan: A free press, secularism, and democracy are the work of foreign powers, religious minorities and godless liberals, and ultimately serve to erode national identity, honor, and security."

Countries that were once subjugated by the Ottoman Empire use terms like "cultural imperialism" to argue against what they consider propaganda concealed as drama. In Greece, for example, a political party seized certain Turkish soap operas on the grounds that they were vehicles for political influence. Indeed, the long-running series *Resurrection: Ertuğrul* describes medieval campaigns waged by Turks against Christian enemies. Focusing on the life of Ertuğrul Bey, father of Osman Bey, the 13th-century founder of the Ottoman Empire, the loaded series tagline is: "A nation's awakening."

İzzet Pinto, CEO of Turkey's Global Agency that distributes its top titles, defended their shows to the *BBC Magazine*: "We are showing our country to millions of viewers. We are showing the beautiful scenery, our lifestyle and traditions. So we have a great influence on people through soft power."

The soft power of television is wielded by all countries, though usually more subtly than in Turkey. Certainly American shows have been influencing global perspectives for decades, and some might argue the portrayals of idyllic American family life in the 1950s collide with the truth. Those family dramas and comedies can be considered soft sales that co-evolved with the various pro-America military dramas and heroic re-creations of American history. This is not to mitigate the weaponizing of TV drama in Turkey but to give it context.

Turkish dramas are different from American shows in structure as well as content. They have two distinct genres: one is the *dizi* (literally "serial, row, sequence" in Turkish). Dizi's episodes are longer than similar serialized shows from other countries — 90 minutes or more per episode. Long and frequent music interludes that comment on events on the screen are typical on dizi shows and establish a sort of Turkish style. The second genre of Turkish TV is the telenovela, with soap opera form and style similar to what we see in other countries, molded to Turkish viewers.

Compared to English-language TV dramas, Turkish ones are much slower, feelings and emotions are often overstated, and scenes are considerably stretched out. A scene from the TV drama *Son* (*The End*), which showed a character crying for four minutes in Turkey, had to be cut down to 30 seconds when it aired on Swedish TV.

The Turkish television market can be brutally competitive. With eight free-to-air channels, and episodes that can run as long as two hours and often begin with hour-long recap episodes, broadcasters are quick to cut underperforming programs. Episodes are expensive and shows don't get series commitments easily. A new show can be killed after just a few episodes.

Internal competition is spurred by the size of the prize. All Turkish dramas have high production value. Outside of the United States, they are some of the costliest productions in the world, with budgets per episode exceeding half a million dollars. That sounds small compared to American shows budgeted in the millions per episode, but Turkish productions invest more heavily in what's visible on screen compared to behind-the-screens costs for "above the line" talent in the U.S. (such as writers, directors, and actors). The Turkish entertainment industry is also heavily aided by the government that is well aware that entertainment exports have helped augment the economy after Turkey's tourism industry was hit following a series of terror attacks and the 2016 attempted coup d'état.

It's interesting that in this Muslim country where outsiders sometimes think of women as silenced, the most popular Turkish series are all written by women (though the production companies that fund them are still predominantly owned by men). Meriç Demiray has written hundreds of pages of TV scripts since the early 2000s, including episodes of *Back Streets*, a long-running crime series that has been continuously on air for nine years. "As a screenwriter, it was wonderful until about ten years ago. Then I had to write a 60-minute episode per week, as opposed to today's 130-plus minutes. It has become a very mechanical and uninteresting process, just a question of keeping the melodrama going," says Demiray. Doesn't this sound like complaints heard from soap writers in Brazil and Mexico? Amazing how global the concerns of writers can be.

The Turkish online site *Hürriyet Daily News* reported in 2017: "Turkish TV series are driven by what will appeal to women, according to TV and film producers meeting at an equal-opportunity committee in Parliament. 'Many companies do not produce detective series because they will not sell,' said a representative from Focus Film, Mehmet Erişti. 'We exploit the drama of women, and they feel safer when they see other women's dramas in those series.' Some 31 percent of managers in Turkey are women . . . Women's role in society has changed."

Within Turkey, the popularity of television dramas has not come out of the blue. These shows are the product of a long tradition of Turkish melodrama in movies, a style that has been adapted to contemporary platforms. Just as Bollywood delivers an escape for a large part of the Indian population who can only dream of such luxurious lives, so too do the Turkish TV series nurture the dreams of large pockets of conservative societies. These dramas may also reflect their viewers' wish to escape into a fantasy world more comforting than the messy reality of Turkey today. In a fiercely polarized country troubled by rising economic strife and roiled by war over the border in Syria, the grand historical melodramas soothe viewers by tapping into a flattering foundational myth of Turkish glory.

Despite being popular with large global populations, Turkish soaps have also faced a backlash, as I mentioned in Greece. In Saudi Arabia, the religious establishment accused the shows of infiltrating "Western values" into local society. In Iran, *Paschalidou* reported, some husbands resorted to ripping out their TV antennas to prevent wives and daughters from being "corrupted" by soaps. The Grand Mufti of Saudi Arabia described a popular Turkish soap opera, known as *Noor* in the Arab world, as being "anti-Islamic" and said that television channels broadcasting the show are "an enemy of God and his Prophet." In Egypt, national satellite networks dropped Turkish television shows from the air in the wake of the 2013 military coup against former Egyptian President Mohamed Morsi. As Egypt moved away from its former ally, Turkey, the networks turned instead to Indian television series to replace them.

Nevertheless, the impact on Middle Eastern culture is compelling. According to *The Fader* site: "Turkish soaps have contributed to the destigmatization of divorce in communities where it has long been taboo; in the United Arab Emirates, their ubiquity was linked to an increase in divorce rates. Samar Shaaban of the United Arab Emirates explained how watching *What Is Fatmagül's Fault?* helped her find the courage to divorce an abusive husband: '[Fatmagül] showed me that a woman can claim her rights. I watched her go to court and win, and [thought] Why can't I do the same?'"

Some of these shows speak to female viewers by featuring unorthodox male leads that are romantic instead of being macho. *Noor*, for example, depicts a romantic love between the heroine and her husband. Women viewers remarked to their husbands on how well the lead character treated his wife — it set a romantic ideal where "women are valued, appreciated, and adored," says Mazen Hayek, spokesman for the Saudi-backed Middle East Broadcasting Centre (MBC). The impact of the show was such that Arab women "started talking to their husbands through Turkish drama." The story was thought-provoking for conservative societies where expressions of love are usually private, adds Abdallah Alsalmi, Middle East media analyst at BBC Monitoring. And because the characters on screen had plenty in common with Arab audiences, it was more controversial as well as easier to relate to, he says.

Turkish dramas are popular throughout the Middle East, says Iranian-American businesswoman Goli Ameri, who has served as a diplomat. "Because they show that you can be Muslim, but at the same time modern — and you know, Turks basically look like everyone," Ameri says. She points to one recent Turkish series that captivated viewers on both sides of the Gaza Strip. "At 3 or 4 PM, when the series was running, the fighting would stop and people would watch the series. It had that kind of an impact."

What does all this mean for American writers? It suggests Turkey is not as far away as it seems. In 2017, *Variety* reported that Netflix acquired more than 400 hours of *dizi*. And Turkey has begun adjusting to Western television by creating shorter episodes. *Variety* wrote: "That in itself is a major game changer. Also, similar to the impact of cable TV shows in the U.S., they can be bolder in content."

In 2015, the Fox Network gave a pilot order to *Runner*, from 21st Century Fox TV. It marked the first Turkish drama series set up at a network by American producers. Fox representatives pitched that *Runner* is to guns what Traffic was to drugs and delves into the traditionally masculine world of arms dealing through the unexpected lens of a woman.

Another drama based on a Turkish series, *Game of Silence* sparked a bidding war and landed at NBC with a pilot commitment. Developed by *CSI* showrunner Carol Mendelsohn, *Parenthood* executive producer David Hudgins and Sony TV, *Game of Silence* centers on a rising attorney on the brink of spectacular success who could lose his perfect life when his long-lost childhood friends threaten to expose a dark secret from their violent past.

That doesn't mean cross-cultural adaptations are easy. Remember our discussion of adapting *Shameless* from the U.K. to the U.S.? Well, now imagine Turkey's adaptation. *Hürriyet Daily News* remarked: "Those who are watching the below-the-belt shenanigans of the Gallagher family in the American series *Shameless* on Turkish TV have been missing out the actual below-the-belt shenanigans. The Turkish Radio and Television Supreme Council (RTÜK) have been making sure with its strict regulations and high penalties that self-censorship is intact on Turkish television. The unapologetic, weekly adventures of the Gallaghers with alcohol, drugs, sex, and swearing have been missing its many racy scenes on Turkish TV, with subtitles altered at times to the point of making viewers miss crucial parts of the story. Not to mention the scenes of smoking digitally altered, which is almost every scene. So when the news of a Turkish remake of *Shameless* going into production came, devoted viewers were skeptical at best. A user on the Turkish social media site Ekşi Sözlük (Sour Dictionary) posted: 'The adaptation will be true to the original except for sexuality, homosexuality, alcohol, drugs, smoking and swearing. Hence, each episode will run about one minute.'"

Still, U.S./Turkey collaboration is on its way, and any new venue can be an opportunity for writers, whether adapting their shows or discovering a market for something you'll create. Watch this space.

ISRAEL

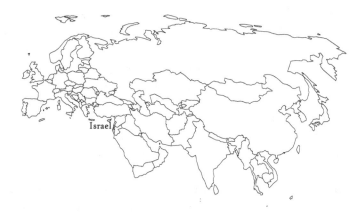

"For those of us who live in Israel, it's no secret that our young TV industry has been a huge success story for a decade. It all began with *BeTipul*, a psychotherapy drama, a highbrow and low-budget TV series, which was made into an HBO drama *In Treatment*, and adapted to more than 20 versions in other countries. A few years later came the success of *Hatufim*, the Israeli series about three POWs who return home after years of captivity, which was turned into *Homeland*, about one such American soldier."

That comment in thejc.com reflects the country's pride in its success in television drama, especially in a kind of partnership that has developed with Hollywood. Since those first two hits on HBO, virtually every Israeli series — not just dramas but also reality and comedy — has been acquired by an American studio. And yet Israel is a country of only 8 million people, larger than Denmark but comparable in being a tiny nation with an outsized impact on world drama. Like Israel, in Denmark, as we discussed in that visit, homegrown stories make the best use of what they have on modest budgets. But there's a difference. Denmark's studios don't aim for

Hollywood — they get there by delivering indigenous authenticity, aimed first at their own people. In Israel, the target is global from the start. Keshet Intl. managing director Alon Shtruzman told *Variety*: "Israel is lacking natural resources. We don't have any gas or oil, and we hardly have any land — it's a small country. So what we sell is brains. The same way we sell technology, whether it's software or hardware, we're also selling media."

Israel didn't get here by accident. Remember the law we discussed in our visit to Brazil that required Brazilian producers on many television shows? Well, the Israeli government also influences television by regulating it. Cable (HOT) and satellite (YES) operators are required to devote 8% of their programming to locally produced shows. As a result, the operators invest in local content. Yoram Mokady, VP Content at HOT, said: "We launched ten shows this year and have only seven on our staff. The result is you have to be willing to take more calculated risks. We seldom do pilots. That means that if I go for a show, I go for the whole season and pay for the whole season and film the entire season. Our dramas cost between $40,000 and $200,000 per episode."

Initially that local requirement was a response to pressure. Remember our discussion of "soft power" and what I called "the weaponization of drama" in our visit to Turkey? Here's another case rooted in politics. During the 1967 Arab–Israeli War, Israeli Prime Minister David Ben-Gurion launched a single, state-regulated channel to "combat Arab propaganda," according to the *Wall Street Journal*. But it wasn't until 1993 that the same channel turned into a commercial enterprise, airing American shows such as *Seinfeld* and *Friends*.

The government quickly realized the popularity of American TV was a threat to local productions, so in the early 2000s, it began regulating the amount of airtime devoted to local and foreign broadcasts. Today, the government mandates that 40 to 50 percent of Israel's broadcast content must be produced locally (not just the 8% requirement for station operators). Given the small size of the Israeli population, those in the entertainment field say the bar for success is set pretty high. "We're dealing with a lot of limitations that actually force us to be more creative," said Lisa Shiloach-Uzrad, a producer with Israel's July August Productions.

Filmmaker Eytan Fox has lived through the evolution of Israeli TV drama. Back in the 1980s, he was in a class at Tel Aviv University with the creators of *BeTipul* that became *In Treatment*. He told thejc.com: "There was nothing for us when we graduated. There were maybe seven films made per year and only one TV channel. A few of us started a little production company and things began to change around us. Suddenly there was commercial TV, then satellite and cable. A new law was passed in 2000 that ensured a specific percentage of revenues would be injected into Israeli cinema. So suddenly all the film schools began to develop and the talent which had been there from the start had a chance to make TV series."

Those accounts make it seem as if Israeli success was foreseen and planned. But like many so-called "breaks" in the industry everywhere, luck and personal connections played a part. *BeTipul* was based on a plot that had to do with living in a warzone. In the original, an Israeli pilot, who was troubled by bombing civilians, sought the help of a therapist. Hagai Levi, who created *BeTipul* (and who later co-created the American series *The Affair*), has questioned the theories of Israel's emergence into television. Actually, according to a *Los Angeles Times* article from 2012, a trip by Noa Tishby, an actress and producer who lives in Los Angeles, opened the floodgates when she traveled to Israel to visit her family. When she arrived, she heard everyone buzzing about *BeTipul*, a series set in a therapist's office. Tishby felt the series would tap into the U.S. market's appetite for high-end drama and she called Hagai Levi. So alien was the idea of a Hollywood sale that Levi at first thought Tishby was calling to angle for a role. "He couldn't believe that it was something we thought we could sell," she said.

So why do Israeli shows adapt so well in America? Morgan Spurlock analyzed, "The barriers of our expectations of things looking beautiful, and that everything has to look like a Kubrick film, have gone. We've become much more forgiving as an audience; it's much more about the story, about people and their stories. That tops everything."

Israeli dramas deal with issues that were not far from real-life events. That creates a passion bred from personal experience in the scripts. "The new wave of Israeli series is heavily rooted in the security situation," says Levi, "and this has to do not only with the worldwide interest, but also that most of the TV series are genre series: action and spy dramas. On the one hand, this corresponds with the needs of the U.S. industry, and on the other, that we have these stories to tell."

Another answer might be the attitude of Israelis to new businesses. According to thejc.com, Israel has had to fight against overwhelming odds for its very survival. This experience combined with the precariousness of day-to-day life seems to have bred a maverick quality into the country's young entrepreneurs. Taking risks is a part of daily life and that translated into an adventurous business mentality that has worked well in Israeli TV production, where creativity is crucial and risk-taking fundamental. Another aspect that works to the Israelis' advantage is that to be produced in Israel, programs have to be delivered on a tight budget. This means that if the idea is good, overseas broadcasters can also develop the format without spending a fortune.

Finally, a sort of common culture might encourage smooth Israeli/Hollywood adaptations. IMDB.com posted: "I know it can sound strange, but when you think about it, the two countries have a lot in common, whether it's in social values or storytelling," Gideon Raff, the creator of *Hatufim* and an executive producer on *Homeland*, said in a Tel Aviv cafe a few days before the *Homeland* finale aired in the U.S. "And Israelis as a people don't really care that much about traditional rules, which fits a little with what's going on in cable television in the U.S. right now."

Whatever similarities the countries may have in content, the methods of production are far apart. While budgets are in the millions for typical U.S. episodes, the average per-episode budget of an Israeli show is about fifty thousand dollars. This financial disadvantage often works in these shows' favor, since the emphasis gets placed on the quality of writing and dialogue — transferable things — rather than on big-name actors or effects. The advantage runs even deeper: because of their limited budgets, Israeli networks only develop series after reading their entire season arc. This allows the writers more creative freedom to begin with, as they are less prone to ratings-related pressures.

Not all is so easy in international adaptations, though, even among friendly nations. In an insightful article in the *New Yorker* in 2012, Ruth Margalit interviewed Gideon Raff, creator of *Homeland*, and revealed the show's complex reception at home. Margalit said Raff conceived of the idea for *Homeland* during his visits to Israel. "When you live far away, home looks a little different every time," he told Margalit. "So I thought about someone who returns home and wants everything to be the same, but it's not — and how everyone at home wants him to be the same, but he's not." Raff was also interested in exploring Israel's unique regard for its captured soldiers, and the prominent place that these soldiers occupy in the public's consciousness.

That soldier in the Showtime series became Brody — a U.S. Marine who had been missing in action for eight years before being rescued in Afghanistan. While the U.S. version focused mostly on the romantic relationship between Brody and Carrie, a CIA operative who believes that Brody had switched sides in captivity, the Israeli version centered around the families of the kidnapped soldiers, and broached issues of posttraumatic stress disorder, uneasy adjustment, and lingering suspicions — issues that had been seen as taboo in a country that places the return of its captured soldiers at the top of its political agenda.

Not all Israelis were pleased with the show's treatment of this sensitive subject. It was an especially fraught time in Israel, where a massive public campaign was underway to pressure the government into striking a deal for the release of Gilad Shalit, who had been captured on Israel's border with Gaza in 2006. Many in the country found the context and the timing of the show troubling. Raff said, "I remember screening the promo and someone asked me, 'How dare you?'"

Acceptance in Israel and adapting to the U.S. were only part of this show's challenges. In the American version of *Homeland*, the series gets a glossy treatment, a romance, and a female lead. In the Spanish language version in production by Televisa in Mexico, this primetime drama becomes a daytime telenovela. "It's the same arc, the same narrative DNA, but developed differently based on the market needs and geopolitical connotations," said Alon Shtruzman, the chief executive of Keshet International. Welcome to the world of international adaptations.

As I compile the television news for you, a new series from Hagai Levi and Noah Stollman (the team behind *In Treatment*) is filming in Israel with American audiences in mind. By the time you read this, will it be yet another Israeli hit? Here's HBO's description: "The series dramatizes the tragic torrent of violence that followed the disappearance of, and intensive search for, three Israeli teens during the summer of 2014. The show follows an idealistic investigator for the Shin Bet (the Israeli equivalent of the FBI) as he deals with the ramifications of violent reactions on both sides of the escalating conflict. A new command position thrusts him into a confrontation that undermines his faith and worldview, leading to a dramatic conflict between his values and the actions of those closest to him."

Check out what happens to that show and many more on the way from this small land that likes its nickname: "Start-Up Nation."

NIGERIA AND SUB-SAHARAN AFRICA

Nigeria

Nigerian writers I've mentored over the past few years, whether in U.S. classes or workshops in Africa, have stood out to me for their ambition, energy, and sophistication about American TV shows. Of course this is not a scientific survey — anyone from Africa who turns up in high-level seminars would have both the financial means and education to take advantage of them, advantages that don't apply to many others. Still, I have a sense that the closest comparison to the state of television drama in Nigeria would be Israel before American and British outlets discovered Israeli dramas. Like Israel, the talent in Nigeria is ready and waiting; like Israel in its earlier years, the infrastructure to create television on the level of the top American shows is only beginning to emerge.

Not that Nigeria lacks a filmmaking presence. Dubbed "Nollywood," by 2009 it had surpassed Hollywood as the world's second largest movie industry by volume, right behind India's Bollywood. And in 2014, the Nigerian government released data showing Nollywood is a $3.3 billion sector, with 1844 movies produced in 2013 alone, according to *Fortune*. However, critics note that while Nollywood has volume, it lacks production value. In a reach for that elusive critical quality, Netflix spent $12 million for the movie rights to the Nigerian novel *Beasts of No Nation* that starred Idris Elba. Yes, Netflix is television, but this was a one-off, not a series, and though it was based on work by Nigerian writer Uzodinma Iweala, it was scripted by an American, and shot in Ghana, not produced by Nigerians.

So much for its entry into the global television market, though several Nollywood movies are available on Netflix (along with just about everything from everywhere).

Within sub-Saharan Africa, though, Nigerian film is prominent, even without much of a presence elsewhere. Nigeria is the most populous country on the African continent, with a fifth of the total population of Africa. A dynamism and relatively greater sense of economic and travel adventure by Nigerians has led to pockets of Nigerians plying their trade. Those many small regional African sales constitute a first market for Nollywood film merchants. Another reason for Nigeria's prominence in Africa is the low level of development of local film industries in many other countries of Africa. The African online site *GBera TV* commented, "The film products from Nigeria over time get to pass and gain recognition in the market, given that they are the closest that can be gotten to satisfy the 'local itch' at the moment."

However, the Nigerian writers I've met have little interest in Nollywood. They aspire to write American-style television. Nigeria had made local TV for decades, but into the 21st century pay-TV platforms and access to the Internet altered the expectations of Nigerian viewers. As American TV series became most requested, Nigerian series became less and less popular. Filmmaker Tope Oshin told *Pulse Nigeria* in 2016, "In the past our TV dramas and soap operas were more popular then because we didn't have a lot of options. The industry was small, the industry was just beginning, there were just a few people who were doing these things. Right now, if you turn on the TV for instance, we have so many local channels, we have so many cable channels, we have so many satellite cable providers as well. So, everybody is not watching the same thing at the same time. There's several soap operas, several sitcoms, so, it's very very difficult for one to become that popular or become what everyone is watching."

Now that Nigerian producers and screenwriters are aware that millennials are obsessed with American TV series, Nigerian creators are attempting series with the kind of drama that would grab the attention of their viewers. Sometimes they try too hard. My heart went out to one young man who had traveled more than 4,000 miles from Lagos, Nigeria for a chance to pitch a drama series in a seminar I gave in Johannesburg, South Africa. So much energy and detailed planning had gone into his show, and uncountable hope. I listened to him, hoping also, but in his desperation to succeed, he had imitated the most clichéd action-adventures he'd seen on American television: "maverick" guys with big guns driving recklessly through Africa shooting other tough guys and blowing stuff up. No one had taught him to develop character first; no one had taught him anything. Yet he'd come all this way. He's bright and willing; if only there was a path forward.

With all the resources in Nigeria, you'd think their time would be coming on the international television stage. In 2017, *Variety* wrote, "Hardly helping matters is the unconventional business model of Nigerian broadcasting, in which producers are forced to buy airtime for their shows — pushing them into partnerships with deep-pocketed corporate sponsors in order to bring their creations to the small screen. It's a system, says [Ambassador Segun] Odugbemi, which has killed innovation among independent producers. Yet guarded optimism remains in a vast country of 180 million with a resilient streak and a reputation for getting things done. Digital migration is expected to herald a host of new broadcasters eager to invest in local content."

Not everyone is looking forward to what they consider "cultural imperialism" that would occur if powerful American broadcasters do invest in making Nigerian television a global commodity. The *Arabian Journal of Business and Management Review* editorialized in 2013: "Local content broadcast in Nigeria is meant to be a conduit through which the mass society experience culture; enhancing cultural learning by promoting and sustaining the moral and community life of the Nigerian people. Television broadcasting in Nigeria (especially private owned) continues to be criticized over the foreign nature of its contents, while its local contents feature a high level of hybridization — an infusion of western and Nigerian culture which do not necessarily compliment the culture of its viewers, rather exposes them to mores and values contradictory to their culture. This raises major concern over the cultural mores and values that would be transmitted to the next generation of Nigerian youths who constitute the majority of television viewers, and are at risk of losing the basic crust of their culture.

"All you can hope for is when a nation holds authentic cultural value that they would be able to resist it. Take India, for example. In spite of their long years of independence, they have one of the biggest film industries. Most of their film productions are in Indian languages. There are certain things you won't find on their films. You won't find people kissing or find people who engage in covert sex advances or escapades because it has become part of their culture. They hold to their cultural values. But in Nigeria, we think modernization means an abandonment of your culture. So, that is not the problem of the television industry but the problem of a nation. Of course, television may begin to assist to revalue the society but the society must accept that certain things have been lost."

Cultural integrity is a critical issue as television becomes increasingly global, partly because streaming is easy and Netflix (as well as other platforms) are available almost everywhere in the world. We heard those concerns in Brazil where laws mandated Brazilian-made shows, in Turkey and Israel, where a positive national image had to be a feature of their shows, and the issue even arose in noticing how *Shameless* was transformed from British to American tastes. Usually the antidote to cultural conquest relies on building indigenous shows that people want to watch. At the base, this comes down to individual creators — writers — you — telling authentic stories with characters the audience will believe.

On a national level, systems exist to encourage the best creative talent.

Yemi Farounbi, a veteran broadcaster, told Nigeria's *Sunday Vanguard*: "Two things to do. The first one is training. If possible, government could help them so that quite a lot of people most especially the freelancers, independent producers can get properly trained in the art of broadcasting. Some of these values that are authentic to Nigeria can be part of their training and these can be reflected in their programs. If you take an American film, you know that the good will always win. Second, we also need to devote more money to program making. We need more of not only soap opera or dramas that are based in contemporary little problems of romance, a man and a woman, we need some epic that even in 50 years, people would love to watch. We need to devote money if we want good programs. And we need the time."

In 2017, Nigeria's government granted "Pioneer Status" to the creative film and television industry. It was a landmark move aimed at transforming the industry to a creative economy and creating jobs. By the time you read this, Nigeria might be on its way to global status in original television.

Meanwhile, throughout Africa, television shows are proliferating via Amazon Video and iRokoTV. Amazon posted this announcement:

> *EbonyLife TV Launches Five All-New Shows on Amazon Video giving the Diaspora new access to homegrown African content!*
>
> **LAGOS, NIGERIA, JANUARY 26, 2017**
>
> EbonyLife TV is thrilled to announce the release of five drama series on Amazon. Amazon Video offers a rich streaming program that lets users watch

programming when and where they want. Watch Amazon Video from your phone, tablet, games console, Smart TV and the Web.

EbonyLife TV broadcasts to 49 African countries, including South Africa and other southern African countries. We have expanded to include Flow Networks in the Caribbean, with viewers in Antigua, Barbados, Curacao, Grenada, Jamaica, St. Lucia, St. Vincent & The Grenadines and Trinidad & Tobago, Cayman Islands and The Bahamas. The channel continues to grow exponentially across the globe with some of our premium scripted programs now available on Amazon.

Even before Amazon, its chief competitor in Africa, iRoko put up its own boast: "iRoko, the world's largest online distributor of African movies and music, is a great illustration of how programmers can experiment, measure and refine their monetization models. When it launched, iRoko was a free service supported by ads, and after some experimentation, rolled out a subscription, ad-free offering of global TV series and movies. It was so successful with its Nigerian TV and movie content that it began licensing deals with major Hollywood studios in order to offer its viewers programming beyond its core Nollywood line-up."

Before we celebrate Africa's emergence in television, take caution with what else is happening there:

CHINA'S PRESENCE IN KENYA

We discussed "soft power" and what I called the "weaponizing of television drama" in our visits to Turkey, Israel, and elsewhere. Those cases all relied on countries trying to present themselves to the world through stories and images they want to promote. Call it best face forward or plain propaganda, the dramas promote an internal national interest. Now comes the use of soft power by an outside entity aimed at persuading a foreign population. It's a calculation by China that Africa, especially central African nations including Kenya, Ghana, Democratic Republic of Congo, and Central African Republic, will be more amenable to its economic plans if the people there have a friendly attitude towards Chinese development. Thus the conquest of Africa by television.

StarTimes, a privately owned Beijing-based media and telecommunications firm, has been gradually overhauling the continent's broadcast infrastructure and beaming Chinese content to millions of homes since 2002. "Privately owned" has a different meaning in China than in Western countries, though. According to Jonathan Kaiman reporting for the *Los Angeles Times* in 2017, "Beijing has invested billions of dollars into soft power campaigns aimed at convincing the world that China is a cultural and political success story."

"There's a huge ideological element" to StarTimes' African operations, said Dani Madrid-Morales, a doctoral fellow at the City University of Hong Kong. "It's a huge effort to get Africans to understand China. Even the selection of TV shows is very carefully done. It's very specific shows that showcase an urban China, a growing China, a noncontroversial view of China."

With 14 million subscribers, StarTimes sells nearly half of Kenya's pay-TV subscriptions for as low as $4 per month. Observers question how much of the Chinese content the subscribers are actually watching, though, since China has strategically attracted those viewers by offering local content on their channels too. Linus Kaikai, a manager at the Nairobi-based National Media Group, said Kenyan audiences have been shifting away from foreign content for years, as local shows grow more popular. So here's the question for the future of Kenyan (and other African) original TV series: Can access to the Chinese technology become a springboard for indigenous television drama some day?

SOUTH AFRICA

South Africa

Flying out of Tambo International Airport in Johannesburg, 10,376 miles away from home, I feel the good people I met in Africa still with me. For three days in August, professional writers, producers, media educators, and broadcast executives came from South Africa, and as far away as Nigeria, Ghana, and other African nations to learn about creating their own scripted television series.

But images also cling to me of rows of one-room houses on the outskirts of the city that have no electricity and no plumbing. For toilets they use "long drops" — extremely deep holes in the ground. Yet, each tiny house — every single one — has a TV dish on its roof. They run on car batteries, I was told. The pay television service costs around 400 Rand per month, roughly $100. That may be a quarter of a month's pay for some of these families. But it's the way to access quality shows — many of them American.

I asked my insightful guide, "Why are they willing to pay for television when they can't afford a toilet?"

"Priorities," she answered.

The stories they watch allow them to escape into worlds they'll never really experience. The best ones also help them frame the lives they have, as the best shows do for people everywhere.

My guide drove me drove past fine houses behind high gates topped by coils of barbed wire. I saw a new high-tech cosmopolitan city, and I saw people not fortunate enough for the one-room houses with dishes on the roofs who are living in hand-built shacks. Maybe they watch the free TV run by the government.

Everyone I met in Joburg was passionate about good television, and frustrated with the limitations they feel their own systems have put on them. A gifted man from Nigeria told me he orders scripts online and reads whole seasons of the best American dramas. Almost everyone in the seminar was current on HBO, AMC, and the networks, and though Netflix did not yet stream to Africa at the time of my visit, they raved about *Orange Is the New Black* that they managed to get anyway . . . I didn't want to know too much about how.

South Africa is a country in transition, and the evolution of television programming there tracks the changes in society. Under apartheid, television was banned for fear it would unleash ideas of revolution under the white regime. No one even heard of *I Love Lucy*.

When apartheid fell in 1994, the Mandela era of freedom produced an artistic flourishing and the first original South African TV dramas were created along with films. The love for Madiba seemed palpable to me because he achieved the impossible: peace, and a path forward.

Since Mandela retired, I was told, the country has still been reeling from centuries of repression. For example, the government-owned and operated free television system uses broadcasting for social engineering aimed at building a black middle class. (*The Cosby Show* is endorsed.) At the same time, in the attempt to mold behavior, it is forbidden to show a couple kissing on screen. A producer told me a door has to close in time to block a view of the offending behavior. This from a president with five wives.

It's a time of dynamic change there, and contradictions.

The British newspaper the *Guardian* newspaper said of South African writer-director Neill Blomkamp, who made *District 9* and *Elysium*, "Given his South African upbringing, divisions infuse Blomkamp's work. Like *District 9*, *Elysium* deals with segregation, although this time the metaphor is not racial but financial. He believes the increase in population and decrease in resources means the whole planet will become one big Johannesburg of fortified communities nestling next to slums. 'Then we'll go beyond that timeline,' he says, 'and it'll either be a singularity discussion or this *Mad Max* group of savages roaming on the horizon, a Malthusian catastrophe.'"

Well, in my limited experience as a visitor, the divisions didn't seem as stark as Blomkamp's movies. In my workshops, the population was equally white and black. Nor is it that simplistic. One man's family was from India, someone else has Lebanese relatives, a few mentioned they're Jewish, and the people from Nigeria, Ghana, Mozambique, the Zulus, and those of other African ethnicities easily sat intermixed and offered their stories.

More than a thousand languages are spoken in South Africa: 23% Zulu, 16% Xhosa, 14% Afrikaans (a cousin of Dutch). For 10%, English is the first language, though English is everyone's second language. Television channels are divided according to languages and cultural groups, so narrowcasting is normal.

The creative challenge is to discover the universals. Among the inventive series pitches, I heard multiple-viewpoint structures from all the cultures. One was set among university students in the midst of the 1990s anti-apartheid revolution, crossing lines of race, age, and nationality. Another was a *Rashomon* type of crime dramedy, whose cast represented the range of Africa.

And I kept hearing the term Pan African. People of South Africa that once was considered a European island in a black continent referred to themselves as Africans. A film crew who interviewed me emphasized they broadcast to all the sub-Saharan countries. This consciousness wouldn't have happened even three years ago, I was told.

Some of the roots of the new Pan African identity may arise from the threats to the land from Chinese mining. The first day I arrived, I heard about the Chinese copper mine that poisoned the farms in the Congo. The animals have died, and the people who fed themselves off the bounty of the earth for thousands of years are starving. One woman told me she looked at a hilltop and noticed a big rat running across. Moments later, she saw a group of men racing after it. They weren't chasing it away; they were trying to catch it to eat.

With those stories (and many more) in my thoughts, I left Joburg. I drove past the fine homes behind tall gates topped with loops of barbed wire, and again I passed the one-room houses each one topped with its own TV dish.

INDIA

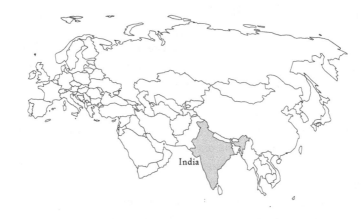

Images of Bollywood with dancers bejeweled like Hindu gods in raucous celebration spring to mind at the mention of Indian media. As an outsider, I expected Indian television to be an extension of their internationally successful movies, but despite a few forays into Bollywood TV, that's not what's happening.

In the past, the influence of Bollywood did overwhelm television. Today the Indian public adores the stars of certain television shows as their own cult figures. The boundaries between these two industries are blurring, and financial interests are forcing production companies to make both feature films for the cinema and soap operas for television. Soap operas (that other countries call telenovelas) dominate India, targeting a rural audience with conservative themes. The picture is not so simple, though, and today's India is as much a land of high technology as rural traditions. It's a divide seen around the world: urban versus rural, the future versus the past, and the cultural polarities play out clearly in television drama series.

Meanwhile, the soaps persist in fierce competition with each other in a market that is increasingly fragmented. With the rapid growth in the number of channels and regionalization, the number of soap operas in India has been increasing. Several dozen are broadcast daily in the country, spread over just three channels — Star Plus, Zee TV, and Colors. The ratings war can be felt every day during filming, according to India's INA Global site. Usually an episode is filmed just a few days before it is broadcast, so the writer may be charged with changing a script at the last moment to compete with some turn in a competitor's plot. We've witnessed this attitude worldwide, of course: if ratings are slipping, blame the writers and expect them to fix the problems instantly. In India, the tricks that producers and writers frequently turn to include bringing back a character, which requires some creative acrobatics when the said character was cremated a hundred episodes earlier; and leaps forward of around twenty years, so that a storyline that is going nowhere can be ditched.

In the first decade of the 21st century, Ekta Kapoor, the creative director of the production company Balaji Telefilms, systematically developed the soap opera concept exploiting the narrative dynamic of *saas-bahu* — "mother-in-law, daughter-in-law" — unavoidable in a country where it is still the norm for three generations to live under the same roof. By 2010, Balaji Telefilms produced the most popular soaps on Indian television, providing 15,000 hours of viewing. It is said of Ekta Kapoor that she turned the Indian housewife into a heroine, thanks to the storylines based closely on the conservative Indian middle class.

The characters are all stereotypical: in each series, there has to be a baddy, who will be easy to spot with his clothing, make-up, gestures, and the music when the character makes his entrance. As in Indian mythology from which the screenwriters must take their inspiration, the forces of good and evil collide. There is little real dialogue between characters in the way Western writers think of scenes. Most speeches are monologues, and most of the scenes end in tears, while the camera revolves around the characters reacting with set, horrified expressions on their faces.

India's *Caravan Magazine* traced what happens to a new writer named Gitangshu Dey as he learned the rules of a job writing for a soap. I found his journey interesting, especially as it compares with the work of beginning screenwriters elsewhere, including the experiences of my former students interviewed in the previous chapter. I'll summarize parts of the *Caravan* article for you:

When Dey entered the industry, he was taught a set of rules to follow. These rules are supervised by different departments of a production house as the script passes through them, like an assembly line. Dey was in fact interviewed by an executive, and not a writer, before he was hired.

He was told the heroine needs to be what they considered an "ideal" figure — an ideal daughter-in-law, an ideal wife, an ideal mother, or an ideal sister. "The moment you take her out of that mold, the popularity plummets," Dey said. But what constitutes "ideal"? Dey explained that the heroine must always be self-sacrificing. "Quiet submission," according to Dey, "is a trait appreciated by the Indian audience."

An ideal heroine contrasts sharply with the evil vamp, who is shown wearing garish make-up, and is dressed in a way a conservative audience finds provocative. The vamp derives sadistic pleasure from creating trouble for the protagonist. Since such characters are one-dimensional, Dey pointed out, the audience can grow bored of them easily. So, after a while, they either die or are thrown out of the family and disappear forever. Soon, fresh evil takes their place.

Dey soon realized the writers' department had limited control over stories. He was also answerable to "creative" executives hired to ensure the production process was oriented towards maximizing ratings, and the production house gave these executives a wide mandate to enforce storytelling rules. One such rule, for instance, decreed that the heroine must be present in at least 70 percent of the scenes in an episode. If she wasn't, an executive could demand that a writer redraft the episode.

Over the years, Dey familiarized himself with formulas for plot twists. He watched old American soaps such as *Days of Our Lives* to learn other popular plot-advancing tricks. For example, in the world of soap operas, an evil double might replace a character, complicating the lives of those around them. Simple miscommunications ruin relationships forever. Streaks of horrible luck are unending. Besides all this, of course, there's always an evil conspiracy brewing against the protagonists.

In August 2015, after eight years of assisting other writers, Dey was hired as the head writer for a show about a love triangle set in Punjab. Apart from executives, he now has to deal with other corporate departments. The research team, for instance, which collects audience responses through surveys, fan emails, and phone calls, has a say in every matter. Recently, he strayed away from a cardinal rule by making his central female character "independent, bubbly, and outgoing." The research team soon informed him that the audience did not like her. She was too "strong-headed."

"So I had to turn the character around a bit," he said. He made her "more caring," and began making her "do things for her family." The heroine needs to be involved in family affairs, he said. "It is expected of her to solve household problems." She gradually became "ideal" again.

But India is changing. According to *The Hindustan Times* in 2016, "Time and again, it dawns on the members of the TV industry that there is a dearth of high-quality shows. But soon, any discussions about the topic take a back seat. They face the huge pressure of delivering numbers. Today, TV shows have to prove their mettle in a month or less. Grabbing eyeballs through sensationalism is the only solution to achieve that target."

That solution is eroding now, partly through the influence of American series. Remember the insight from Anna dos Santos Israel in the overview that began this whole chapter? Anna said that growing up in Brazil, she watched the major American television dramas, and they informed her tastes and ultimately her writing. Something similar is beginning in India.

A senior producer, on condition of anonymity, says, "The urban youth are hooked on to American television. They watch these on various online platforms or download them. The younger generation doesn't watch Indian TV shows at all. Women and kids in rural households are hooked to our TV shows. Producers and broadcasters are simply catering to this demand. Channels want regressive themes as that helps them rake in advertisers. The audience suffers instead as they have no option but to watch the shows aired. It's a vicious circle."

Well, not quite a closed circle. Some production companies are venturing shows "inspired by" American hits. They usually fail, but the effort continues. A show called *Yudh* was supposed to have been inspired by *Breaking Bad*. Despite having an all-star cast, *Yudh* was replaced by *Indian Idol* (a singing show) after a mere 20 episodes. In another case, a well-made crime drama series, *Powder* attempted to be an Indian adaptation of *The Wire*, but that failed too. Indian critics said the audiences were not yet ready for a drama that packed that big a punch.

That's not the end of the story, though. Enter Netflix and Amazon, and even the queen of Indian soaps is looking at American-style fare through streaming in an effort to win over the millennials. Now, Balaji Telefilms, the production house behind some of the country's biggest soap operas, has entered the fray with its over-the-top service, ALTBalaji. Its lineup features a gay romance and a contemporary adaptation of the classic Bengali novel, *Devdas*. But while the 1917 book was about the life and times of a wealthy man, ALTBalaji's protagonist is a rebellious 21st-century woman.

So why is the soap opera magnate venturing into digital entertainment? The answer lies in India being the world's fastest growing smartphone market, with 300 million users currently. As the Internet becomes faster and cheaper in the country, the smartphone has become the dominant screen for many Indians. As a result, young Indians no longer have to watch what they did on their family TV whose remote controls were with their grandmothers.

Original content is the buzzword for other over-the-top services, too. Amazon Prime Video has said it has 18 India originals in the pipeline, ranging from sports drama to mythological fiction.

Netflix is competing for the same audience. In a 2017 visit to the country, Reed Hastings, CEO of Netflix, said: "There are around 300 million smartphone users in India. But we are targeting mostly the high end — 10 or 20 million — for whom our pricing is not a problem." Pointing out that India is "hugely important" to Netflix because "it's one of the strongest Internet markets." Hastings added, "India has seen the highest growth among all the Asian markets."

The new platforms are groundbreaking for writers. Datta Dave, a partner in India's first talent agency representing writers, said, "Experienced feature film writers are given the opportunity to be showrunners, which essentially elevates them to a producer role. Up-and-coming writers get the chance to contribute to writers' rooms. There's a renewed respect for the profession, which is a wonderful step toward creating better content." In 2018 Amazon brought in a U.S. showrunner to teach Indian writers episodic structure and character development. Series creator Rangita Nandy said: "Amazon gives us wings. We can develop content we always wanted to do without worrying about censorship or the box office. All of us are doing pieces we've wanted to make but haven't had the platform for."

CHINA

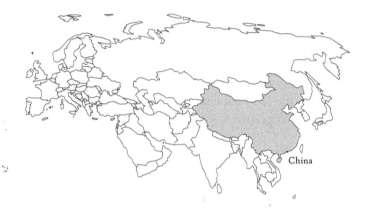

China

I was thrilled to discover the Chinese publication of the third edition of this book translated into Chinese in 2016. It's a beautiful looking book. But I was surprised because I wasn't aware the Chinese leadership was interested in writing American-style drama series, many of which don't fit their media rules. I should have realized that the progress of China on the global scene, not just economically but also in its reach for greater cultural appreciation, would bring along an effort to create more impactful drama series. The many Chinese students entering USC's School of Cinematic Arts are enthusiastic. In my classes, students who are actually from China (not just Chinese-Americans) have been fluent not only in English but in American shows that many of them have already watched. Likely, this is a result of the Internet prevalence in China that had around 731 million Internet users as of 2017.

But it's a quandary: how does a society combine the free forward motion of creating original shows with government censorship of media? According to a report on CNN.com: The state-run Xinhua news agency said shows should refrain from content that expresses "overt admiration for Western lifestyles," jokes about Chinese traditions, or defiles "classic materials." "They should also avoid putting stars, billionaires, or Internet celebrities on pedestals; or sensationalizing private affairs, relationships, or family disputes." Here's what else is on China's blacklist:

Cleavage — Actresses' cleavage was ordered to be cropped out of a Tang dynasty period drama by China's censors. After *The Saga of Wu Zetian*, a TV drama about China's only female emperor, attracted large viewership, it was abruptly pulled for "technical reasons." The show returned a few days later with a lot less skin. Censors ordered the show's editors to crop the footage to hide any cleavage, resulting in much tighter shots on stars' faces, and widespread outrage online.

Drinking and smoking — The "General Rules for Television Series Content Production" were drafted in order to "thoroughly implement (Chinese President) Xi Jinping's speech at the national forum on literature," in which he stressed that art must serve a social purpose. Some of the first things to be hit by the new rules were shows that promote "smoking and drinking, fighting, and other unhealthy behavior."

Homosexuality — Guidelines from 2015 categorize homosexuality as an "abnormal sexual behavior" unfit for China's TV screens, alongside incest, sexual abuse, and other "perversions." *Addiction*, a popular web drama about romantic relationships between teenage boys, was pulled despite attracting almost 10 million views in its first 24 hours of release.

These attitudes are remnants of decades when Chinese TV was designed to dispense traditional values to the masses. Wartime dramas full of marauding Japanese and deceitful nationalists who massacred Communist forces underlined the ruling party's heroic narrative that it was the only force that could defend and unite China.

But early in the 21st century, many Chinese satellite TV channels turned profits by peddling locally made copies of foreign hits. The government reacted and ruled that nearly all primetime slots must be reserved for "self-innovated TV programs with Chinese cultural inheritance and characteristics [that] can better carry the Chinese Dream themes, the socialist core values, as well as patriotism and Chinese fine traditions," according to Xinhua.

In visits to previous countries, we've observed various efforts to limit the influence of foreign shows, beginning with Brazil and including everywhere else that is trying to build their own television industry. In China, the rules extend to the Internet, so the *Beijing News* reported in 2014 that the number of foreign TV shows carried by Chinese websites couldn't exceed 30% of the number of domestic TV shows carried the previous year.

Besides restricting percentages, the Chinese government uses subtler methods aimed especially at the way most U.S. dramas are produced. Until 2015, popular U.S. TV shows — everything from *Two Broke Girls* to *Mad Men* — had been available online with Chinese subtitles within hours of their stateside broadcast. The exploding popularity of online video sites in China, with paid rights, was a boon for foreign producers, who for years struggled to combat piracy activities.

But China's State Administration of Press, Publication, Radio, Film and Television said that instead of portals being allowed to post foreign shows episode-by-episode as they are made and broadcast overseas, they would have to clear an entire season of shows with censors before the programs could be put online. TV programs made in China are typically broadcast only after the entire series is recorded and reviewed by censors. But unlike Chinese TV series, most U.S. programs do not film an entire season before broadcasts begin. The new requirement could drive Chinese viewers to look for pirated versions, according to industry observers.

If you're not daunted by all that and you still want to produce an original show in China, here's a cautionary tale as it was told to the *Wall Street Journal* in 2016. Gao Mantang, a veteran TV screenwriter who is behind several hit shows, was asked to get permission from six central government departments when producing *Family On the Go* (2012), a drama that tells the story of self-made business-people in a coastal Chinese city famous for its entrepreneurs.

Mr. Gao said he was told to get permission from China's Ministry of Foreign Affairs for a character in the drama who is a migrant worker and travels abroad, and the State Administration for Industry and Commerce for two scenes showing a street vendor getting caught by local market regulators. He was also told to speak with the National Energy Administration, the Ministry of Land and Resources, and the Propaganda Department of the Communist Party's Central Committee about a lead character who moves to northern China to extract oil, and the Ministry of Commerce about a mention in the drama of "a clueless farmer who travels to France to start a small business." "These government departments have no branch to take care of censorship, so we had to carry our discs and knock on each of their doors," said Mr. Gao, describing the censors and broad-casters as "evasive." As we'd say in America, "Oy."

Funny thing is American shows are as popular in China as ever. Anyone from China who I ask is up to date on *Game of Thrones*, for example. In Chinese, the title literally means "Games of Power." Intrigue has been a recurring theme in Chinese history, making power struggles a natural crowd-pleaser. In addition, China has its own medieval fantasy lore, and, as everybody knows, its own dragons, making *Game of Thrones* a big hit. There is definitely a niche audience for more explicit shows like this, though access to these shows is generally limited to pirated DVDs and streaming sites.

House of Cards is a hit because of the popularity of scandal stories in Chinese culture, and because Chinese people find the spectacle of American democracy entertaining. The Chinese government is frequently mentioned and plays a role in the plot, which has also made the show popular with the government. Now here's an interesting cultural difference: While American audiences consider Frank Underwood a scoundrel, to Chinese audiences, he is an ambitious, even admirable character.

All five seasons of *Breaking Bad* are available for free in high definition with Chinese subtitles on several Chinese streaming sites. A Chinese blogger who uses the handle "bloggerMing" posted, "I once tutored a Chinese middle school student who avidly watched *Breaking Bad* as a way to learn English and because his favorite subject was chemistry, which made Walter White somewhat of an inspiration to him. While I found it odd that a thirteen-year-old was taking chemistry advice from a drug lord, I started watching myself and found Chinese subtitles a great way to pick up some vocabulary." Like *House of Cards*, *Breaking Bad* — whose title is trans-lated in China as "Fate-Defying Drug Master" — is popular with Chinese audiences who are interested in its dark super realism.

We've been discussing international co-productions since the beginning of this chapter, and it's the logical way around Chinese restrictions. Where there's a will for Chinese audiences to enjoy American shows (and busi-nesses to profit on both sides) a way will be found . . . besides piracy. For several years, American companies have been partnering up with Chinese companies so the movies and television they make will not be considered foreign. Co-productions require a certain amount of Chinese financing, scenes shot in China, and Chinese actors. China's laws forbid local movie companies from partnering with foreign filmmakers intent on "damaging

China's national dignity, honor, and interests, or harming social stability or hurting national feelings," but within those limits is plenty of potential.

Around the world we've also noticed Netflix streaming all kinds of shows on "over the top" platforms — that is, bypassing national broadcast networks to deliver shows directly to Internet subscribers. In 2017, originals like *Stranger Things* and *Black Mirror* were among the first Netflix programs to appear on the Chinese Internet platform iQiyi, but Netflix cautioned that its expectations for the deal were modest. There are still hurdles the pair will need to contend with before Netflix's originals can join the platform. iQiyi reportedly has 500 million monthly viewers and is in the midst of transitioning from an ad-supported model into an on-demand subscription service, like Netflix, so the partnership is possible.

This is only the beginning of the story of China's emergence in television on the global stage. We already discussed China's presence in Africa. China's leaders, and its cash-rich companies, want more than just domestic success. After all, Bollywood has exported its productions across the developing world. Tiny South Korea has managed to capture part of the global TV market with its gauzy costume dramas. Chinese leaders may ask themselves 'Shouldn't we be able to project our own soft power?' Even as President Xi has restricted artistic freedom at home, he has urged China to export its values and promote a "global creative industry."

And that brings us to you, the writers, the makers of stories who have the craft to deliver them on screen. Any time an industry is growing and changing opportunities open. As the global entertainment market seizes on of the importance of being able to write towards the vast Chinese audience, initiatives arise to find voices that can speak to that population. Where I teach, scholarships have recently been created for China-themed (or at least China-sensitive) pilot scripts, and pathways in the media for Asian-American screenwriters have multiplied. China, with all its contradictions, may be a formidable dragon, but it's one you may be able to ride.

SOUTH KOREA

The "Korean Wave" of television drama (*Hallyu* in Korean) splashed like a tsunami over Asia in the early 21st century, though it didn't seep onto American shores until later. International sales of Korean shows generated $180 million for broadcasters and producers back in 2009 and have since enjoyed even more growth, according to the Korea Communications Commission. Locally, it prompted pop culture-driven international tourism,

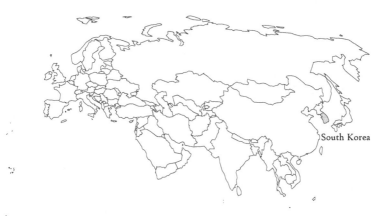

South Korea

known as "drama tourism," involving visits to shooting locations and efforts to meet Korean celebrities. Globally, the attractiveness of the Korean Wave expanded cultural diversity in an industry dominated by U.S.-derived content, where cultural globalization plays a huge role in which shows are popular enough to get distribution deals.

Korean TV drama series are also part of the story about Chinese television that I left out of the previous section so I could tell you about it here. By 2013, China had begun purchasing remake rights to Korean television dramas. Chinese television stations, as well as online and mobile platforms, also started hiring Korean producers and writers as an alternative to importing Korean dramas in order to bypass restrictions on foreign entertainment products mandated by the Chinese State Administration of Press, Publication, Radio, Film and Television.

Peak "K-drama" fever in China was reached in 2015 with a military romance, *Descendants of the Sun*, which chronicled the star-crossed relationship between a soldier and surgeon and was viewed more than 440 million times on the video-streaming site iQiyi.com. Apparently, the strict rules on broadcasting foreign dramas were relaxed for *Descendants of the Sun*, whose production was reportedly partly funded by Chinese investors.

An editorial carried by the Chinese Communist Party newspaper *People's Daily* praised it as "an excellent advertisement for conscription" showcasing South Korea's "national spirit" and "communitarian culture," and suggested China create similar television serials. The pressure escalated, with powerful entities asking why China, a country with a much larger audience, could not make such popular TV dramas. What's wrong with China's television dramas? Possibly, the clampdown on foreign television shows after 2015 wasn't so much about keeping Hollywood at bay as competing with its neighbor to the east. In a way, the success of Korean series in China heralded their demise (or at least reduction) in what had been their largest market.

Why are South Korean TV series so popular? To American tastes, the shows might be described as frothy. Aside from the military themes in *Descendants of the Sun*, K-dramas tend to be romantic and love oriented, with what has been called "overflowing aestheticism," and storylines that play to young women's fantasies. Both male and female protagonists are written to be vivacious, complemented by extravagant plots and popular music, also aimed at young viewers.

The success is calculated. South Korean TV dramas are examples of the effective implementation of Seoul's "culturally oriented" national strategy. On the one hand, the South Korean government has employed policies and pumped in funds for the development of their cultural presence. On the other, it has taken measures to encourage non-governmental capital — private investment, American-style.

The gauzy romances might feel like soap operas (telenovelas). They're not because they don't air daily, though they seem to have a similar psychological pull. At the same time, Korean producers are working on the more substantial kinds of dramas exemplified by *Descendants of the Sun*. It has the familiar ingredients of the top K-dramas: a convoluted plot, A-list actors, and an exotic location — in this case Greece, standing in as the fictional, war-torn Mediterranean country Uruk. Korean analysts say the military theme has resonated because the armed forces play a big part in South Korean society, with the constant looming threat of war with the North, and where conscription is mandatory for male citizens.

Screenwriters drive Korean TV dramas. In other places we've visited that rely on scripts for daily soap/telenovela scripts, writers are also at the heart of production. But the Korean model is closer to the current American cable and streaming form, with 16 episodes per season. According to a professor in communication studies at Hainan Tropical Ocean University in China, "South Korea has reframed its cultural industrial model and value chain, forging a 'cultural industrial community' made up of the government, businesspeople, and academic circles, which has helped establish a cultural pattern in which scriptwriters form the core of the series-making teams and TV dramas drive the development of related industries." In non-academic talk, he's saying 'writers rule.'

That's not to say television writers have it easy in South Korea that employs a "live-shoot" schedule like what we observed in India. Most Korean TV series start airing after shooting just a few episodes. Production gets busier as the shows rush to the end. Actors have been known to receive scripts right before filming starts on all-night shoots, while editors often struggle to deliver a final cut on time. The result is usually lower-quality episodes as a series reaches its climax. The brunt of the pressure falls on the writers, though.

Business partners that care especially about ratings favor the live-shoot model because it allows series the flexibility to adapt to real time audience feedback. Sometimes popular characters are mandated to receive increased screen time. But guess who has to change plotlines to satisfy audience expectations? The writers, of course. It's not a system that would be accept-able in countries like the U.S. or U.K. that have effective writers' guilds (unions), but it has succeeded so far in South Korea.

Writers (and everyone else) also have to contend with censorship. The regu-lating bodies reserve the right to block content that is deemed "subversive" and "harmful to the public order." This includes: pornography, nudity, materials harmful to minors, cyber defamation, sexual violence, content that praises North Korea, and antimilitary content.

Weapons such as knives are always censored on broadcasts. While large swords in ancient dramas aren't blurred, small knives that are intended to be used as weapons in certain scenes are blurred out. The Korea Commu-nications Standards Commission has issued a censor for anything that might cause excessive shock, anxiety, or disgust to viewers. Cigarettes are common in South Korea, but cigarettes are one of the most censored items on television, as they aren't seen as "family friendly" enough to show on broadcast. Korea is still conservative when it comes to tattoos. And in order to make shows "family friendly," stations will often times either pixelate tattooed areas of celebrities or ask them to wear tape to cover up their ink.

Yet, American shows that do all those things are prevalent in South Korea, and South Korea has maintained a good trading relationship with the United States. Half of the ten most popular U.S. exports to Korea are crime procedurals, such as *NCIS* and two from the *CSI* brand, *Cyber* and

Crime Scene Investigation. If you consider the nature of K-dramas, it's not a surprise that ABC's soap-meets-procedural *Scandal* was South Korea's favorite American show in 2015. That and other shows from Shondaland (Shonda Rhimes's production company) have romantic fun that fits the Korean appetite as they twist and turn in cliffhanger plots.

As for adaptations, it seems American shows have taken over and drawn huge viewership, especially after the success of *The Good Wife*, which was the first American show remade in Korea. Meanwhile, their version of CBS's *Criminal Minds* will be airing in Korea by the time you read this.

In the future, those adaptations of traditional network broadcasts will seem small in comparison to the rising tide on the Internet. This is especially relevant after Chinese investment withdrew from South Korean TV dramas. Korean productions need investment from somewhere else and telecom giants and Internet content service operators are competing to secure more exclusive, original series, with Netflix also jumping into the game.

That's not without a challenge. For a country that boasts the fastest Internet speeds in the world and one of the most highly connected populations — with 77.8% of all citizens identifying themselves as internet users and over 84% of all homes having internet access — many credit South Korea as being ahead of the curve when it comes to Internet culture. With Internet technologies, perhaps. However, the South Korean government still regulates and censors the Internet that they so often brag about.

Nevertheless, Netflix is making its first Korean original series *Love Alarm*, and announced an original 12-episode drama series that will be adapted from a popular South Korean online comic series. In 2017, American and Korean media firms invested in streaming Korean TV dramas to Americans, and Netflix signed a deal with South Korean cable TV network JTBC to provide its dramas to Netflix subscribers. Netflix also collaborated with South Korean film director Bong Joon-ho in producing *Okja* that was released on Netflix in 2017.

U.S. broadcast networks aren't far behind. According to *Variety* in 2017, DramaFever, the Warner Bros.-owned subscription VOD service specializing in Korean dramas and other international fare, will premiere its original K-drama series *My Secret Romance* both in the U.S. on its streaming platform and in South Korea on cable channel OCN. It marks the first time that DramaFever will stream a show in the Americas simultaneously with its overseas broadcast. Around the same time, ABC premiered *Somewhere*

Between, based on the Korean drama *God's Gift*, the first U.S. remake of a Korean drama. And the American version of *Good Doctor* — a Korean hit TV series — also ran on ABC.

That may sound better than it is, and previous adaptations of Korean dramas have failed here. "It's not surprising that these American remakes aren't immediately happening," said Korean pop culture critic Kim Bong Seok. "Korean dramas remain a niche genre outside of the country. Series like *My Love From Another Star* feature elements of fantasy that appeal to Asian viewers, while their conservative depictions of romance and family values and the toned-down violence resonate with Middle Easterners. The melodrama seems to strike a chord with telenovela-watching South Americans." But not with the larger U.S. audience, at least so far.

Michel Rodriguez of The Format People described Korea as being "on the edge of the international TV industry," but it's there on the edges where some of the best out-of-the-box thinking can be found. Once upon a time, Israel, Scandinavia, and Turkey were on the peripheries of the global TV industry but were busy coming up with ideas that were unlike those being developed by the mainstream — and look where they are now.

Given South Korea's global positioning, the popularity of its other cultural contributions like K-pop, and the growing acceptance in the major TV markets of ideas from anywhere, we might have seen only the initial stages of the Korean drama wave.

NORTH KOREA

We can't really visit North Korea, but we'll peek over the DMZ that divides it from the South. Views from space reveal a country with no electricity at

night, an island of darkness next to the brightness of South Korea. Without electricity, you can't have television. But as you'll see, this becomes a story not so much of oppression as an emerging resilience among North Korea's young citizens . . . and we'll get to that part.

In my visit to Africa outside of major cities, I noticed satellite TV dishes on the tops of shacks that lacked plumbing. At that time, power came from car batteries. Similarly, in 2002, a friend traveled to remote rural areas of China where people had never met a Westerner. He told me the farmers there lived in tiny one-room shacks, but at night he could see blue lights in all the windows. Those people couldn't even use car batteries because none existed where they were (though now they do, of course). So how were they watching TV? It turned out they used wind-up generators, and it was the job of children to keep them turning. And guess what they were watching — American sitcoms from the 1950s like *I Love Lucy*. Of course, today Chinese media is far more sophisticated and prevalent, as we've seen. But I digress with these memories for perspective on the resolve of human beings and the significance of television shows in their lives all over the world.

It is estimated that 55 of every 1,000 North Koreans have access to televisions. And if they are wealthy enough to own one, it is only able to play the four North Korean television stations (three if you're outside of the capital Pyongyang). Television purchases must be authorized by the police and spot checks are carried out to ensure that they have not been modified to receive foreign transmissions. In North Korea, watching something other than the government-approved television programming will likely result in you and your family being sent to a labor camp, or worse.

Writing for *The Kernel* section of the online magazine the *Daily Dot*, James Cook reported in 2013: Every evening in North Korea, families gather in front of their television sets to watch the carefully planned mix of television available on Korean Central Television, the only official source. North Koreans are treated to one film a day. They all seem to have the following plot: hardworking North Korean man meets hardworking North Korean woman; their hardworking North Korean friends are shown doing hard work; sweeping panorama shots of the North Korean countryside are shown as patriotic music plays, and eventually the two main characters sit on a hillside and thank the eternal president for finding each other.

In 2015, the *Guardian* reported that North Korea's constitution dictates that the Republic should nurture its "socialist culture," meeting the worker's demand for "sound" emotion to ensure that all citizens can be builders of socialism. "Every drama for television and radio has to be ratified by the highest authority, even in its initial planning stage," said former KCTV writer Jang Hae-sung in a video for the South Korean Institute for Unification Education. The prevalent values in North Korean dramas are loyalty to the leader, economic awareness, and self-rehabilitation, he adds.

Jwawoomyong (*The Motto*), a North Korean drama on KCTV, mirrors those values. In one episode, a father agonizes that he has failed the party after his construction project falls apart, but is restored by the memory of his endless devotion to the party.

A Day in Exercise, which aired on KCTV in 2015, tells a story of a young military officer who dares to break custom for the sake of effectiveness in battle. His actions make his platoon soldiers miserable. In one scene, he deliberately tampers with his soldiers' rifles right before shooting practice to ensure they check their rifles at all times. But when the young platoon leader suffers injuries during battle, he regains his strength by looking at the latest copy of state newspaper the *Rodong Sinmun*, featuring the supreme leader's face on the front page.

It's unlikely that we'll see any significant changes in the North Korean broadcasts any time soon. "There are certain limitations in what the North Korean broadcasting system can express," says Lee Ju-chul, researcher at the South Korean national broadcasting system KBS. "Throughout the decades there has been little change in the contents and there will be little chance for a revolution in TV if there's no revolution in North Korean politics first," he said.

And that brings us to the first awakenings — not as much a revolution as a building awareness. And, yes, North Korean official television won't change until official North Korea changes. But it's not as if television has to wait. In fact, it can be an engine of change. That's in the hands of a young generation.

According to libertyinnorthkorea.org, North Koreans who are now in their 20s and early 30s came of age after the collapse of the state-socialist economy — an era of marketization and eroding state relevance — and that is the only North Korea they remember. They are the "Jangmadang Generation" (*jangmadang* is North Korean for "market") that grew up in an era where people had to fend for themselves. Many of them never relied on the state for work, food, wealth, status, protection, or information. Traditional ideology seems hollow and irrelevant to them, and they are more influenced by foreign media. This demographic is only going to grow with time and they will be crucial in pushing for change in the future.

An op-ed in the *New York Times* in 2016 said that an estimated two-thirds of the population depends on the hundreds of street markets for food and other goods, including foreign media. Human smugglers, drones, DVDs, thumb drives, helium-filled balloons, and airborne leaflets are all used to get information. The distribution networks have become so sophisticated that people in some parts of the North can watch popular South Korean dramas just 24 hours after they have aired in Seoul. People working for defector-led nongovernmental organizations in South Korea receive text messages from their North Korean contacts with specific requests for foreign TV shows.

Liberty in North Korea says marketization is increasing the proliferation of mobile phones, televisions, radios, DVD players, and South Korean dramas and Chinese films to watch on them. It is possible to buy cheap Chinese DVD players for around $20, and DVDs themselves are available for less than a dollar and are commonly shared or even rented. USB drives are also growing in popularity, and are used with computers and the newer DVD players that have a USB input port. This makes it easier to share and watch foreign media without being detected, because USB drives are so easy to conceal.

Until you're caught, that is. In 2014, *Al Jazeera* reported that Kim Jong Un, North Korea's ruler, ordered the creation of the so-called "114 teams." These teams, consisting of political police and officials of the ruling party, were charged with one task: They had to make sure the North Korean people would not watch South Korean melodramas and thrillers, or Hollywood blockbusters. In other words, their task was to put an end to the booming illegal market for the sale of foreign bootleg DVDs.

By 2016, the *International Business Times* reported that North Korea had executed three women for circulating a South Korean television drama based on a true story of a North Korean dancer who defected to the South in the 1990s. Three other people were shot to death in North Korea when they were caught watching a South Korean television dramas on their mobile phones, according to a report in the *Daily NK*, a Seoul-based publication run by North Korean defectors. They were killed to send a message to others about what happens when people "get caught up in corrupt and depraved ideologies and go against the Party to watch such video content," a source claimed, citing a party official. Even members of the government are not exempt. London's *Daily Mail* reported ten senior members of North Korea's ruling party had been executed after they were caught watching soap operas.

Still this resistance through television goes on, almost like a kind of soft power guerilla war, according to defectors. Former North Korean diplomat Thae Yong-ho told TheStar.com.my of South Korea, "It depends on the class, but there is not one North Korean who hasn't seen a South Korean drama or movie as far as I know. It's no longer easy for the regime to cut off Hallyu. . . . The Kim regime appears stable from the outside, but is rotting from the inside. . . . We (North Koreans) hail Kim Jong-un during the day and watch South Korean dramas at night under blankets."

CBS News reported the story of Hyeonseo Lee, a young defector who fled the North in 2008. "Because of drama(s), many North Koreans left North Korea," she told CBS News at her college campus in Seoul. North Koreans, she said, are "curious about South Korea. They want to come here because what they learned (from North Korea propaganda) and what they saw (on TV) is completely different." After fleeing to China and then South Korea, Lee made a harrowing journey back into her homeland to extract family members. As her mother set eyes on the South Korean capital for the first time, she was stunned by something that Seoul's residents take for granted: traffic. She had always assumed the car-clogged avenues in the television dramas were fiction, arranged by collecting every car in the country in order to shoot a scene.

In 2017, *NPR* quoted a survey from the Washington-based research group *Intermedia* that discovered: of a group of 350 North Korean defectors, refugees, and travelers, 92 percent said they watched foreign content on a DVD player. The black market has grown, they suggest, because government officials benefit from it. State salaries are so low that border guards can easily be bribed. Demand is so high that some Chinese companies manufacture products geared to the North Korean market. There's even a device called the "Notel," a portable media player with a USB input. Users plug two things in at once: the illicit media on a USB stick, and in case of inspection, a state-approved propaganda disc.

As I write this in 2017, the future of North Korea is unknown. Maybe the day will come when the romances of South Korean television freely fill the air in the North, as the refugees dream. Or maybe by the time you read this the situation will have become even worse. All I can offer you as writers is perspective. The next time you get maddening script notes from a showrunner or executive, imagine what life might be like if the penalty for a rejected script is not that it won't be shot, but you might.

JAPAN

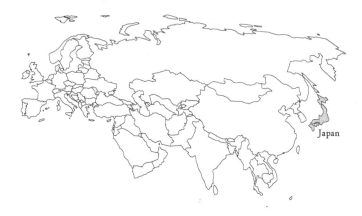

Japan

Though it's just a few hundred miles between North Korea and Japan across the narrow Sea of Japan, the countries are worlds apart. If North Korean television can be represented as a dark dungeon, Japanese TV feels more like Hello Kitty.

The easiest place to start is with anime (the serialized animated versions of comic books/graphic novels called *mangas*). Anime is like a gateway drug into Japanese culture. But more and more in America, *otakus* (anime fans) are discovering a form of Japanese television because of its sheer wackiness and anime-like humor. It's called J-drama (Japanese drama). One subset of this fandom is the subbing community. Subbers are fans, often groups of fans, who translate the original shows from Japanese into another language and distribute them via the Internet, usually without legal permission.

According to CNN's *Geek Out!* blog, adapting manga or anime to live-action drama has been successful, capitalizing on fans of the stories in their original form. Some of the most popular J-dramas are these types of adaptations, such as *Great Teacher Onizuka*, which told the story of a gang member-turned-teacher and his students. The show *Gokusen* was also set in a school, and documents a young idealistic teacher's attempts to straighten up a class of delinquents. As Japanese spend so much of their life on education, high school dramas are especially popular.

Most Japanese dramas fall into three genres: procedurals, office dramas, and school dramas. Historical dramas, an additional form, tend to be rare, usually based on "Taiga" novels that describe the rise and fall of an era through the stories of a character or a clan. Trailing far behind is romance, which often appears as a slice-of-life/growing-up-story/ensemble. In Japanese dramas, friendship often supplants romance and the main relationship for the leads is friendship. Other J-dramas feature over-the-top comedy springing from the *shōjo* (a genre of Japanese comics and animated films aimed at a young female audience, characterized by personal relationships) and *shōnen mangas* (a genre of Japanese comics and animated films aimed at a young male audience, characterized by action-filled plots). These are written for teens and feature quirky characters, fantasy sequences, and credulity-stretching plots.

According to DramaFever.com, Japanese dramas are concerned with capturing a sense of life as it is — hence all the school and office dramas — and with portraying "outsider" characters, people rejected by society either because of their looks, personality, or heightened intelligence. They aim at portraying the magic of daily life and the epic feel of adolescence.

Similar in length to what Americans are used to on cable and streaming, Japanese shows run 48 to 60 minutes per episode, with eight to thirteen episodes per season. But unlike American television, very few primetime fictional series in Japan receive more than a one-season contract at a time. After that season the show's performance is judged, and if it makes financial sense, producers will commission a second season, which may not be ready to air until years later. In 2014, *Japan Today* criticized this stilted production schedule for "making it almost impossible to craft the kind of sustained, complex narratives that Western viewers have enjoyed in shows such as *Breaking Bad* and *The Sopranos*."

In a way, Japan's industry reminds us of the 20th-century network era in the U.S. when only four broadcast networks competed for the entire audience. That led to LOP (Least Objectionable Programming) that created bland, imitative shows, as discussed in earlier chapters. Today Japan's broadcasters tend towards a similar risk-averse attitude because of the comparatively small number of TV channels in Japan. There are roughly a half-dozen national networks, but cable is all but nonexistent, and satellite TV doesn't offer the variety it does in the U.S. Recently, Netflix, Amazon, and Hulu are entering Japan. But as of 2015 a smaller number of options still meant a less segmented market with less niche programming, keeping the pressure on all networks to attract the widest audience possible by choosing content with the broadest appeal, which in turn means doing the same things as your competitor.

Whatever may be the internal limitations of Japanese traditional networks, U.S. producers are making the most of its anime library. In 2017, Tomorrow Studios, Marty Adelstein's joint venture with ITV Studios, developed a live-action adaptation of the cult Japanese animated series *Cowboy Bebop*. Considered one of the best anime series of all time, 26 episodes of *Cowboy Bebop* aired in Japan from 1998–1999. It has done well internationally, garnering several anime and science fiction awards, and is credited with helping to introduce anime to Western viewers. In the U.S., it initially aired on Adult Swim. Tomorrow Studios also partnered with Shueisha on the series adaptation of Japanese comic series *One Piece*, the best-selling manga series in history.

But the big news in Japan as everywhere has been the impact of streaming. Netflix has been ramping up its original content in Japan, where it competes with Amazon Video and Hulu. In 2017, Japan's public broadcaster NHK picked up the Netflix original drama series *Hibana: Spark*. Based on a prize-winning novel, the 10-episode series was written by comedian and screenwriter Naoki Matayoshi, and tells the story of a pair of comedians. *Hibana* will be the first series that debuted on an Internet platform to broadcast on NHK, Japan's largest terrestrial broadcaster.

The *Japan Times*, however, wrote it was skeptical that Netflix would succeed. They warned: "It's important that the team has artistic freedom, and they're not restrained by what the sponsor is going to think or other 'administrative' people around them," Greg Peters, president of Netflix Japan insists they will have that freedom, "so they can realize the potential in their work, which I think makes something globally attractive. Our job is to be 'creator-enabling'; the team's job is to have a vision, and then execute it. Ours is to enable them and then get out of the way. And I think the creators are excited by it and enjoy the freedom." Indeed, Katsuaki Yamaji, director of content business at Yoshimoto, an entertainment conglomerate, agrees that Netflix's creative process has allowed for a solid adaptation of Matayoshi's novel. "We like the 'creativity first' attitude that Netflix has," he says. "We were able to express the story while staying true to the original work."

Meanwhile, Hulu told *Variety* they plan to be a one-stop shop for Japan with U.S. drama series. According to Hulu executives, they premiere in Japan two to three weeks after the U.S. airdate, with that time used to localize the content. Hulu also had several Japanese-language originals in development in 2017 and announced, "We are developing several high profile scripted series."

Also jumping into the Japanese ring, Amazon's ambitious original content plans for Japan are part of "a winning strategy," James Farrell, Amazon's head of content for the Asia Pacific region told *Variety*. "We've had success with all types of content, from anime to variety, and from TV series to movies," Farrell says. The best performing Japanese Amazon original series include the 12-part drama series *Happy Marriage* and the sci-fi comedy series *Businessmen vs. Aliens*.

Japan Today remains skeptical, though. They editorialized in 2017, "The claim is interesting given how slow Japanese consumers have been to adopt digital delivery of movies. Companies including Tsutaya now offer movies online, but still see video shops and home deliveries of DVD as their dominant business."

By the time you read this, will streaming platforms from the U.S. have dominated J-dramas? If so, what does that tell us about the impact of television drama on cultures around the world?

FLYING HOME

Returning to Los Angeles after this breathless tour of more than 15 nations, I'm overwhelmed by the scope of television drama being made around the world. But, no, I haven't personally watched all these — no one could. If our minds are already boggled by the abundance of shows now available in the U.S., imagine what a challenge it is to comprehend the profusion of international television in addition. From 30,000 feet above the Pacific, I'm reaching for a more insightful conclusion than simple "muchness."

A sprit of global connectivity — humanity beyond borders — has always attracted hope for the future. On a single day in the summer of 1967, the then-new Beatles song, *All You Need Is Love* beamed around the world by satellite to 400 million people who experienced it simultaneously through a BBC-TV special *Our World*.

Now in less innocent times, we're learning to celebrate differences almost as much as unity, and one of the lessons of this tour (for me, at least) has been the diversity of TV dramas overseas. Writing in the *New York Times Magazine* in 2017, Mary Kaye Schilling observed that viewing crime dramas allowed her to drop into "the unique emotional worlds" of *Case* in Ireland, *Spiral* in France, and *Department Q* in Denmark.

Schilling also notes in her review of various international crime dramas that the casts seem more real. In *Bordertown* from Finland and *Braquo* from France, the actors look older than is permitted here with under-eye bags, splotchy skin, and crooked teeth, and she delights in shows with romantic leading men who are balding, out of shape, and middle-aged as in *The Break* from Belgium, *The Bridge* from Denmark and Sweden, and *Nobel* from Norway. She also celebrates detective *Saga Norén* of *The Bridge* for smelling her armpits before pulling on a "fresh" T-shirt from her desk drawer. True, we could believe Jessica Jones might do that on her Marvel show on Netflix, but it's unimaginable on most network broadcasts in the U.S. where "Hollywood" standards sanitize our characters. So the international models can be refreshing for us as writers searching for the most authentic characterizations.

After all these travels, though, my profound realization turned out not about the indigenous shows but the prevalence of Netflix as a transformative global phenomenon. That's somewhat true also of Amazon Video, but Netflix really is everywhere, speaking the language of the people. As of 2017, it had over a million paid streaming subscribers and made massive investments in new shows. The company says it plans to spend $8 billion on content in 2018 alone. According to the *Los Angeles Times* in 2017, Netflix now counts more overseas subscribers than domestic ones. For example, the South Korean movie *Okja*, and the series *3%* from Brazil are designed to appeal both to local audiences and to viewers worldwide.

That's not to say anyone is rooting for the centralized power that a single platform may provide, however magnanimous. But we do need help navigating these extremely crowded waters. Critic Walter Iuzzolino offers himself as that curator with his limited *Walter Presents* series from the U.K. (available in the U.S. by subscription). His first offerings include a Norwegian thriller set in an illegal underground clinic in an old Oslo bomb shelter, and a Dutch Mafia drama in the *Sopranos* mold, but with a woman at the head of the family, each show subtitled in English.

Iuzzolino told *Emmy* magazine he sees his series as something of a mission. "The wave of cultural conservatism that's sweeping Western society is strange and unsettling," he says. "So now there's an argument for real windows onto other worlds, other cultures and other societies. More than ever, being isolated culturally is a bad thing." And I agree.

CHAPTER NINE

THE FUTURE
IS NOW

I was charmed by the streetlights. How quaint, I thought, that they still had them in this time. Oh, wait. I'm in this time. A momentary time-traveler's panic swept me: how will I get home? Of course, I reconciled myself that I actually do live in this era, and I was standing at my own front door.

No doubt I was influenced by research for this book. Television all over the world today feels like the moment after the Big Bang with creation spinning out at near-infinite speed. And a new crop of TV executives sound like they're riding these atomic broncos shouting "whoopee!"

Translating all this down to earth: more quality dramas and comedies of more kinds in more lengths are being made in more ways on more platforms in more countries.

It's part of "The Great Convergence," long-anticipated and now arrived. In theory, it comes from melding television with the Internet, but in practice it's so much more because this is not a mere technological change.

Someone asked if I think all the TV outlets and shows will kill each other off, if competition will whittle them down to a top few, as happened with traditional networks. Apparently not. It seems that the entities are defining niche audiences and other ways to identify themselves in the crowd. In the past, the only option was to reach the broadest audience with material that would offend no one. But the freedom to program for distinct and passionate interests has freed writers and producers to make series that would have been impossible in the past. For example, Apple Inc. has struck a multiyear deal with Oprah Winfrey to produce original content for its devices, including "Apple TV." The battle for talent among tech titans and traditional studios just keeps heating up.

As for ways of succeeding, when people ask is it this way or that or some other way, my answer is simply yes. It's all of them. Everything is happening at once and everything is possible.

That's not the future. That is now. We are in a vortex of change where all times are simultaneous. That's not only because we can stream 13 hours of *Orange Is the New Black* at once, or binge 60 hours of *The Wire* new-to-us more than a decade after it went off the air, or discover shows made in Korea or Turkey or Denmark or Israel as readily as those made in America. And it's not only that we can instantly be on Mars through a rover's lens.

On television, the future is an eternal now. If you try to picture the street-lights extending into infinity, the possibilities go all the way to the stars. Here are a few new ways to go with them.

INTERACTIVE TV

Interactive television isn't really new. Way back in the 1950s *Winky Dink and You* (on CBS) involved viewers in storytelling, pioneering interactive programming at the same time television itself was pioneered. Children sent away for a kit that had crayons and a plastic screen that stuck to the TV tube with static electricity. When a character needed help, children would be asked to get him out of trouble by drawing on the screen. For example, if he needed to cross a river that had no bridge, the viewer would draw a line so he could escape. The grownup host encouraged kids to invite a friend over to watch the program; sharing the experience was essential to it. So helping Winky Dink in his adventures became an early expression of "participation television."

Unlike theatrical movies, the very nature of television has always involved audiences on an intimate level in a personal space, while at the same time creating a virtual community beyond geographic bounds. Those charac-teristics account for TV's continuing power as much as the quality of the shows; that's why television transcends any particular device on which shows are watched. None of that is new.

But now, interactivity is positioned on the frontier. This is beyond what I discussed in the section about Amazon Studios' crowd-sourced script development. In the Amazon model, individual writers commented on and contributed to another writer's pilot. That's a limited kind of interactivity targeted at affecting someone else's project. A second model of interactivity is fan fiction that predates television, in which audiences who love characters in a book, play, movie, or TV show, imagine further adventures for them. But now this is different. The next step in interactivity minimizes the individual sense of ownership, replacing it with what some describe as a "democratic" creative process, and others describe as anarchy. Some people think this is a step to blending with A.I. (artificial intelligence), a future in which we are all melded with machines. Some call it the "hive mind."

"The hive mind" comes from an idea that all humans are one entity, like a beehive or an ant colony, and that our inventions that make us proud of ourselves are really the products of group consciousness. Everyone plays his or her part as an individual, and is important in that sense like an individual ant or bee, but in the big picture no individual matters. Or each of us matters to the extent we are unique aspects of the whole, but on our own, no hive, colony, or culture could exist. An example often cited is guessing how many tiny items are in a jar. Experiments have shown that no individual guesses the correct number. But with a large enough number of participants, averaging everyone's guess always results in an accurate count.

Can we behave like bees or ants? Should we if we can? Proponents of making art collectively don't address that. The arguments, instead, are that more interesting products emerge when more voices are heard; and it's the wave of the future, like it or not. A generation sharing openly on social media and willingly surrendering privacy online will demand participation in its entertainment on every level. At least, that's the theory.

But since we're "interacting," I'll share an alternate perspective. In a Q&A with Chris Willman in the *Hollywood Reporter*, T Bone Burnett let loose. Though the award-winning music producer refers mostly to the music industry, these excerpts reflect an attitude towards crowd power that is also shared by many producers of television.

"The worldwide web was supposed to give everybody access and democratize everything. It was supposed to create a level field and increase the middle class and everybody had more access and more information. But now anybody can say anything and nobody cares. This is the problem of ubiquitous data.

"And what's happened in reality is that the power's been consolidated in very, very few companies, and the middle class of musicians really has just been wiped out. I mean the Internet has been an honest-to-God con.

"The Internet went into: 'Everything wants to be free, give your stuff away, pass it around, we don't care about the definitive version — the hive mind will take care of it. Leave it to the wisdom of the crowd, that'll work it all out, and everything will be fine in the end.'

"The car industry gets decimated and people go into apoplexy. The recording industry gets destroyed and people seem to be sanguine or happy about it, almost, because they're getting everything for free. If somebody had come down from Silicon Valley 30 years ago and said 'I've got this new technology, and you're gonna be able to see all around the world, transfer your stuff all over the world, you're gonna be able to send things, you'll be able to see your friends, you'll be able to hear music — all you have to do is give up your privacy and your royalties,' everybody would have said, 'Get the f— out of town! Right now! Get out of here!' Instead, these guys came down with their shtick, and everybody went, 'Well, how can we make money from this great new technology?' 'Oh, you're not gonna make *money* from it. Everything's gonna be free. Just give us the intellectual property we can send around in our pipes, everybody will subscribe, and then we'll be rich. Not *you*, though.' [*Laughs.*] 'Don't ask us what we're doing with the money. Just make the stuff and send it to us for free.' That's how much of a straight-up con it's been. People in Hollywood, we should go up there with pitchforks and torches to Silicon Valley now. Unfortunately, that's [how sophisticated] our response would be — pitchforks and torches.

"Promoting yourself and crowdfunding and all that kind of stuff, that's no way for an artist to live. When I go to one of these conferences and people ask me, 'How do I market myself on the Internet?' and all that kind of stuff: Look, your *fans* will market you on the Internet. But if you want to be a musician, practice eight hours a day. I don't believe in crowdsourcing because you'll end up doing the same thing over and over again. People tend to want artists to do the same thing, and it is incumbent upon artists to do something that the audience doesn't want — yet. I'll tell you this. *I won't follow an artist who will be led by his audience. Because I don't want to have to follow an artist that I have to lead.*"

TRANSMEDIA

On the far side of Interactive Television, beyond the whirlpools of artists who are led by crowds, lies the land of "Transmedia."

What does that mean, I asked Jay Bushman, who has two Emmy awards, the first two ever given for original interactive content, both for his role as a transmedia producer. The award went to *The Lizzie Bennet Diaries* that had 100 episodes, each around 5 or 6 minutes long, on a main YouTube channel, and also 150 shorter episodes across five different channels, and an uncounted number of tweets, posts, and other communications that were intrinsic to the series.

Bushman answered: "We have a joke that you put two transmedia creators in a room and pretty soon you'll have three definitions of transmedia.

"One branch is rooted in franchises. That's most of what you see in the press — you have movies, and video games that tie into that, and books, and it's all part of the same story world. But we already had a word for that: continuity.

"You see the Marvel example: You have the *Iron Man 3* movie, *The Shield* TV show, the comic books. But each piece of that is a discrete entity. You can watch the *Iron Man* movie and not have watched *Thor*; *Iron Man 3* is an entity unto itself. You can watch *The Shield* series and each episode is a story unto itself.

"I approach transmedia from a different perspective. I use multiple channels, multiple formats, multiple media, and have each piece part of a larger whole but none of the individual pieces stands alone. So it becomes a multimedia experience where you get part of the story here but you have to switch to another place to get another part. By putting all those individual pieces together, you create something larger than the whole. It's a singular experience.

"That's still trying to find its feet as a repeatable model. It's difficult. People get used to consuming media in one way. There's a whole culture built around making television shows or making comic books. But when you try to make a single story that uses all these elements where you have to cross from looking at something on your website to looking at something on your phone or twitter to get a single experience it can be challenging to frame that, challenging to sell that, really challenging to make money on that.

"I've taken those ideas and tried to apply them to making dramatic fictional series. In *Lizzie Bennet Diaries*, everything is scripted. It's a ton of work. How do we make one cohesive story that takes place on YouTube and on your Twitter feed and on your social media feeds and place it in the world. We scripted all that too.

"Early on, as my price for being on the show, I needed to be a member of the writing staff and sit in the writers' room with everyone else to break stories and make decisions at that level so the transmedia elements would be tied in tightly to everything else.

"Traditionally what happens on television shows is they write the show and bring in another team to do what they call ancillary material. There are two conflicting paradigms here. One is that you have your core creative team and bring in specialists to do this other stuff. But what have we been taught from the very beginning as writers? If it's not essential, cut it. So what happens when you bring in other people to bolt on other stuff that is not essential? Because it's not essential, it's not enjoyable, it's not fun, and it's treated as ancillary content, which means it's not important. The big crusade for me is to get this material elevated past the level of ancillary, to be tied into the world in a larger sense.

"When people start talking about interactive content, they leap to 'choose your own adventure' user-generated content, giving up story control to the audience. I don't believe in that. One of the tenets we talked about was 'Hamlet isn't a better play if you let the audience choose the ending.' Go to your bookshelf at home and look at all the books you own, and count how many of them are 'choose your own adventures.' The answer is going to be zero because 'choose your own adventure' is not going to be emotionally satisfying. When multiple endings are possible, no individual ending is important.

"We were looking for ways to use this interactive conduit but still be able to tell emotionally engaging stories. I developed a working theory based in part upon thinking done by others. There is a continuum. On one end is the three-act structure based on Aristotelian philosophy, with a diagram of tension we've all seen. At the other end of the spectrum is The Magic Circle. This is game storytelling like *World of Warcraft*. The game creators make a universe with rules and stories, but the audience experiences things in their own time, their own way, and everyone has a different experience within this world. The storyteller's basic job in this paradigm is to define what's inside the circle, and what's outside. Everything inside the circle is the story; everything outside the circle is not.

"I looked at this continuum, and asked what if we put the two ends together. I started working with an idea I call Through-Line and Magic Circle. You have a story world, an environment, and in the middle of this world is a through-line story, an anchor story that doesn't change. To my mind Magic Circle stories only become emotionally engaging if they have a through-line to play off.

"That's the model *Lizzie Bennet Diaries* is built on. We have a through-line — the story of *Pride and Prejudice*, the story of Lizzie Bennet and her sisters and Mr. Darcy and how they come together. But around that story, we have created a world and invited the fans in to play little parts in this surrounding world. The characters can converse with this audience, and it makes this story world real, immediate, and continuous.

"We told that story over the span of an entire year with two video episodes per week at minimum, but social media and transmedia content was three, four times a week or more. That created a world that was always there to the audience. You could be out doing something else, pick up your phone, and oh, look, there's Lizzie tweeting about something. The characters were always available to the viewer. No matter what time of day, something was going on. If you missed something today, you could catch it tomorrow, and things kept going while you missed it. It had a lived-in feel. That's the power. It gives the audience a sense of ownership of the world and these characters.

"In order to get to that you have to commit to this world building. A lot of stuff that gets done by network and cable shows functions like one-offs. For example, *Breaking Bad* created a website for Sol, the lawyer. But that's a one-time joke — you look at it and go Ha, and the experience is over. But we created a world where each piece leads to something else. It's a world to live in, not just a one-off tactic to provoke a response. The response we want is for you to engage in the story world."

MICKEY MOUSE

I began the discussion of interactivity with the 1950s, and I'll "bookend" it referring to the 1950s again with the quintessential transmedia character: Mickey Mouse. He'd already been around as a cartoon for decades by the time Disneyland opened in 1955; in the years since *Steamboat Willie* (in 1928), Mickey appeared in movies such as *Fantasia* (1940), in animated TV series, and on merchandise and games. But in 1955, Mickey walked off the screen into Disneyland where a costumed performer interacted as a living being.

And that changed everything. Not that people hadn't dressed up as fantasy characters before — humans performed rituals dressed as animals for eons, and historical reenactments and role-playing have been common for a long time. But mutating an original screen creation to become a living interaction presaged a likely next evolution in entertainment.

Futurists speculate that "experience" will be the new watchword. Places formerly known as theme parks will be rebranded "experience parks." Virtual reality, augmented reality, and holograms will move characters off the screen into your room where you will seem to inhabit the space where a scene plays out. That will cause a new definition of "off screen" and impact how much is written for action that is now out of frame or in a background.

What matters here is not future tech. This is about going beyond platforms so that human beings are in touch with other humans. It's a different way to think about the "hive." We don't do well in isolation. Probably when early humans became separated from the group they were eaten, and we never forgot how bad that felt. Unfortunately, new media has the ability to separate us into units staring into personal screens — all the people meeting for lunch, looking at their phones instead of each other. So now we're in the throes of a pushback through mass "friending" and frantic connections on social media. But that's not enough. As a species, we seem to need to touch each other, to know each other in more than 140 characters.

And that brings us full circle to storytelling, and how you fit into the picture.

CONCLUSION

The keys to the future are on your keyboard.

In a time of far-reaching change, the specific shows, even whole channels and the methods of distribution that I mentioned in this book will be different by the time you're reading this. The frontier will move, as it always does, and no matter how fast you travel, you will not exceed the speed of the light emanating from the many kinds of screens in the distance.

Everything I've shared with you, and the insights contributed by the writers, producers, and executives quoted, as well as our journey around the globe, can be the basis for your own continuing journey.

No matter where you go and how far, your own stories remain the ticket to ride. Your characters and their relationships will evolve, as will their challenges, fun, and fantasies. To the extent your stories are authentic, they will resonate with your audience, however you define an audience. Whether you see yourself as part of a collective global spirit or an individual creator, you are a voice in the most powerful communications medium on earth. You are a witness to the human condition. You are the one who forms a tale of these times.

The keys to the future of television are on your keyboard.

ABOUT THE AUTHOR

Pamela Douglas is an award-winning writer with numerous credits in television drama.

Previous editions of this book have been adopted by network mentoring programs and published in translation in Germany, Spain, Italy, France, China and Taiwan. She is also the author of *The Future of Television: Your Guide to Creating TV in the New World* (MWP 2015), and has lectured and given seminars internationally on creating for television.

She has been honored with the Humanitas Prize for *Between Mother and Daughter* (CBS), an original drama that also won nomination for a Writers Guild Award. Multiple Emmy nominations and awards, and awards from American Women in Radio and Television went to her other dramas. She was a creator of the series *Ghostwriter*, and wrote for shows including *Star Trek: The Next Generation* that was named one of the top 100 shows by the Writers Guild of America.

She has also been a member of the Board of Directors of the Writers Guild of America, West.

At the School of Cinematic Arts of the University of Southern California she is a tenured professor in the John Wells Division of Screen and Television Writing, where she teaches writing TV drama.

She consults internationally to professional TV writers and producers, and has lectured in Africa, Europe, Asia, and throughout the United States.

Further information is available at PamDouglasBooks.com, and she can be contacted at pamdouglaswords@aol.com.

SAVE THE CAT!®
THE LAST BOOK ON SCREENWRITING YOU'LL EVER NEED!

BLAKE SNYDER

BEST SELLER

He's made millions of dollars selling screenplays to Hollywood and now screenwriter Blake Snyder tells all. "Save the Cat!®" is just one of Snyder's many ironclad rules for making your ideas more marketable and your script more satisfying — and saleable, including:

- The four elements of every winning logline.
- The seven immutable laws of screenplay physics.
- The 10 genres and why they're important to your movie.
- Why your Hero must serve your idea.
- Mastering the Beats.
- Mastering the Board to create the Perfect Beast.
- How to get back on track with ironclad and proven rules for script repair.

This ultimate insider's guide reveals the secrets that none dare admit, told by a show biz veteran who's proven that you can sell your script if you can save the cat.

"Imagine what would happen in a town where more writers approached screenwriting the way Blake suggests? My weekend read would dramatically improve, both in sellable/producible content and in discovering new writers who understand the craft of storytelling and can be hired on assignment for ideas we already have in house."
> – From the Foreword by Sheila Hanahan Taylor, Vice President, Development at Zide/Perry Entertainment, whose films include *American Pie, Cats and Dogs, Final Destination*

"One of the most comprehensive and insightful how-to's out there. Save the Cat!® is a must-read for both the novice and the professional screenwriter."
> – Todd Black, Producer, *The Pursuit of Happyness, The Weather Man, S.W.A.T, Alex and Emma, Antwone Fisher*

"Want to know how to be a successful writer in Hollywood? The answers are here. Blake Snyder has written an insider's book that's informative — and funny, too."
> – David Hoberman, Producer, *The Shaggy Dog* (2005), *Raising Helen, Walking Tall, Bringing Down the House, Monk* (TV)

BLAKE SNYDER, besides selling million-dollar scripts to both Disney and Spielberg, was one of Hollywood's most successful spec screenwriters. Blake's vision continues on *www.blakesnyder.com*.

$20.95 · 216 PAGES · ORDER NUMBER 34RLS · ISBN: 9781932907001

THE WRITER'S JOURNEY
3RD EDITION

MYTHIC STRUCTURE FOR WRITERS

CHRISTOPHER VOGLER

BEST SELLER
OVER 170,000 COPIES SOLD!

See why this book has become an international best seller and a true classic. *The Writer's Journey* explores the powerful relationship between mythology and storytelling in a clear, concise style that's made it required reading for movie executives, screenwriters, playwrights, scholars, and fans of pop culture all over the world.

Both fiction and nonfiction writers will discover a set of useful myth-inspired storytelling paradigms (i.e., "The Hero's Journey") and step-by-step guidelines to plot and character development. Based on the work of Joseph Campbell, *The Writer's Journey* is a must for all writers interested in further developing their craft.

The updated and revised third edition provides new insights and observations from Vogler's ongoing work on mythology's influence on stories, movies, and man himself.

"This book is like having the smartest person in the story meeting come home with you and whisper what to do in your ear as you write a screenplay. Insight for insight, step for step, Chris Vogler takes us through the process of connecting theme to story and making a script come alive."
> – Lynda Obst, Producer, *Sleepless in Seattle, How to Lose a Guy in 10 Days;*
> Author, *Hello, He Lied*

"This is a book about the stories we write, and perhaps more importantly, the stories we live. It is the most influential work I have yet encountered on the art, nature, and the very purpose of storytelling."
> – Bruce Joel Rubin, Screenwriter, *Stuart Little 2, Deep Impact,*
> *Ghost, Jacob's Ladder*

CHRISTOPHER VOGLER is a veteran story consultant for major Hollywood film companies and a respected teacher of filmmakers and writers around the globe. He has influenced the stories of movies from *The Lion King* to *Fight Club* to *The Thin Red Line* and most recently wrote the first installment of *Ravenskull*, a Japanese-style manga or graphic novel. He is the executive producer of the feature film *P.S. Your Cat is Dead* and writer of the animated feature *Jester Till*.

$27.95 · 300 PAGES · ORDER NUMBER 76RLS · ISBN: 193290736x

THE COFFEE BREAK SCREENWRITER: 2ND EDITION
WRITING YOUR SCRIPT 10 MINUTES AT A TIME

PILAR ALESSANDRA

Got ten minutes? Write your screenplay.

The writer receives guidance and tips at every stage of the often intimidating writing process with a relaxed, "ten minutes at a time" method that focuses the writer and pushes him or her forward. At each step, writers are encouraged to "Take Ten" and tackle an element of their script using the templates and tools provided. "What You've Accomplished" sections help writers review their progress. And "Ten-Minute Lectures" distill and demystify old-school theory, allowing the writer to unblock and get writing.

- A "how to" workbook packed with over sixty 10-minute writing tools, taking the writer through brainstorming, storytelling, structuring, outlining, scene work, page craft, and pitching.
- An approach honed and proven in Pilar's fifteen years of teaching through her "On the Page" feature and television classes.
- The book for a busy world. Perfect for texters and tweeters, this book uses short, focused bursts of writing to move forward on a screenplay or television pilot.
- A ready launching point for compatible software, cellphone applications, workbooks, and online courses.
- Additional second-edition content that adds television — currently the hottest medium in which to write — to the mix.

PILAR ALESSANDRA is the director of the writing program On the Page®, host of the popular On the Page Podcast, and author of "The Coffee Break Screenwriter." Pilar started her career as Senior Story Analyst at DreamWorks SKG and, in 2001, opened the On the Page Writers' Studio in Los Angeles. Her students and clients have written for *The Walking Dead*, *Lost*, *House of Lies*, *Nip/Tuck*, and *Family Guy*. They've sold features and pitches to Warner Bros., DreamWorks, Disney, and Sony, and have won the prestigious Nicholl Fellowship, Austin Screenwriting Competition, and Warner Bros. TV Writing Workshop. Pilar has trained writers at ABC/Disney and CBS and traveled the world, teaching in London, Beijing, Warsaw, Lisbon, and South Africa. www.OnThePage.tv

$26.95 · 270 PAGES · ORDER #236RLS · ISBN 9781615932429

THE COFFEE BREAK SCREENWRITER...
BREAKS THE RULES
A GUIDE FOR THE REBEL WRITER

PILAR ALESSANDRA

March to a different drummer! Take risks. Make bold choices. Break the rules! But do it purposely and strategically, using *The Coffee Break Screenwriter . . . Breaks the Rules* as your guide, and create a script readers will remember.

Pilar Alessandra's popular book, *The Coffee Break Screenwriter,* taught writers how to outline quickly, write efficiently, and rewrite creatively. It is the "go-to" book for getting one's story on the page. But now that same writer may be doing a final pass on a project, working with a producer, or coming up with a new project only to be hit with . . . RULES! Should the writer respond to this random list of do's and don'ts pertaining to structure, characters, dialogue, and formatting? Nope.

Who says you have to follow the screenwriting rules? In this book Pilar reviews the rules writers assume they should follow, discusses why they're there in the first place, and then shows you ways to creatively break them!

Rules evaluated include those addressing:
· storytelling devices like *flashback* and *voiceover*
· character rules such as *empathy* and *backstory*
· dialogue faux pas such as writing *on the nose*
· structural issues such as *nonlinear writing* and *act-break placement*
· formatting sticking points involving *emotion* and *visuals*

PILAR ALESSANDRA is the director of the writing program On the Page®, host of the popular On the Page Podcast, and author of "The Coffee Break Screenwriter." Pilar started her career as Senior Story Analyst at DreamWorks SKG and, in 2001, opened the On the Page Writers' Studio in Los Angeles. Her students and clients have written for *The Walking Dead, Lost, House of Lies, Nip/Tuck,* and *Family Guy.* They've sold features and pitches to Warner Bros., DreamWorks, Disney, and Sony, and have won the prestigious Nicholl Fellowship, Austin Screenwriting Competition, and Warner Bros. TV Writing Workshop. Pilar has trained writers at ABC/Disney and CBS and traveled the world, teaching in London, Beijing, Warsaw, Lisbon, and South Africa. www.OnThePage.tv

$12.95 · 104 PAGES · ISBN 9781615932825

THE MYTH OF MWP

In a dark time, a light bringer came along, leading the curious and the frustrated to clarity and empowerment. It took the well-guarded secrets out of the hands of the few and made them available to all. It spread a spirit of openness and creative freedom, and built a storehouse of knowledge dedicated to the betterment of the arts.

The essence of the Michael Wiese Productions (MWP) is empowering people who have the burning desire to express themselves creatively. We help them realize their dreams by putting the tools in their hands. We demystify the sometimes secretive worlds of screenwriting, directing, acting, producing, film financing, and other media crafts.

By doing so, we hope to bring forth a realization of 'conscious media' which we define as being positively charged, emphasizing hope and affirming positive values like trust, cooperation, self-empowerment, freedom, and love. Grounded in the deep roots of myth, it aims to be healing both for those who make the art and those who encounter it. It hopes to be transformative for people, opening doors to new possibilities and pulling back veils to reveal hidden worlds.

MWP has built a storehouse of knowledge unequaled in the world, for no other publisher has so many titles on the media arts. Please visit www.mwp.com where you will find many free resources and a 25% discount on our books. Sign up and become part of the wider creative community!

Onward and upward,

Michael Wiese
Publisher/Filmmaker

CPSIA information can be obtained
at www.ICGtesting.com
Printed in the USA
JSHW022005160820
7295JS00003B/9